Sunset
Complete
Home Storage

By the Editors of Sunset Books and Sunset Magazine

Supplying maximum storage in a minimum of space, this organized wall closet easily accommodates his wardrobe alongside hers. Architect: N. Kent Linn. Interior design: Joan Simon. Closet interior: The Minimal Space.

LANE PUBLISHING CO. • Menlo Park, California

Cover: "A place for everything" is the objective of good storage planning, and places can be found throughout the house: tucked under the basement stairs (top left, from *Garage, Attic & Basement Storage,* page 60); built into a kitchen work center (top right, from *Kitchen Storage,* page 26); and concealed in a bedroom headboard (bottom, from *Bedroom & Bath Storage,* page 10). Design by Susan Bryant. Photography by Gene Hamilton (top left), Tom Wyatt (top right and bottom).

Editor, Sunset Books:
Elizabeth L. Hogan

Second printing April 1990

A Storehouse of Ideas

Most of us live with many more possessions than we can comfortably manage without an organized storage system. Properly placed, belongings stay tidy, safe from damage, and conveniently accessible. This handbook can help you make the most of your home's storage space, allowing you to tailor it to your specific needs. In the process, you'll also discover potential storage areas that you never knew existed.

Our storage anthology combines three top-selling Sunset titles that focus on areas of the house where demand for storage is usually the greatest—kitchen, bedroom, bath, garage, attic, and basement. With the ideas and practical tips in this three-in-one handbook, you can soon shape up these and other areas of your home so that whatever you need will be easy to find, right at your fingertips.

Contents

KITCHEN STORAGE

Bustling with activity and brimming with equipment, kitchens require well-organized storage to function smoothly. Here you'll find hundreds of practical and attractive designs for kitchen drawers, shelves, cabinets, racks, pantries, desktops, islands, and more. There's even a reference list of cabinet and storage manufacturers at the end of this section.

BEDROOM & BATH STORAGE

Serenity and privacy are important qualities of bedrooms and baths. Look through this section for innovative, good-looking designs that maximize the storage potential of these quarters. You'll see ideas for underbed storage, super-efficient closets, and exciting new organizers to help you streamline your own bedroom and bath.

GARAGE, ATTIC & BASEMENT STORAGE

Garages, attics, and basements tend to attract a miscellany of bulky items, from camping gear to potting soil, and from outgrown clothing to woodworking tools. Now you can design a hard-working storage plan for these spaces, following the dozens of ideas in this section.

Sunset

Kitchen Storage

By the Editors of Sunset Books
and Sunset Magazine

*Special shelf for food processor or mixer swings up to
convenient work height (see page 31).*

Lane Publishing Co.
Menlo Park, California

Dishes ride on slide-out shelves for easy access (see page 31).

Thanks...

to the many architects, designers, and home owners who shared their ideas with us, especially Michael Goldberg, C.K.D., of The Kitchen Specialist; Stewart Fair at Kitchens by Stewart; Julie Ball of Great Kitchens at Boucher's; Del Brandstrom of The Refacers, Inc.; Rick Sambol of Kitchen Consultants; California Kitchens; Stacks & Stacks; and Crate & Barrel.

We extend special thanks to Phyllis Elving for her careful editing of the manuscript.

Cover: Designed for efficiency, remodeled kitchen features cooking island, generous counter space, and abundant storage. Design: Allen Sayles, Architectural Kitchens & Baths. Cover design by Susan Bryant. Photography by Stephen Marley.

Photographers: Glenn Christiansen: 8, 9 bottom, 11 top, 19 bottom, 29 bottom left; Peter Christiansen: 37 top left and right; Stephen Cridland: 18 top; Renee Lynn: 15 bottom left and right, 24 top, 42, 43, 48; Jack McDowell: 1, 2, 3, 17 top, 21 right, 23 top, 27 left, 29 top left, 31 top left and bottom right, 32 right, 33 top and bottom right, 34, 36, 37 bottom left; Stephen Marley: 15 top, 18 bottom, 20, 21 left, 22, 31 top right, 44 left and bottom right, 46; Don Normark: 9 top; Norman A. Plate: 7, 13, 16; Chad Slattery: 10 bottom, 40 bottom; Rob Super: 25, 33 bottom left, 40 top, 41 top left; Russ Widstrand: 4, 5, 10 top, 14 top, 17 bottom, 19 top, 27 right, 28, 30, 31 bottom left, 32 top and bottom left, 35, 37 bottom right, 38 left, 41 bottom left and center right, 44 top and center right; Tom Wyatt: 11 bottom, 12, 14 bottom, 23 bottom right, 24 bottom, 26, 29 top right, 38 right, 39.

Photo styling: JoAnn Masaoka Van Atta: 1, 4, 5, 11 bottom, 12 top, 15 bottom left and right, 17 bottom, 18 bottom, 23 bottom right, 24, 26, 27 bottom, 28, 29 top left, 30, 31 bottom right, 32 bottom left, 33 bottom right, 35, 38 left, 42, 43, 44 left, 46.

Editor, Sunset Books: Elizabeth L. Hogan

Second printing April 1990

Book Editor
Don Vandervort

Coordinating Editor
Gregory J. Kaufman

Design
Roger Flanagan

Illustrations
Bill Oetinger

Contents

Pivoting pull-out reclaims lost space in corner of base cabinets (see page 36).

The Organized Kitchen

Thanks to sky-high real estate values, two-income life-styles, and an influx of new technology, the kitchen has assumed a new identity in recent years. Today's kitchen is the hub of the household—a place of community where we gather with family and friends. And it is a dynamic workspace, filled with high-tech machines to dice onions, brew espresso, extrude pasta, extract juices, and handle scores of other chores.

To meet the challenge of its new identity, today's kitchen must be carefully planned. Filled with gear and yet open to the household and its guests, it needs to provide abundant storage. To maximize every valuable cubic inch of space and every valuable moment in our busy lives, that storage must be both space-efficient and easily accessible.

One thoughtfully organized kitchen is shown on these two pages. You'll find scores of other ideas in this book to inspire and aid you in transforming your own kitchen into an equally efficient workspace.

Essence of efficiency
Large storage island is just the beginning of this kitchen's efficiencies. Clutter-free, spacious, and organized for easy use, this kitchen was designed for a busy family. Kitchen design: Laurie Candelora.

Baking center and pantry

Generous drawers behind large doors provide capacious storage for foods. Pull-out counter is handy near microwave and ovens. Above ovens, trays and baking pans stay organized between vertical dividers.

Cabinet organizers

Custom oak spice shelves mount to inside of cabinet door. Below cabinet, tambour door rolls up to reveal food processor.

Full-feature island

Cutting board pulls out for chopping next to preparation sink. Large drawers below hold breads and cereals. Cabinets and drawers all around island offer abundant storage.

Hard-working shelves and drawers

Access to corner cabinet's full depth is made possible by corner carousel fitted to inside of angled double door. Drawers beneath cooktop hold pots, pans, and lids. Doors close to conceal drawers for neater kitchen lines, but they could be eliminated for quicker access.

Storage Components

Cabinets are a kitchen's key storage components. They create the personality of a kitchen and provide the structure for most of its organization and storage. For this reason—and because they represent the largest single investment in a new kitchen—it is important to study the many options available before purchasing new cabinets.

What materials do you prefer? Your choices include warm hardwoods, European-style laminates, painted veneers. Will you buy stock cabinets at the local lumberyard, order custom modular cabinets, or have cabinetry hand-crafted by a custom cabinetmaker? Your decisions will depend upon the look you want for your kitchen and how much money you're willing to spend to achieve that look.

Several other kitchen components supplement the storage provided by cabinets. Open shelving offers both visible display and quick access. Islands provide countertop space and centralized storage. Storage walls and pantries house paraphernalia and foods en masse. And carts roll about the kitchen, keeping frequently needed items within arm's length.

You'll find examples of typical cabinet options and ideas for other storage components throughout this chapter. For information on outfitting cabinets with hard-working hardware, see page 26. And for information on planning, selecting, and buying cabinets, see the Design Workbook beginning on page 46.

A harmony of kitchen elements
Cabinets, shelving, and islands or peninsulas are key storage elements contributing to a kitchen's appearance and efficiency. Sleek white laminate cabinets in this kitchen complement home's contemporary style. Custom elements include wine rack and, below, appliance storage area behind roll-up tambour door. Design: David Knox, Zephyr Architectural Partnership.

Cabinets: Design Choices

Basic building blocks of kitchen storage

Custom color

Bright red lacquered cabinets reach to ceiling; matching panels cover refrigerator. Lacquered finishes offer glossy elegance, but they're not for everyone—they are quite expensive and unforgiving of scratches and dents. Design: Robert Schatz, Plus Kitchens.

Kitchen curves

Undulating perimeter cabinets wrap around figure-eight island. Curves, which generally enhance price as well as appearance, are easiest to form with laminates. Architect: William P. Bruder. Cabinetmaker: Laurent Construction.

Craftsman's touch

Custom kitchen contains features you won't find in a stock-cabinet catalog. Cabinet faces have raised beaded panels, large-radius corners. Paneling also covers appliance faces, cabinet sides, sink soffit, and flared hood above cooktop. Design: Rob Boynton, Midland Cabinets.

Wood Cabinetry

Bringing nature's richness and warmth to the kitchen

Country fresh

Light-stained oak combines the warmth of wood with the pale tones characteristic of contemporary kitchens. Cabinets feature raised-bevel panel doors, large drawers beneath cooktop, and built-in microwave oven. Kitchen design: Kathy Grundhoffer. Cabinets: Kitchens by Stewart (Wood-Mode).

Rustic pine

Knotty-pine cabinets, owner-built from glass and blemished lumber, create a rustic mood. Glass doors display contents yet discourage dust. Chopping blocks set into gray-blue ceramic tile counter beside sink and cooktop take heavy use in food preparation. Design: Fred Spencer and Karen Brooks.

Sleek and contemporary

Even-toned custom wood cabinetry is of bleached and oiled vertical-grain clear fir. Countertops of white plastic laminate provide contrast. At the closed end of the U is a raised breakfast bar. Architect: Robert Anderson. Interior designer: Sheryl W. McKinsey.

Upscale elegance

Dark mahogany, marble, brass, and stainless steel distinguish this older home's kitchen. Matching custom panels mask refrigerator. Dark woods can express old-world warmth and character. Design: Osburn Design.

Laminate Cabinets

Crisp, clean lines and easy-care surfaces

Softened lines

Off-white laminate cabinets, typical of contemporary "Euro-style" kitchens, are durable and easy to clean. Generally a less-expensive choice than hardwoods, laminates lend themselves to curved surfaces. Architect: William B. Remick. Interior designer: Jane Howerton Interiors.

A study in black and white

Gleaming polished granite countertops reflect white-white cabinets in crisp, ultramodern kitchen. Though laminates are available in hundreds of colors and textures, white can be the most striking choice in the right setting. Rich slate tile floor enhances the contrast. Architect: Rob Wellington Quigley.

Warm gray

Cabinets and island of medium-gray laminate combine with deep purple tiles to convey richness, warmth, and comfort. Angled walls add interest at far end. Island doubles as counter and storage. Architect: Gary Gilbar.

Cabinet Variations

Unusual materials and slight twists expand your options

A place for plaster

Unusual? You bet! Though most of this kitchen's cabinet surfaces are laminates, the island and part of the wall that houses ovens have a plaster finish. These surfaces blend with the surrounding walls, complementing the contemporary Southwest theme. Design: Finnegan/ Widstrand Company and City Cabinetmakers.

Best of both worlds

Combining wood and laminates can take advantage of both materials' benefits. Laminates on large surfaces are relatively inexpensive and easy to maintain. Using wood for trim or smaller surfaces adds a touch of natural warmth. Design: European Kitchens & Baths.

Popular alternative

Painted wood cabinets are an excellent, inexpensive alternative to hardwood and laminate cabinets. Walls and cabinets can match precisely; a color change is just a stroke of the brush away.

Face-lifting for a new look

Centerpiece of this kitchen remodel was refacing—rather than replacing—existing cabinets. Configuration of cabinets before remodel, left, suited owners' needs adequately, but resurfacing them with a whitewashed wood laminate gave a lighter, updated look—at considerably less cost than installing all new cabinetry. Design: Del Brandstrom, The Refacers, Inc.

Open Shelves

Simple, inexpensive—and indispensable—storage solutions

Quick access

Doors of upper cabinet fall short to allow open shelves, an ideal parking spot for frequently used dishware or kitchen paraphernalia. These basic frameless white cabinet boxes, typically made of painted or laminate fiberboard, have bleached wood doors— one of several style options. Bought knocked down, cabinets were assembled and installed by owner.

Cookbook storage, hidden lighting

Cookbooks and metal canisters stay out of the way but still within easy reach on this handy shelf. Fixtures mounted to underside of shelf provide light for baking counter below. Architects: Fisher-Friedman Associates.

Reference center

Open-shelf cabinet houses bound cooking magazines, cookbooks, and even a small television. This cabinet was manufactured to match the balance of the kitchen's cabinetry. Kitchen design: Kathy Grundhoffer. Cabinets: Kitchens by Stewart (Wood-Mode).

Hard-working Islands

Expanding kitchen counter space, stretching storage

Heart of the kitchen

Generously sized island adds to kitchen in two ways: by providing storage in its base and by offering abundant counter space, relieving storage needs elsewhere. Handsome Italian granite slab surface is both an excellent surface for pastry and candy making and a grand piece of horizontal art. Design: Don Atwood. Craftsperson: John Hall.

Multipurpose island

For on-the-go meals, cooking, and easy-access storage, island plays a major role in this kitchen. To accommodate normal chair height, counter steps down. Interior design: Ruth Livingston.

Preparation center

Broad counter, storage drawers, and small food-preparation sink make this island an activity hub. Cabinets, island, and countertop are all of white laminate. Architect: Martin Bernstein. Cabinetmakers: City Cabinetmakers.

For one or more chefs

Great for food preparation and display, generous island in expansive kitchen also houses a cooktop and numerous storage cabinets. Corners are angled to allow free traffic circulation. Architect: Kenneth Kurtzman, Kurtzman and Kodama, Inc. Interior decorator: Caryl Kurtzman.

Storage Walls

Floor-to-ceiling cabinets devoted to storage

Cupboards for dining gear

Everything from table leaves to coffee cups is kept in floor-to-ceiling cupboards along wall separating dining room from kitchen. Table leaves, folding chairs fit between blocks of wood nailed to top and bottom of cupboard compartments. Shelves fill in remaining space. Design: Pennington & Pennington.

Built-in storage

Recessed into dining area wall, shallow cupboards offer adjustable shelves for storing kitchen's overflow. Casseroles, tableware, baskets, and groceries hide behind tall doors. Antique cabinet at left houses more dishes and table linens. Interior designer: Joan Simon.

Flexible food cabinet

Sparkling white double doors swing open to reveal a flexible food storage system in frameless cabinet. Drawers are roomy enough for tall bottles of soda and a big basket brimming with oranges. Shelves adjust on metal tracks to accommodate jumbo-size food packages. Architects: Fisher-Friedman Associates.

A whole wall of storage

The beauty of these cabinets lies in their natural finish, clean lines, and almost unlimited storage capacity. Spacious shelves behind cabinet doors hold packaged foods, canned goods, and dishes; vented tip-out bins are filled with fruits and vegetables. Large baskets and crockery fit in space between cabinets and ceiling. Architect: Robert C. Peterson.

Walk-in Pantries

Satellite rooms lead the race for space

Joint venture in wine and food storage

Walk-in pantry features wine "cellar" on far wall and a cooler to keep wines at proper temperature. Pantry shelves are fixed at various heights. Ladder brings top shelves within reach. Design: Gordon Grover.

This one has it all

Walk-in pantry (at left) holds everything but the kitchen sink. Shelves on walls adjust to accommodate kitchen equipment of different heights; hooks hold molds and small cooking utensils. Packaged foods and canned goods fit in single rows on shallow door shelves. Especially convenient are counter for preparing food and storing appliances, undershelf baskets for fruits and vegetables, and storage place for stool. Architects: Sortun-Vos.

Hidden mini-pantry

Behind sliding louvered doors, a roomy pantry houses food, appliances, and other kitchen gear. Pantry interior is lined with open shelving. Architect: Peter C. Rodi, Designbank.

Kitchen Carts

Counter space and storage on the move

Ready-made rolling storage

Coated-wire cart topped with laminate work surface glides across the kitchen for easy table-setting. Pull-out baskets and hardware are sturdy enough to allow storage of dishes as well as table linens; such commercially available carts are adaptable to all sorts of kitchen storage needs.

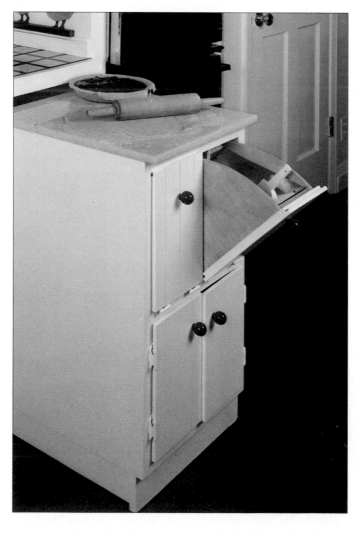

Stowaway

Compact baking center comes out of hiding, rolls to any part of the kitchen, then tucks away neatly in a counter end when work is done. The marble top is great for pastry and candy making; metal-lined tilt-out bins below hold flour and sugar. Baking gear stores in the lowest compartment. Architect: William B. Remick.

Roll-around multipurpose cart

For flower arranging— or any other purpose— this cart rolls out from underneath counter to become a work island. Shelves and drawers provide storage for infrequently used items. Design: Plus Kitchens.

More than a butcher block

Beneath lavish array of gleaming cookware is a butcher block table fitted with casters. Modified to include a lift-out metal bin with cover, sliding blade-storage tray, wire basket, and even towel pegs, island moves from one kitchen work center to another. For a home where children are present, knives and food processor blades would be best kept elsewhere. Architect: Peter W. Behn.

Outfitting Cabinetry

When planning your kitchen's storage scheme, imagine your cabinets as empty boxes, perched on the floor or mounted on the wall. Then consider how you might outfit these boxes to provide the most efficient and accessible storage for your kitchen. Starting with a "blank slate" is often the best way to see your kitchen's storage potential.

Numerous accessories can be used to extend the usefulness of cabinetry: doors in several styles, fixed and movable shelves, drawers and baskets, carousels and lazy Susans, specialty pull-outs, space-saving racks, and more. This chapter illustrates some of your choices.

Though you can buy accessories such as shelf supports, drawer glides, and space-saving racks at home-improvement stores, many specialty pull-outs and organizers are sold only to cabinetmakers, manufacturers, and dealers. If you're ordering new cabinets, you can page through catalogs that show options. If you're updating your existing cabinetry, ask dealers or cabinetmakers whether they can order specialty hardware for you.

Supercenter

Mild-mannered cabinets (above) conceal super powers of storage and organization (right). Built for a serious pastry cook, this baking center features everything needed in one well-thought-out unit. The granite top is both pastry slab and landing place for hot dishes; beneath it, a bread board and oven coexist with a wealth of storage that leaves no space untapped. Design: Carlene Anderson, CKD.

Pull-out pantry

Gliding smoothly on heavy-duty hardware, one of a pair of birch and alder pull-out pantries keeps food storage centralized in the middle of the kitchen. Dividers above ovens keep cooking and serving trays organized. Architect: Michael D. Moyer, The Architectural Design Group.

Dynamic duo

Small drawer front drops down to reveal pull-out chopping block. Beneath it, waste bin slides out when you pull open cabinet door. These features are typical of specialty hardware available through cabinet dealers. Cabinets: Wood-Mode.

Cabinet Doors

Options that affect your kitchen's form and function

Potpourri of doors

Cabinets at left are outfitted with three different styles of doors. Tambour door retracts into curved corner cabinet, glass doors display crystal and glassware, and raised-bevel panel doors cover everything else. Above, round-cornered cabinet, part of the same custom modular system, has door shaped to flow with the curve. Cabinets: Wood-Mode.

Roll-top appliance nooks

Ideal for appliance garages at countertop level, tambour doors stay out of the way when open. Be sure tambours are counterbalanced properly so they don't drop shut when you let go.

Disappearing doors

Doors can be mounted on sliding hinges so they pivot open, then slide into cabinet to remain out of the way. Side-mounted doors work well for television cabinet, as shown here. Doors can be top-mounted, too— an excellent solution for countertop appliance cabinets. Architect: William B. Remick.

Glass sliders

Bridge of black laminate cabinets spans concrete island. Glass doors keep glassware in view but dust-free. Instead of swinging out into the kitchen where they might cause an accident, these doors slide in grooves. Architect: Ted Tokio Tanaka.

Interior Shelves

The cabinet's most basic organizers—some typical choices

Standard adjusments

Adjustable shelves in manufactured cabinets typically rest on metal pins inserted into holes drilled in cabinet sides. This system is both adjustable and inconspicuous.

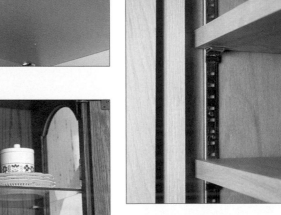

Tracks and clips

Screwed to cabinet's inner walls, track-and-clip system is highly adjustable. For a do-it-yourselfer, mounting tracks is much easier than aligning and drilling hundreds of holes for shelf pins.

See-through shelves

An elegant alternative to standard shelving, glass shelves are an excellent choice for display case or for high, light-duty shelves where you may want to identify contents from below.

Modified shelving

Particleboard shelves, edged with wood trim, are notched to receive cabinet's door-mounted spice rack when door closes. Shelves sit on dowel pegs pushed into holes drilled in groups of four.

Pull-out shelves for amplified access

Shelves mounted with drawer glides are a popular option in today's kitchen. Particularly in base cabinets, pull-out shelves allow you to reach items at very back quickly and easily. Architect: Woodward Dike.

Shelves or shallow drawers?

Concealed behind cabinet door, stack of shallow drawer/shelves keeps placemats organized. Low fronts leave contents highly visible and serve as drawer pulls. Architect: Bo-Ivar Nyquist.

Rising to the occasion

Spring-up shelf serves as storage area when down, work surface when up. Though hardware is relatively expensive, such a shelf is very handy for food processor or heavy mixer and can be adapted to most cabinets.

Adjustable pull-out

Special mounting tracks and brackets make this drawer-style shelf adjustable in height. Trade-off is loss of about 3 inches in shelf's width to accommodate hardware.

Drawers

Convenient, full-access storage solutions

Drawers galore

Long bank of drawers serves as primary storage in this kitchen. Drawers are efficient containers that offer full access to contents. Custom drawers like these are expensive; stock drawers, available in standard sizes at building supply centers, are more economical and can be adapted to fit most cabinetry—though often with some loss of storage space. Design: Pat Larin Interiors and City Cabinetmakers.

Drawers and more

Drawers come in all shapes and sizes. Cabinet door next to top oven is actually front of four-shelf drawer unit. Bottom cabinet houses two more drawers. Both units provide quick access to food and easily visible storage. Architect: Michael D. Moyer, The Architectural Design Group. Interior designer: Joan Simon.

Large-scale drawers

Beneath cooktop, wide drawers are sized to fit contents—cutlery and utensils on top, pots and pans below. Wide drawers require sturdy, heavy-duty glides and dual drawer pulls.

Touring a designer's kitchen

Bank of drawers (above) proves more efficient than regular cabinets with shelves. Two drawers are sized to hold standard boxes and metal container for flour. Carousel trays provide access to corner storage. Below sink (above right), large roll-out drawers disclose a trash can and cleaning supplies. Drawer beneath cooktop (right) holds pots; lids rest in a vertically divided drawer below. Jars in spice drawer are tilted for easy access. Design: Carlene Anderson, CKD.

Coated-wire baskets

Easily visible through coated wire, dishes can be removed from both sides of two-way cabinet. Place-mats and napkins lie flat in adjacent drawers. Baskets are often a less-expensive alternative to drawers and are better for storing foods that require ventilation—such as potatoes and onions. Architect: Gilbert Oliver. Interior designer: Nancy Brown, ASID.

Drawer Organizers

Keeping contents orderly and easy to find

For the ardent cook

An army of knives stands at the ready, sheathed in a series of knife blocks set in deep, full-extension drawer. On one flank, slanted racks in shallow drawers keep entire inventory of spices visible. In a home where children live or visit, child-safety latches should be added to knife drawer (see page 44). Design: Gordon Grover.

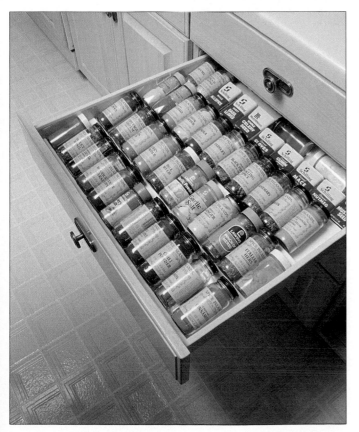

Three typical organizers

Most cabinet manufacturers offer drawer organizers as options. Here are three examples. At top left is a plastic flatware tray, exactly fitted to the drawer. Above, a wooden knife block organizes miscellaneous cutlery in shallow drawer. At left, spices rest on tiered, angled drawer divider. Cabinets: Wood-Mode.

Carousels & Lazy Susans

Hardware for reclaiming lost and hard-to-reach cabinet space

Semicircular swing-outs

Making the most of space that would otherwise be lost in a "blind" corner, coated wire shelves swing open, then pull out to provide complete access to contents. Kitchen design: Bob Easton Design Associates.

Cabinet roundabout

Difficult corner cabinet can be handled with an L-shaped door that opens both sides of corner. Built-in lazy Susan pivots for complete access. Raised edges on shelves prevent spills. Architect: Ron Yeo.

Pivoting appliance garage

Tiled, 10-foot-long island terminates at low wall where appliance garage swings out of semicircular storage unit separating kitchen counter from dining area. Architect: Craig Roland, Roland/Miller/Associates.

Upper-cabinet lazy Susan

L-shaped door pivots into corner cabinet to reveal three attached rounded shelves that maximize use of corner's depth. This, like other carousels and lazy Susans, is an option available from manufacturers.

Floor-to-ceiling lazy Susan

Taking a good idea to its logical conclusion, corner lazy Susan measures 12 feet from top to bottom. Three sections, reached through separate doors, turn independently of one another. Each ¾-inch plywood tray measures 36 inches in diameter and has an aluminum lip. Middle section stores most-used equipment, bottom section is for less-used items, and top—reached via ladder— is for kitchen gear that's seldom needed. Architect: William B. Remick.

Cabinet Pantries

High-density food storage in the center of your kitchen

Generous food drawers

Hidden behind tall cabinet doors, five large oak drawers mounted on heavy-duty guides are filled to capacity with food. Shortened drawer fronts allow a quick scan of contents. Of all cabinet pantry options, drawers give you the most high-density storage for your money. Kitchen design: Kathy Grundhoffer. Cabinets: Kitchens by Stewart (Wood-Mode).

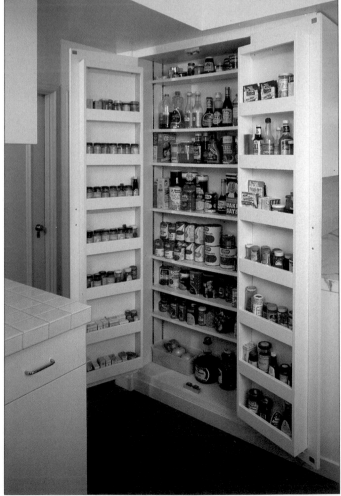

Narrow-and-wide pantry

Tall doors open to reveal a shallow pantry that divides available depth between doors and cabinet. Most goods are displayed in single ranks for simple selection and inventory. Architect: Hiro Morimoto/Atelier Architects.

Pull-out rack

When space is deep and narrow, pull-out rack on heavy-duty rollers offers effective storage for cans, bottles, and boxes. Architect: Steven Goldstein.

Fold-up pantry system

Unfolding like a child's puzzle, this pantry makes maximum use of standard cabinet dimensions. Door-mounted shelves, two-sided swing-out shelves, and more shelves at the back of the cabinet ensure access to every bit of space. Similar pantries are available through cabinet manufacturers. Design: Sarah Lee Roberts.

Specialty Accessories

Stretch your kitchen's usefulness with specialized fittings

The no-office office

At one end of contemporary kitchen, typewriter swings out and up from base cabinet. Files hang in special file "drawer" in cabinet at right; phone sits on counter. When not in use, this minimal home office completely disappears into cabinetry. Architect: Gilbert Oliver.

Instant table

Disguised as part of the cabinetry, tabletop pulls out of base cabinet. You can buy similar tables that, when fully extended, will seat up to five people.

Concealed laundry center

Sophisticated European fir cabinetry with black plastic laminate counters hides a pull-out ironing board and, in adjacent tall cabinet, a washer and dryer. Architect: Gilbert Oliver. Interior designer: Nancy Brown, ASID.

Wrinkle-free linens

Simple rack, built like a bottomless drawer with large dowels running from front to back, keeps table linens suspended in cabinet. Design: Wood-Mode.

Cleanup accessories

Beneath the kitchen sink, wire rack with adjustable shelves pulls out for easy access to cleaning supplies. When you open right-hand door, lid automatically lifts as trash can pivots out. Slim space in front of sink—normally wasted—holds narrow metal tray for sponges and scrubbers. Such accessories are available for many manufactured cabinet systems.

Space Extenders

Store-bought racks and holders that maximize storage

Shelving maximizers
Dinnerware, cups, and mugs stack on and hang from coated-wire shelf organizers. Several styles are available; shown here are a combination mug rack/shelf, a cup stacker, a shelf organizer for dinnerware and cups, and a shelf doubler.

Hanging shelves
Simple coated-wire hanging shelves slide onto existing shelving to reclaim lost space. Those shown here store placemats and napkins, adding much-needed shelf space quickly and inexpensively.

Undercabinet space-savers

Space beneath upper cabinets is maximized with specialty racks that store knives and stemware. You can buy similar racks to hold spices or cookbooks. Cabinet-mounted can openers, coffee makers, and other small appliances provide another way to take advantage of under-cabinet space.

Wire utility racks

For kitchen garbage bags or miscellaneous items, you can mount coated-wire racks to cabinet walls or doors. Door-mounted rack holds folded grocery bags as well as garbage sack.

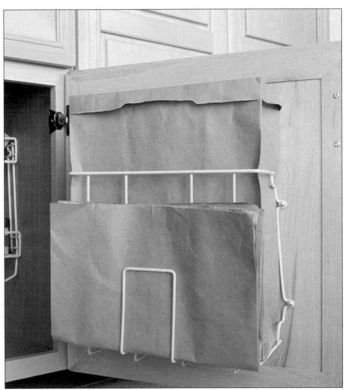

Organizers for pans and lids

Avoid jumbled pans and lids by filing them in wire organizers that sit on cabinet shelves or pull-outs. These inexpensive racks, and a potpourri of others similar to them, are available at home improvement centers.

Safety Hardware

Where small children are present, remember to childproof

Childproof latch

Spring-loaded latch screws easily onto doors or drawers. When door closes, latch hooks to underside of cabinet stile, allowing door to open only far enough for adult finger pressure to release it.

Padlock for doors

Where cabinet knobs or pulls pair up, simple plastic lock—similar to a bicycle padlock—secures them together. An adult presses plastic button to release lock.

Handy extinguisher

Be prepared for fire: mount a fire extinguisher near kitchen's exit, above small children's reach and at least 6 feet from kitchen range.

Child-safe cooking area

Wire corral (from a children's store), stuck to countertop with suction cups, keeps small fingers from reaching pots or burners. Pot handles are turned inward to prevent spills. Wall-mounted rack hangs utensils well out of reach. Plastic plugs seal off unused electrical outlets; latches lock doors shut. Design: Lizette Wilbur.

Complete Kitchen Safety

More often than not, the kitchen is the heart of the home, a place where both adults and children spend much of their time. Because it is essentially a work center, filled with machines, utensils, appliances, and other potentially dangerous tools, this is where accidents are most likely to occur. Small children are particularly susceptible; more children's lives are lost in home accidents than in all childhood diseases combined.

The following are a few important steps you can take to help ensure your family's safety in the kitchen. But be aware that childproofing requires a comprehensive approach. Children, in their boundless curiosity, inevitably will find the few hazards left unprotected. For more detailed information on making your entire home and yard safe for small children, see the Sunset book *Making Your Home Child-Safe.*

General Safety

Whether or not you have small children, consider taking these important precautions:

■ Install a smoke detector between the kitchen and living areas, and keep a Class A-B-C fire extinguisher handy. If a small fire starts, first remove everyone from danger; then use the extinguisher. But if a fire is out of control, stop using the extinguisher and get everyone out of the house.

■ Reduce fire potential by storing flammables away from heat. Clean the entire cooking area frequently; grease buildup can be dangerous, yet it often goes unnoticed on concealed surfaces.

A grease fire in a cooking pan on the stovetop is extinguished by placing a lid over the pan and turning off the heat. Lack of oxygen snuffs out the fire. *Never try to put out a grease fire with water.* To put out an oven fire, just shut the oven door and turn off the heat.

■ At the kitchen range, loose sleeves can catch fire easily; so can dishtowels used as pot holders. When cooking, wear trim-fitting clothes and use pot holders designed for the purpose.

■ Natural and LP gas are scented to alert you to leaks. For a major leak or service interruption, evacuate the house, turn off the main gas valve, and immediately call your utility company from a telephone outside your house. For minor leaking caused by a blown-out pilot, ventilate the room thoroughly. Then relight the pilot according to the manufacturer's instructions, or call your utility company.

Sparks can ignite gas— don't turn on electric switches or appliances if you suspect a leak.

■ To avoid carbon monoxide and nitrogen dioxide poisoning, make sure that your gas range has a hood fan or other exhaust fan that vents fumes to the outdoors. Never use a gas oven to heat your rooms, and never cook with charcoal indoors.

■ Use properly grounded outlets with adequate fuses or properly-sized circuit breakers. Don't overload circuits (hot plugs are a warning sign). Avoid outlet "extenders," or "cube taps" and extension cords.

■ Unplug appliances immediately after use. Keep appliances away from water; never touch water while you're using them. Always unplug appliances for cleaning or repairs.

If You Have Small Children...

When there are young children in the household, you should take several basic steps to minimize the possibility of their being injured in your kitchen.

■ Keep baby out from underfoot when working in the kitchen. A playpen or feeding table set a safe distance from the range and other hazards protects baby while allowing companionship with the cook.

■ Pick up and store anything that might be hazardous to your baby— small, sharp, breakable, or poisonous objects.

■ Remove dangerous items from any cabinets within your child's reach. In most kitchens, the place to start is under the sink. Move frequently used supplies, such as dishwasher detergent, to an upper cabinet with an easy-access latch (see photos on facing page). Put garbage in a container with a hard-to-open lid— or store it under the sink and install a child-resistant latch on that door.

Most kitchen cleansers and related chemicals are packaged in bright containers that may make them look edible or drinkable to a small, curious child. Don't leave any of these products within reach. And never store them in containers that originally held food or drink, such as soft-drink bottles.

Move liquor to a cabinet with a child-resistant latch or to an out-of-reach spot. Keep knives safely beyond your child's reach— yet convenient to you, so that you'll be sure to put them away again after use.

■ Don't let electrical cords dangle over countertop edges where they might be pulled. Put away all kitchen utensils after use. Small appliances should be unplugged when not in use and stored out of reach. Always remove and put away any sharp blades.

Design Workbook

Imagining your dream kitchen isn't enough. You want to make it *happen.* As anyone who has ever experienced a remodel will tell you, making the leap from fantasy to reality takes work.

Your first task—whether you're modifying your existing kitchen or building a new one— is to begin planning. Cabinets, appliances, counters, islands, pantries, plumbing, wiring—a variety of elements must be orchestrated carefully to create a kitchen that truly meets your family's needs.

Start with the main ingredient—the storage— and then work out the other components. On the facing page, you'll find some guidelines for basic kitchen planning. Turn to pages 48-53 for information on selecting and buying cabinets. For the complete story on planning and designing your kitchen, see the Sunset book *Kitchen Planning & Remodeling.*

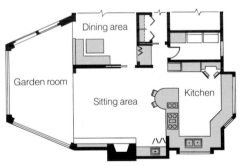

Planning pays off

Thoughtful kitchen design is keyed to family's living patterns. Layout creates comfortable work areas and small table for quick breakfasts; cabinetry provides storage that's efficient and accessible yet inconspicuous. Plan (above) shows how kitchen relates to the part of the home where family spends most of their time. Architect: Donald King Loomis. Interior designer: Ruth Livingston.

About Kitchen Planning

A few important fundamentals

Whether you're hiring a professional designer to plan your kitchen or doing the planning yourself, it's a good idea to consider a few basic design concepts in the early stages. This will help you to identify your needs and get a handle on what work will be involved.

If the scope of your project calls for it, work with a professional designer. Architects, interior designers, kitchen designers, and some kitchen showroom salespeople are experienced in designing kitchens; look under "Kitchen Cabinets" in your phone book. Cabinetmakers also often provide a design service when custom-building cabinets. Whomever you choose, be sure they are qualified in this specialized field. Ask for references, and visit actual installations they have designed. See page 51 for more about getting help.

Start your planning by taking graph paper and a tape measure in hand and drawing a basic floor plan of your existing kitchen, measuring as exactly as possible (within ⅛ inch). Include dimensions of walls, windows, and doors; indicate placement of existing cabinets, appliances, and lights. You'll need this floor plan for developing and communicating your ideas.

Though there is no formula for "the ideal kitchen," the guidelines discussed on this page have proven to be important in creating efficient, workable spaces.

Take Inventory

To determine the best storage for your kitchen's contents, first take an inventory of everything stored in your cabinets now. Then consider what else you would store if your kitchen were larger or more efficient. List all the various items, giving a rough idea of the space requirement for each. Then, as you develop kitchen plans, assign each item a space.

Divide & Conquer

When you're planning your kitchen, it's helpful to divide the room according to the functions to be performed in each different area. Though kitchen spaces are interrelated, it's easiest to examine their design elements separately.

Four centers are basic to most kitchens: sink, cooking, refrigerator, and preparation. In addition, you may want to include a planning/work center or possibly an entertaining center with a second sink.

Sink center. Besides the obvious—a sink—this center may include a dishwasher, garbage disposer, and trash compactor, as well as cabinets and drawers. This is where food is rinsed and trimmed, wastes and recyclables are disposed of, dishes are washed and stored.

Provide storage space for chopping board, food preparation utensils, trash, and dishwashing and cleaning supplies. Stow dishes and glassware as close as possible to the dishwasher for easy unloading.

Cooking center. The range—or separate cooktop and oven— is the focus of a cooking center, which may also include a microwave or convection oven and various electric cooking appliances. You may have more than one cooking center; the cooktop is handy to have central in the kitchen, but ovens may be more out of the way.

Near the appropriate appliances, store pots and pans, roasting racks, cooky sheets, and muffin tins. Keep cooking utensils and pot holders within easy reach.

Refrigerator center. This center may consist of not only a refrigerator and several cabinets, but perhaps also a floor-to-ceiling pantry wedged between refrigerator and adjacent wall. If you store nonperishable food items near the refrigerator, putting groceries away is a snap. Tuck plastic wrap, foil, plastic bags, and freezer containers into a nearby drawer or cabinet.

Preparation center. If you have enough room, design a food preparation center with storage for small appliances—food processor, toaster, mixer, and electric can opener, for example. Locating this center near the refrigerator and/or sink simplifies mixing and serving chores. Keep cookbooks and recipe boxes nearby. Store canisters, mixing bowls, and small utensils close at hand, and you'll waste little motion preparing meals.

Consider Layout

Locate the major appliances— sink, range or cooktop, and refrigerator— so that the resulting work triangle is out of the traffic pattern. For efficiency, position these three elements so that the distance between any two of them (measured from center front to center front) is at least 4 feet but no more than 9 feet. Keep the sum of the triangle sides to less than 26 feet.

Allow sufficient space between counters and around eating areas. You'll need at least 48 inches between opposite work counters; between a counter and an island, 36 inches may be ample. If two or more people are likely to share the kitchen, you may want to expand these dimensions. Be sure to plan adequate counter space for preparing foods, unloading groceries, processing dirty dishes, setting out dinner, and so forth.

Place tall appliances or cabinets on the ends of a run of counter to avoid interrupting the work flow. Allow clearance for swinging cabinet doors and front-opening appliances (for example, you'll need 20 inches in front of a dishwasher for loading).

Selecting Your Cabinets

Understanding what's available and figuring your needs

Professional help

In showroom of sample kitchens, professional designer demonstrates features of faceframe cabinet door. Kitchen cabinet showrooms are the best places to view a variety of styles; often they offer complete design services.

You've planned, figured, drawn, and considered. Now it's time to get down to business. You must select and order your new cabinets. Why is making a decision so difficult?

Cabinets have a greater impact on a kitchen's design than any other element. You know you'll live with your decision on a daily basis for years to come. And there are *so many* styles to consider.

To make the decision easier, you need to arm yourself with some basic knowledge. The information on these pages will show you the two ways all cabinets are constructed and the three possible ways you can buy cabinets. Basic cabinet units can be modified and organized in many different ways to create a functional kitchen. Your own particular space and budgetary considerations will help determine what's best for you.

Traditional or European-style?

One of the first choices to make is between traditional "faceframe" cabinets or European-style frameless cabinetry. As a rule, manufacturers specialize in one style or the other (though some manufacturers make both).

Faceframe cabinets. Until recently, traditional American cabinetmakers have masked the raw front edges of each cabinet box with a 1 by 2 "faceframe." Doors and drawers in such a cabinet fit in one of three ways: flush; partially inset, with a notch; or completely overlaying the frame. These are referred to as "flush," "offset," and "overlay," respectively.

Because the frame covers the edge, thin or low-quality panels or wood can be used in the sides of faceframe cabinets (thus reducing price). But the frame takes up space; it reduces the size of the opening, so drawers or slide-out accessories must be significantly smaller than the cabinet's width. In addition, typical door hinges for faceframe cabinets are visible from the front.

European-style frameless cabinets. Europeans, whose kitchens are often so tiny that all space counts, have been making "frameless" cabinets for years. Recently, American manufacturers have begun manufacturing these modular cabinets because of the system's popularity.

On frameless cabinets, a simple narrow trim strip covers raw panel edges, which butt directly against each other. All hardware (for doors, drawers, or accessories) mounts directly to the interior sides of the boxes; hinges are almost always invisible from the outside. Doors and drawers usually fit to within ¼ inch of each other, revealing little of the trim. Interior components— such as drawers— can be sized practically to the full interior dimension of the box.

Thanks to absolute standardization of every component, frameless cabinets are unsurpassed in versatility. Precise columns of holes are drilled on the inside faces. These holes are generally in the same places, no matter whose cabinets you buy, and components plug right into them.

The terms "system 32" and "32-millimeter" refer to the basic matrix of all these cabinets: all the holes, hinge fittings, cabinet joints, and mounts are set 32 millimeters apart.

Another big difference: frameless cabinets typically have a separate toe-space pedestal, or plinth. This allows you to set counter heights specifically to your liking, stack base units, or make use of space at floor level.

Stock, Custom, or Custom Modular?

Cabinets are manufactured and sold three different ways. The type you choose will affect the cost, appearance, and workability of your kitchen.

Stock cabinets. Buy your kitchen "off the shelf" and save— if you're careful. Mass-produced standard-size cabinets are the least expensive option, and they can be an excellent choice if you clearly understand the cabinetry you need for your kitchen. As the name implies, the range of sizes is limited.

Even so, you can always specify door styles, which direction doors swing, and whether side panels are finished. And you can often get options and add-ons such as breadboards, sliding shelves, and special corner units. Most stock systems also have cabinets that can be ordered for peninsulas or islands— with doors or drawers on both sides, and appropriate toes paces, trim, and finishes.

You may find stock lines heavily discounted at some home centers. But buying such cabinets can be a lot like doing your own taxes: no one really volunteers much information that will save you money or clarify your options— and if you make a mistake or get bad advice (even from a salesperson), you're the one who's liable. Knowledgeable people who can help you select stock cabinets tend to be the exception, not the rule.

Custom cabinets. Many people still have a cabinet-maker come to their house and measure, then return to the cabinet shop and build custom frame carcasses, drawers, and doors.

Custom cabinet shops can match old cabinets, size truly oddball configurations, and accommodate complexities that can't be handled with stock or modular cabinets. Such jobs generally cost considerably more than medium-line stock or modular cabinets.

Many cabinet shops take advantage of stock parts to streamline work and keep prices down. They buy door and drawer fronts from the same companies who make them for stock manufacturers. And cabinetmakers are using the same fine hardware (usually German) and tools (multiple-bit drills, metric hinge setters, and precise panel saws) developed for modular systems.

Some cabinet shops specialize in refacing existing kitchen cabinets. This can be an excellent, less-expensive choice than replacing the entire cabinet system, with results that look essentially the same as if you had done just that. Companies that will reface your existing cabinets also often buy mass-produced parts for the job.

Custom modular cabinets. Between stock and custom-made cabinetry are "custom modular cabinets" or "custom systems." Custom modular cabinets can

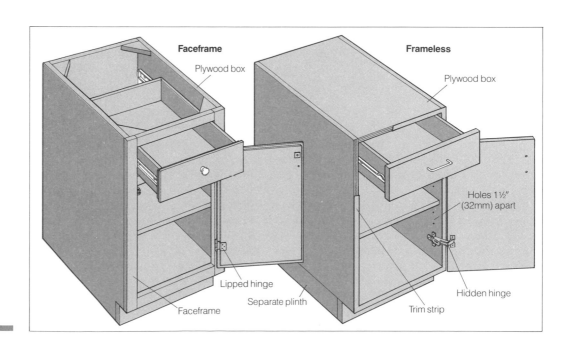

Traditional and European cabinets

Traditional faceframe cabinet (near right) has a wooden frame that covers the cabinet's front edges. European-style frameless cabinet (far right) eliminates frame— a simpler, more flexible system that takes better advantage of space.

Faceframe
Plywood box
Lipped hinge
Separate plinth
Faceframe

Frameless
Plywood box
Holes 1½" (32mm) apart
Hidden hinge
Trim strip

Comparing Cabinets

	STOCK	CUSTOM	CUSTOM MODULAR
Where to buy	Lumberyards, home improvement centers, appliance stores, some showrooms (most stock is made in this country).	Few shops have showrooms; most show pictures of completed jobs. Be safe; visit not only the shop but some installations, too.	If you know a brand name, check the yellow pages. These cabinets are mainly showroom items, but some are found in stock locations and department stores.
Who designs	You should, because the clerk helping you order may know less about cabinet options than you do. Don't order if you're at all unsure.	You; your architect, builder, or kitchen designer; or the maker (but be careful; cabinetmakers aren't necessarily designers).	The better (and more expensive) the line, the more help you get. Top-of-the-line suppliers design your whole kitchen; you just pick the style and write the check.
Cost range	Less than the other two choices, but you'll still swallow hard when you see the total. Look for heavy discounts at home centers, but pay attention to quality and craftsmanship.	Very wide; depends, as with factory-made boxes, on materials, finishes, craftsmanship, and options you choose.	A basic box can cost about what stock does, but each desirable modification or upgrade in door and drawer finishes boosts the cost considerably.
Options available	Only options may be door styles, hardware, and which way doors swing—but check the catalog; some lines offer a surprising range.	You can often—but not always—get the same options and European-made hardware that go in custom modular cabinets.	Most lines offer choices galore—including variations in basic sizes and options for corner spaces. Check showrooms and study catalogs.
Materials used	Cheaper lines may use doors of mismatched or lower-quality woods, composite, or thinner laminates that photo-simulate wood.	Anything you specify, but see samples. Methods vary by cabinetmaker; look at door and drawer hardware in a finished kitchen.	Factory-applied laminates and catalyzed varnishes are usually high quality and durable. Medium-density fiberboard is superior alternative for nonshowing wood.
Delivery time	You may be able to pick up cabinets at a warehouse the same day you order. Wait is generally (but not always) shorter than for other types.	Figure five weeks or longer, depending on job complexity, material and hardware availability, number of drawers, finishes.	Five to eight weeks is typical, whether cabinets are American or imported, but don't be surprised if they take up to six months. Order as soon as you know what you want.
Installation & service	Depends on where you buy; supplier may recommend a contractor. Otherwise, you install yourself. Service is virtually nonexistent.	In most cases, the maker installs. Buy from an established shop and you should have no trouble getting service if anything doesn't work right.	Better lines are sold at a price that includes installation and warranty (one of the reasons price is higher). Some cabinets are virtually guaranteed for life.
Other considerations	You often pay in full up front, giving you little recourse if cabinets are shipped wrong. Be sure order is absolutely correct and complete.	Make sure the bid you accept is complete—not just a basic cost-per-foot or cost-per-box charge.	With some manufacturers, if cabinets are wrong, you'll wait as long for the right parts to arrive as you did in the first place. Check.

offer the best of both worlds. They are manufactured, but they are of a higher grade and offer more design flexiblity than stock cabinets. Not surprisingly, they cost more, too.

Custom systems offer a wide range of sizes, with many options within each size. A good modular shop can do all but truly custom work, using its own components to build a kitchen from finished units. By modifying modular components, you come close to custom cabinetry.

You can change practically everything on these basic modules: add sliding shelves; replace doors with drawers; set a matching hood unit over the stove; add wire baskets, flour bins, appliance garages, and pull-out pantries.

The key to the versatility of these systems is that, if necessary, basic dimensions can be modified to fit virtually any kitchen configuration. Heights, widths, and depths can be changed so that you can adjust units to practically any size.

Though frameless modular cabinets (see pages 48-49) are sized metrically (standard cabinet depth is 60 centimeters— about 24 inches), virtually all lines are now sized for American appliances. And sizes break into about 3-inch increments, with custom dimensions available.

What Options Are Available?

Perhaps more options exist for corners than for any other kitchen cabinet space. If you don't use specially designed cabinets in corners, you'll lose a lot of valuable space. The simplest corner butts one cabinet against another, providing inconvenient access to the corner. Better options include diagonal units with a larger door, double-door units that provide full access to the L-shaped space, and lazy Susans or other slide-out accessories that bring items from the back up to the front.

Many hardware options are available to add to the versatility of kitchen cabinets. You'll find examples throughout this book, particularly on pages 26-41.

Judging Quality

To determine quality in cabinetry, look closely at the drawers; they take more of a beating than any other part of the cabinet. Compare drawers in several lines of cabinets, examining the joinery of each, and you'll see differences.

Drawer guides and cabinet hinges are the critical hardware elements. Check for adjustability of both; you should be able to reset and fine-tune them with the cabinets in place. Some frameless cabinets also have adjustable mounting hardware, so you can relevel them even after they've been hung on the wall. Determine whether drawer glides allow full or only partial extension of drawers. Check to see that doors and drawers align properly.

Getting Help

The cabinets are only part of the puzzle. When you buy cabinets, some of what you're paying for is varying degrees of help with kitchen design.

A kitchen designer will help you figure out how you'll use your kitchen. Some retailers will have you fill out a questionnaire to help determine what's wrong with your current kitchen, how often you do any specialty cooking, whether your guests always end up in the kitchen, whether you buy food in bulk, and other clues in reaching a design solution.

A showroom with many lines of cabinets will give you a better idea of what you want—and the designer a sense of what you're after. Pick a look, and then shop for it; compare features, craftsmanship, and cost. If you're serious about buying, make an appointment with a showroom (try to make it for a time when the place won't be too busy). Some showrooms will also carry the other kitchen components you'll need, such as counters, appliances, sinks, and fixtures.

Some designers may represent a particular line of cabinets, so shop around to get an idea of what's available. Once you become serious, be sure that you like the particular line of cabinets a showroom designer handles.

Your current floor plan is the best aid you can offer a designer (see page 47). Some staff designers in showrooms will do the new cabinet plan for you, applying the charge against the purchase price of cabinets. In fact, some retailers offer a complete kitchen planning service when you buy their cabinets. Some showrooms even use computer renderings to help customers visualize the finished kitchen— and prices for different cabinet configurations are just a keystroke away.

Your budget will affect more than your choice of cabinets. Often you can pay less for some lines by shopping where design services aren't necessarily included. But keep in mind that as you step down in price, you must take on more and more responsibility yourself; *you* have to guarantee the accuracy of every step in the process.

Figuring Costs & Ordering

There are no figures under "Cost range" in the chart at left. Why? Because so many factors influence the final price. The kitchens shown in this book have cabinets that range from about $400 to more than $80,000.

The range of styles—and prices—makes buying cabinets much like buying a car. Like car makers, every manufacturer or cabinetmaker picks a market position, then offers various styles and options that jack up or bring down the price. If you're looking for the cabinet equivalent of "transportation," you can pay a lot less than someone looking for something sportier.

Know your budget. You'll quickly find out what kinds of cabinets you can afford. With your plan in hand, you can get a base price for standard cabinets relatively easily. But options will drastically alter the quote—so the same basic cabinet can end up costing a lot of different prices. Be sure to obtain quotes based on a fully specified room sketch listing the options desired in each cabinet.

Within each line of cabinets, basic costs are determined by the style of the doors and drawers. The basic frame carcass will be the same within a line no matter what door style you choose. Wood choices can also affect price.

In many showrooms, you can get a general idea of costs by asking dealers for the prices of components in sample kitchens. A good showroom has an advantage over most custom shops: you can see many of the possibilities set up in one place.

Even if you're buying manufactured cabinets, consider getting an estimate from a custom shop for comparison. Such a shop can match practically any style or can come up with a pattern or finish not available in a modular or stock line. A cabinetmaker will come to your home to measure your kitchen and give you a price quotation; generally there is no charge for this.

As with stock and custom modular bids, make sure your plan is specific enough to obtain a reliable quote and to eliminate any misunderstanding as to what you're ordering.

Typical Cabinets

Stock and modular cabinets come in many styles—here is a representative variety

Just as appliances come in standard sizes, so do cabinets. Look around your kitchen; you'll see base cabinets that sit on the floor and wall cabinets that screw to the wall. All kitchens contain some combination of these two, and most include a few variations that don't quite fit in either category. Illustrated on these two pages are a few of the many different styles and configurations of stock and modular cabinets.

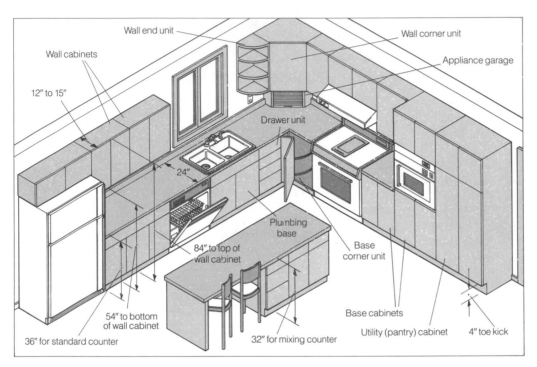

Wall end unit
Wall cabinets
12" to 15"
Wall corner unit
Appliance garage
Drawer unit
24"
Plumbing base
84" to top of wall cabinet
Base corner unit
54" to bottom of wall cabinet
36" for standard counter
32" for mixing counter
Base cabinets
Utility (pantry) cabinet
4" toe kick

Basic units of cabinetry

Typical kitchen utilizes base cabinets, upper wall cabinets, and upper and lower corner and end units. In addition, you can get 7- or 8-foot-tall utility cabinets, special bases that hold a kitchen sink, and matching facades for dishwasher, refrigerator, and other appliances.

Straight upper wall cabinets

Wall cabinets come in singles, doubles, and various specialty configurations. Typically 12 (or 15) inches deep, they can vary in width from 9 to 60 inches. Though the most frequently used heights are 15, 18, and 30 inches, wall cabinets range from 12 to 36 inches high, or more.

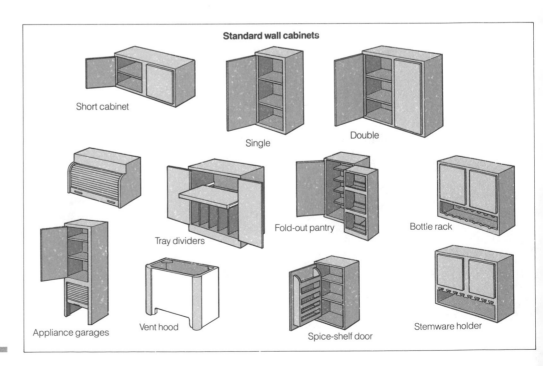

Standard wall cabinets

Short cabinet
Single
Double
Tray dividers
Fold-out pantry
Bottle rack
Appliance garages
Vent hood
Spice-shelf door
Stemware holder

Upper corners and ends

Special cabinets take advantage of areas where upper wall cabinets terminate or turn a corner. End cabinets offer simple shelves or narrow enclosures. Corner cabinets may have angled or curved doors, tamboured appliance garages, or lazy Susans. These cabinets are sized to match other wall cabinets.

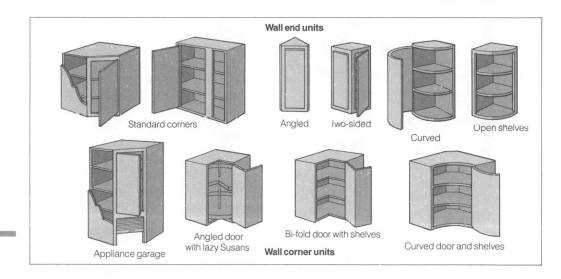

Wall end units

Standard corners Angled Two-sided Curved Open shelves

Appliance garage Angled door with lazy Susans Bi-fold door with shelves Curved door and shelves

Wall corner units

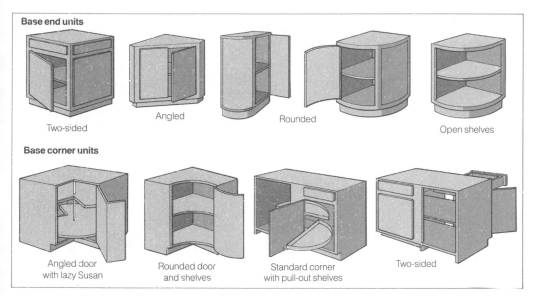

Base end units

Two-sided Angled Rounded Open shelves

Base corner units

Angled door with lazy Susan Rounded door and shelves Standard corner with pull-out shelves Two-sided

Base corners and ends

Corner base units come in at least a dozen configurations; a few are shown here. Lazy Susans and diagonal units use space efficiently. End cabinets may offer storage accessible from both front and side.

Base cabinets

When complete with a toe kick or plinth, base cabinets normally measure 34½ inches tall; the counter adds another 1½ inches. In width, they range from 9 to 60 inches, increasing in increments of 3 inches from 9 to 36 inches and increments of 6 inches after that. Standard depth is 24 inches. Typically, a base cabinet offers one shelf and a drawer above a door, but—as you can see— many options are available.

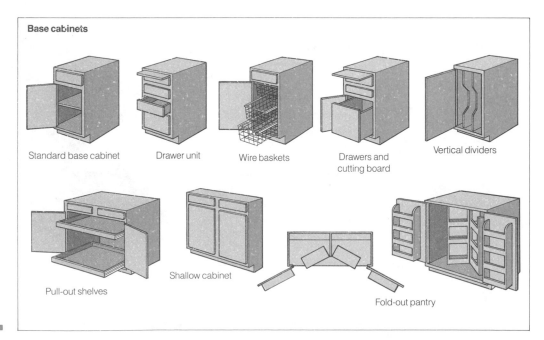

Base cabinets

Standard base cabinet Drawer unit Wire baskets Drawers and cutting board Vertical dividers

Pull-out shelves Shallow cabinet Fold-out pantry

How To Store...

What is the best way to store a food processor? How about large bowls or pans? What about onions? Every element that goes into the kitchen should be stored appropriately— but what is appropriate for the variety of utensils, foods, and other items we store?

This chapter focuses on the best ways to deal with the foods and paraphernalia we pack into our kitchens. Alphabetically, it offers an item-by-item catalog of both standard and creative answers to specific kitchen storage needs.

Appliances

Sometimes small appliance storage involves no more than pushing a blender into a corner. But with the proliferation of kitchen appliances, counters can be overrun in no time with toasters, coffee makers, can openers, juicers, blenders, and so on. Less-used appliances, such as waffle irons and slow-cookers, often disappear into the forgotten recesses of cabinetry. Shown on these two pages are a few better ways to store small appliances.

Convenient base-cabinet storage

Small appliances, particularly those needed infrequently, can be stored in corners of base cabinets— just be sure to provide easy access for handling their large, bulky shapes. Interior corner offers lazy Susan, end cabinet opens on two sides. Large, lower drawers can hold smallest appliances.

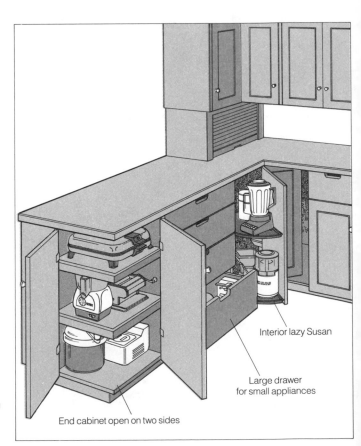

Interior lazy Susan

Large drawer for small appliances

End cabinet open on two sides

Pull-outs, swing-ups, and space savers

At left, lift mechanism brings heavy appliances up to counter height, adds to work surface; accessories store below it. Sliding lid on deep upper drawer serves as surface for mixer or appliance stored inside. Below, a number of kitchen appliances are available in space-saving versions. Cabinet- and wall-mounted styles mount easily; built-ins are a bit more challenging.

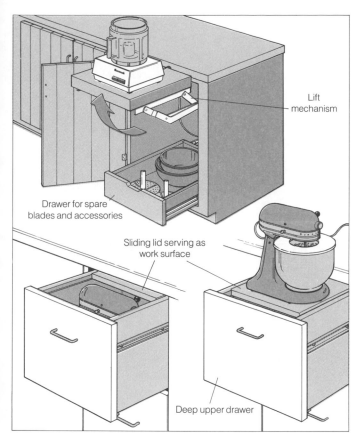

Lift mechanism

Drawer for spare blades and accessories

Sliding lid serving as work surface

Deep upper drawer

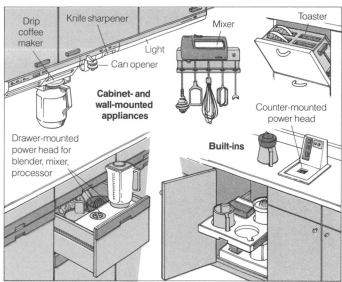

Drip coffee maker

Knife sharpener

Light

Can opener

Mixer

Toaster

Cabinet- and wall-mounted appliances

Counter-mounted power head

Drawer-mounted power head for blender, mixer, processor

Built-ins

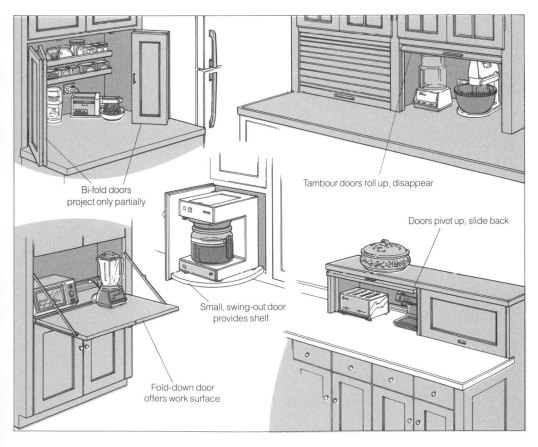

Bi-fold doors project only partially

Tambour doors roll up, disappear

Doors pivot up, slide back

Small, swing-out door provides shelf

Fold-down door offers work surface

Appliances behind doors

Doors that work best for enclosing small appliances are those that stay out of the way when they are open. Bi-folds, tambours, fold-downs, and pivoting/sliding doors are favorites. Stock hardware is available for all.

Bottles

What are the best ways to store soda, liquor, vinegar, oil, and other products that come in tall, awkwardly shaped, breakable bottles? On these two pages, you'll find helpful storage ideas for bottled products.

Wine requires a little extra consideration. To store it properly, place wine on its side and keep it at a relatively cool, constant temperature (around 60°F/16°C), away from bright sunlight and vibration. In an air-conditioned house, location is less critical than in a house with fluctuating temperatures. Don't worry about jug wines or other wines you intend to drink soon after purchase—just place them upright, anywhere that's cool.

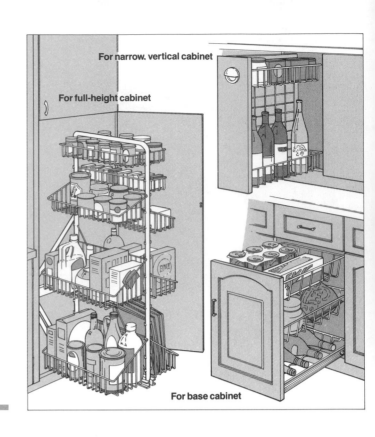

Pull-out racks

For efficient storage of bottles and all sorts of other goods, cabinetmakers and manufacturers can install coated-wire pull-out racks in various configurations.

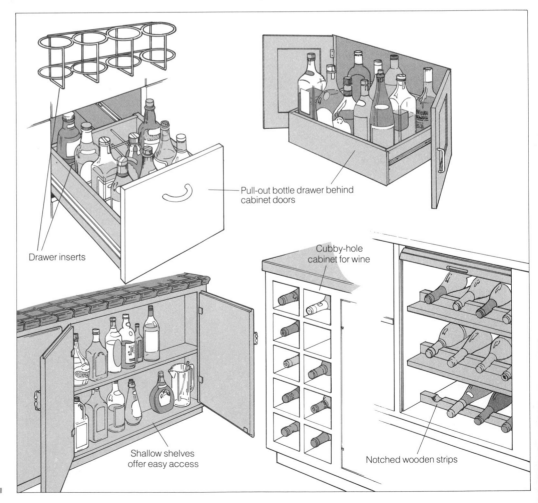

Bottle drawers and shelves

Store bottles deep in your cabinets by placing them in drawers. Drawer inserts available through some cabinet shops keep bottles organized and upright. Shallow shelves also provide easy access to bottles. For horizontal wine storage, you can buy stock cubbyhole cabinets or add notched wooden strips to shelves.

For narrow, vertical cabinet

For full-height cabinet

For base cabinet

Pull-out bottle drawer behind cabinet doors

Drawer inserts

Cubby-hole cabinet for wine

Shallow shelves offer easy access

Notched wooden strips

Easy-to-make wine racks

Wine bottles stay organized and accessible in these three easy-to-make racks. At upper left, 6-inch lengths of 4-inch-diameter PVC pipe are glued together and installed in a base cabinet. At right, store-bought shelf tracks and brackets support 1 by 2s cut to hold wine bottles. Stacking, modular rack at lower left is made by cutting half-circles and interlocking ⅜-inch by ¾-inch notches in pine 1 by 4s.

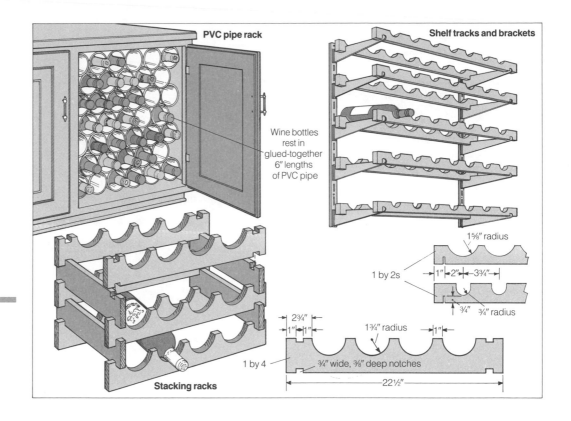

PVC pipe rack

Shelf tracks and brackets

Wine bottles rest in glued-together 6" lengths of PVC pipe

1⅝" radius

1 by 2s

1" 2" 3¾"

¾" ¾" radius

2¾"

1" 1"

1¾" radius

1"

1 by 4

¾" wide, ⅜" deep notches

22½"

Stacking racks

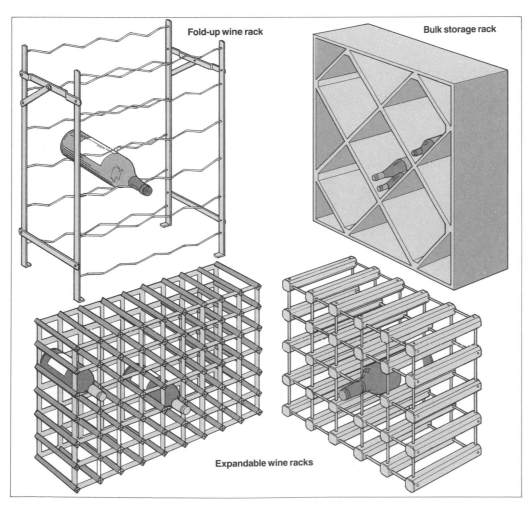

Fold-up wine rack

Bulk storage rack

Expandable wine racks

Wine racks you can buy

Many styles of wine racks are sold at specialty and department stores. Some, like fold-up version at upper left, hold a given number of bottles; others expand to grow with your collection. Model at upper right lets you stack bottles within cubicles for maximum use of space.

Cleaning Supplies

Is the cabinet under your kitchen sink a catchall for jumbled sponges, dishcloths, scouring pads, detergent, and cleanser? Are mops and brooms tangled together in a closet? Cleanup is rarely fun, but you can make it less of a chore through effective organization and accessible storage of supplies. Here are a few ideas for organizing your cleaning gear.

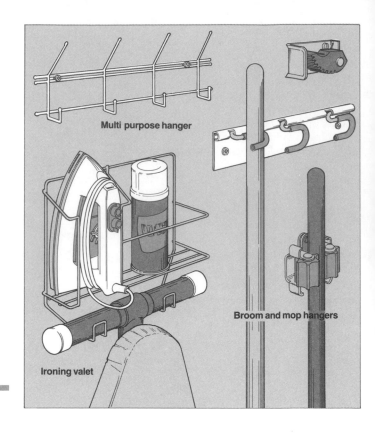

Multi purpose hanger

Broom and mop hangers

Ironing valet

Cleanup hang-ups

Simple organizers make broom closets or utility cabinets tidy. Available at hardware stores and home-improvement centers, special hangers hold broom and mop handles, cleaning supplies—even ironing gear.

Ultimate undersink cabinet

To maximize the awkward space beneath the kitchen sink, turn it into a cleanup center with pull-out trash can and wire storage bins and door-mounted racks for paper towels, grocery bags, dishtowels, and cleansers. Tilt-out tray in front of sink holds sponges and scrubbers. If you have small children in your home, don't forget to add childproof latches to cabinet doors.

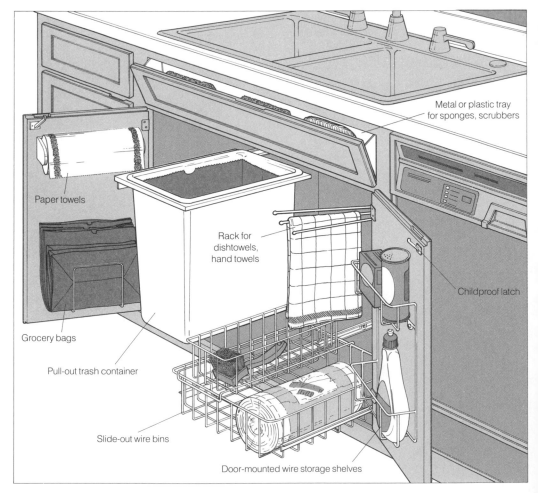

Metal or plastic tray for sponges, scrubbers

Paper towels

Rack for dishtowels, hand towels

Childproof latch

Grocery bags

Pull-out trash container

Slide-out wire bins

Door-mounted wire storage shelves

Holding the bags

Grocery bags stay put if slipped between vertical dividers in a narrow cabinet. Or you can build a simple rack into wall between studs or buy a wire holder to mount on a cabinet door.

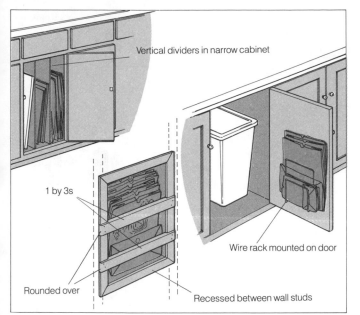

Vertical dividers in narrow cabinet

1 by 3s

Rounded over

Wire rack mounted on door

Recessed between wall studs

Cleanser carryalls

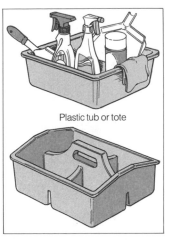

Plastic tub or tote

Household cleaning supplies can be stored under the sink in a small plastic tub or utility tote, then moved en masse to wherever they're needed on cleaning day.

Paper towel holders

Keep paper towels handy by mounting a holder to the underside of a cabinet or onto the backsplash wall, fitting one inside a cabinet (accessible by means of a slot cut in the bottom shelf), or setting out a freestanding model on the countertop.

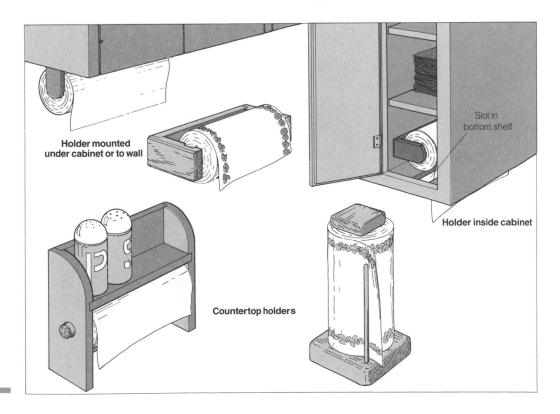

Holder mounted under cabinet or to wall

Slot in bottom shelf

Holder inside cabinet

Countertop holders

Cutlery & Flatware

When the vegetables are chopped and butter begins to melt in the pan, you don't want to have to go on a spatula hunt. If you seem to be burning butter frequently in pursuit of the right cooking implement, perhaps it's time to organize your utensils.

An efficient kitchen has drawers divided to keep flatware and cooking utensils tidy. Knives are stored safely, conveniently, and in a way that won't dull their edges. Many cabinet manufacturers now offer drawers with dividers as part of their stock cabinetry. In addition, you can buy any of a number of divided trays or baskets to slip into drawers.

Valuable silver should be stored in a secure place—perhaps a compartment behind a false kick-space panel. Wherever you put silver, enclose it in layers of flannel or special tarnish-retardant cloth to block air flow and cut down on the need for polishing.

Store-bought knife racks

A purchased knife rack can be mounted on the wall or on the inside surface of a cabinet door, or a knife block can sit on top of the counter near your preparation area. Look for these and similar models at department, cookware, and cutlery stores.

Wall- or door-mounted rack

Freestanding blocks

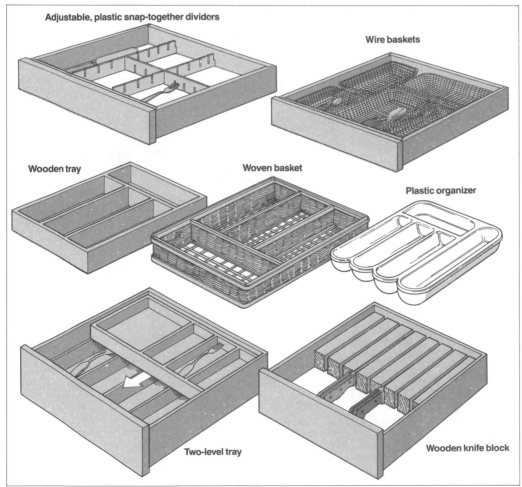

Adjustable, plastic snap-together dividers

Wire baskets

Wooden tray

Woven basket

Plastic organizer

Two-level tray

Wooden knife block

Drawer organizers for flatware and knives

Compartmented organizers keep flatware, knives, and other utensils sorted and help minimize scratches and dulled blades. You can choose from a wide variety of such dividers, from woven baskets to custom two-level trays.

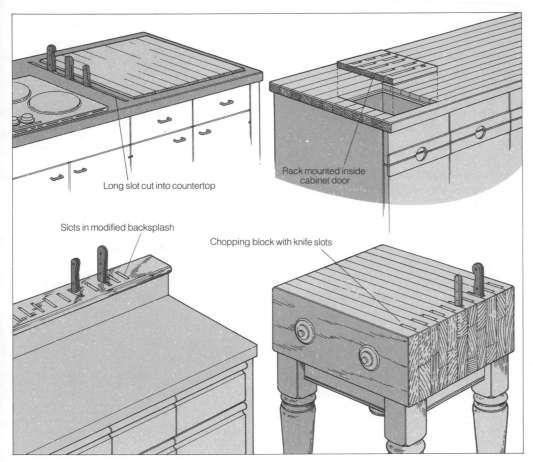

Long slot cut into countertop

Rack mounted inside cabinet door

Slots in modified backsplash

Chopping block with knife slots

Drop-in knives

To minimize countertop clutter and still keep knives where you need them, build a knife block into the counter. Or you can use specially made chopping blocks or modifications to countertops to provide convenient storage. Just be sure blades extend down into unused space, so they can't cut anyone.

Knife holders you can make

Here are two knife racks you can make yourself— a freestanding wooden knife block and an acrylic-covered wall rack.

For the block, use a radial arm or table saw to cut grooves down the entire length of a 4-foot 2 by 8, making them half the desired finished depth. Cut the board into four equal lengths and, with grooves aligned, glue, clamp, sand, and apply oil or other clear finish.

Wall rack is easy to assemble from 1 by 2s and a ⅛- or ¼-inch clear acrylic sheet.

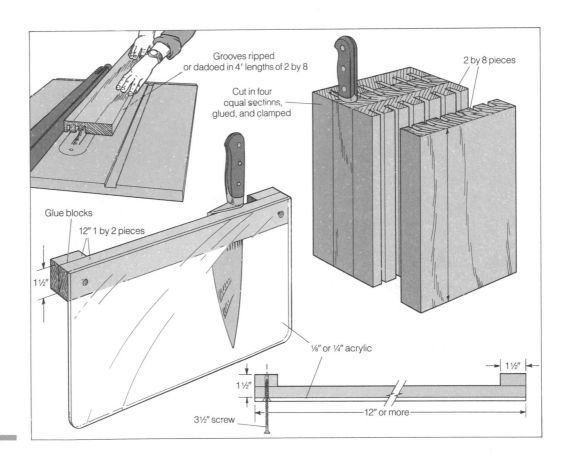

Grooves ripped or dadoed in 4' lengths of 2 by 8

Cut in four equal sections, glued, and clamped

2 by 8 pieces

Glue blocks

12" 1 by 2 pieces

1½"

⅛" or ¼" acrylic

1½"

1½"

3½" screw

12" or more

Dishes & Glassware

Store everyday dishes and glassware in cabinets that are convenient to the dishwasher, refrigerator, and serving areas. Shelves in upper cabinets are usually most convenient. Some people prefer base-cabinet drawers for dishes—but remember that they can chip or crack if drawers are slammed or moved too abruptly.

It's often best to store tableware used mostly for entertaining near the dining room. You may want to display china, crystal, and silver behind glass doors. If so, consider glass shelves for unobstructed viewing.

Custom shelving to organize dinnerware

The more fitted shelving is to its contents, the more efficiently it utilizes space. Here are examples of custom shelving that both organizes and displays its contents.

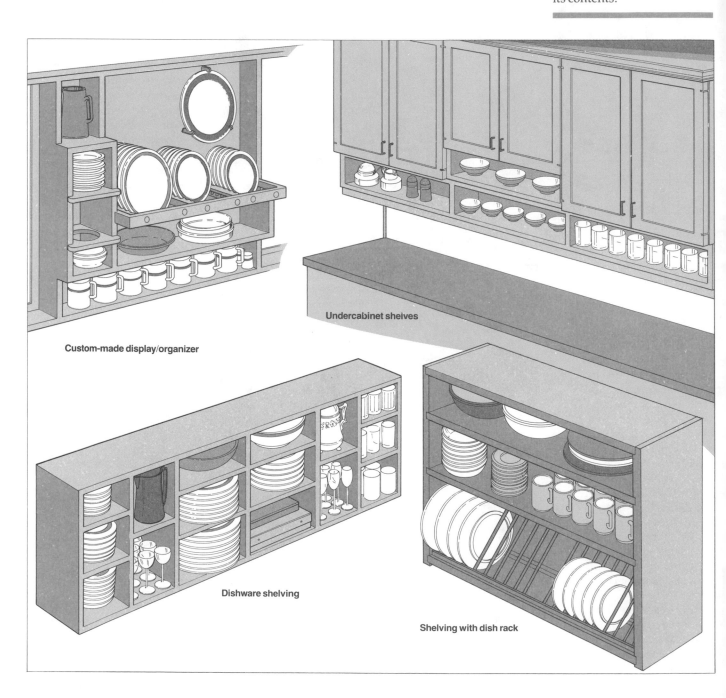

Custom-made display/organizer

Undercabinet shelves

Dishware shelving

Shelving with dish rack

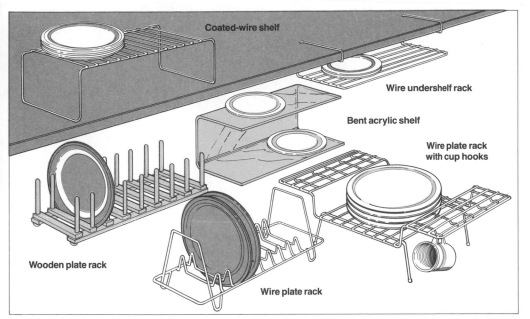

Coated-wire shelf

Wire undershelf rack

Bent acrylic shelf

Wire plate rack
with cup hooks

Wooden plate rack

Wire plate rack

Shelf maximizers

Numerous products are available for extending the storage capacity of standard shelves. These organizers can double or triple usable space, protect dishes, and make access easier.

For more examples, see pages 42 and 43.

Stemware hangers

Inexpensive and effective commercially available hangers for stemware can be mounted to the underside of upper cabinets, onto cabinet sides, or directly to walls. (Also see page 43.)

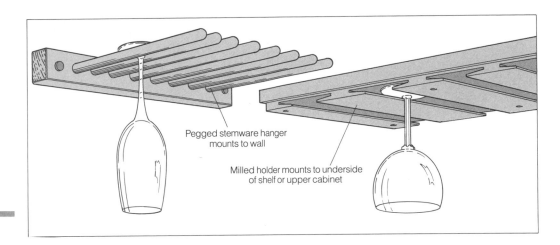

Pegged stemware hanger mounts to wall

Milled holder mounts to underside of shelf or upper cabinet

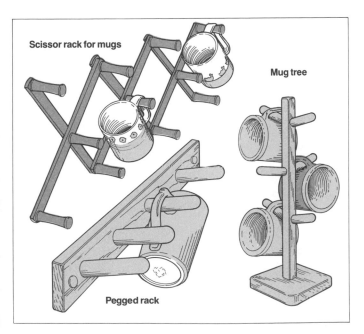

Scissor rack for mugs

Mug tree

Pegged rack

Mug racks

Mugs can take up considerable cabinet space. Instead of setting them on shelves, hang mugs from inexpensive wall- or door-mounted racks. You can buy a "scissor" rack that holds many mugs, a Shaker-style peg rack, or a freestanding mug tree.

Foods: Boxed & Canned

The average American kitchen is stocked with more canned and boxed foods than any other type of edibles: canned soups, vegetables, fruits, meats; boxed cereals, crackers, pastry mixes; and many more packaged foods. Not only are these products easy to serve —they're easy to store and long-lived if unopened. Canned meat, fish, vegetables, and soups last up to 2 years in dry, relatively cool cupboards. Unopened cereals and boxed goods typically last from 3 to 12 months in cool, dry, vermin-free storage. On these two pages, you'll find a number of ways to get the most from your cupboards when storing boxed and canned foods.

Shelves and drawers for boxes and cans

Shelves, drawers, and drawer-like baskets are common facilities for storing boxes and cans. Upper-cabinet shelves, typically 12 inches deep, allow easy access to a single line-up of boxes.

By slanting deep shelves and adding a lip to the front edge (upper right), you can create deep storage that automatically feeds cans toward the front when you pull one out—a method that works well if you store multiples of certain foods or drinks.

For deeper lower cabinets, pull-outs work best. Baskets or drawers with short fronts allow you to locate goods before pulling them out.

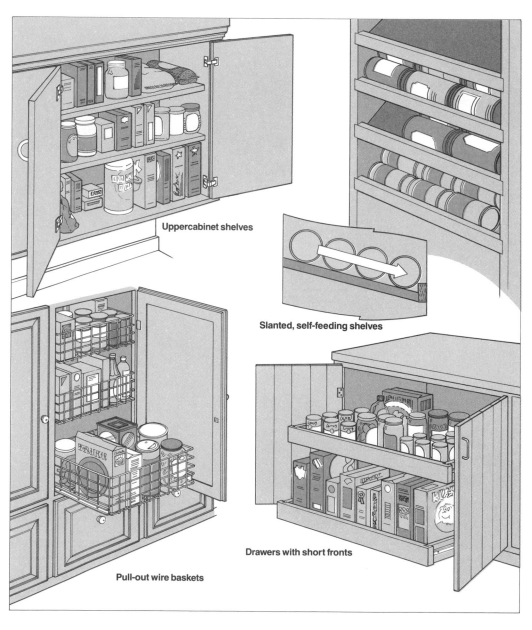

Uppercabinet shelves

Slanted, self-feeding shelves

Pull-out wire baskets

Drawers with short fronts

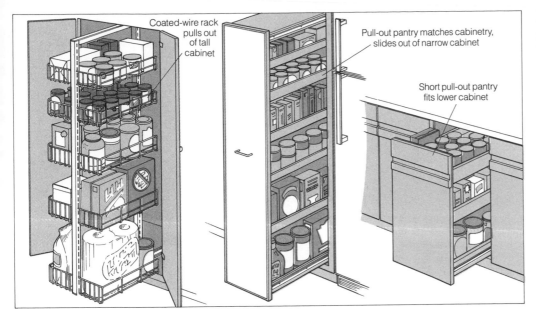

Coated-wire rack pulls out of tall cabinet

Pull-out pantry matches cabinetry, slides out of narrow cabinet

Short pull-out pantry fits lower cabinet

Pull-out pantries

Sliding smoothly on ball-bearing glides, pull-out pantries offer efficient storage for cans and boxed foods. Coated-wire rack has adjustable shelves, fits in tall, narrow space. Narrow wooden rack matches cabinets. Short rack in deep cabinet uses space that would be hard to reach without pull-out hardware.

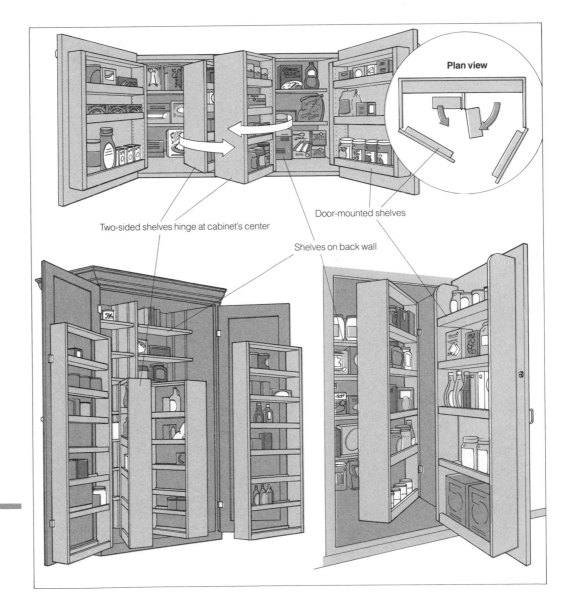

Plan view

Two-sided shelves hinge at cabinet's center

Door-mounted shelves

Shelves on back wall

Fold-out food storage

Loaded with storage for boxes, cans, and jars, fold-out pantries have several layers of shelving—mounted on the back wall, attached to the door, and pivoting on hinges at cabinet's center. Such systems are relatively expensive but worth the money if storage space is tight.

Foods: Dry Goods

Rice, flour, pasta, cereals, and other similar foods will keep for a long time if properly stored. Most dry goods last about a year (the rising agent in self-rising flour may degenerate after about 6 months). But because of the threat of insects spreading among grains and other dry goods, the best storage is in sealed containers where the foods remain isolated and dry. Keep foods near where you will use them.

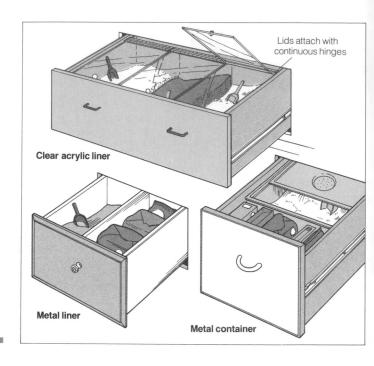

Lids attach with continuous hinges

Clear acrylic liner

Metal liner

Metal container

Drawers for dry goods

Metal or plastic liners in drawers can provide convenient, sealed storage for dry goods. Some types of drawer liners are available as stock items. Others, such as the clear acrylic liner shown at top, must be custom fabricated.

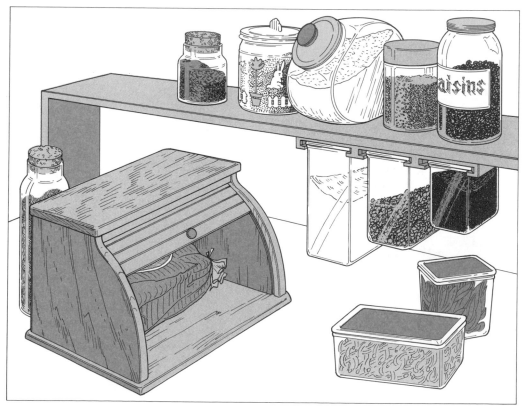

Storage containers

Airtight cannisters, clear plastic stackable containers, jars with tight-fitting lids—you'll find a wide variety of storage containers made for storing pastas, beans, nuts, and other dry goods. The classic bread box keeps breads dry and close at hand.

Foods: Produce

The refrigerator is a kitchen's main facility for storing produce, but not the only one. Fruit baskets, coated-wire baskets, and even old-fashioned cooling cupboards vented to the outdoors are a few other possibilities. Different fruits and vegetables may require different storage conditions—listed below are a few guidelines.

■ Though chilled storage isn't mandatory for fruits and vegetables, most produce lasts longer in the refrigerator. Refrigerate most fruits and vegetables unwashed (so they remain dry), in plastic or paper bags. Though most vegetables stay freshest in plastic bags, some (corn, chives, mushrooms, whole squash, and lettuce, for example) keep best wrapped in paper towels first. Be sure to seal cut melons in plastic bags—they give off ethylene gas, which can hasten spoilage of other produce in the refrigerator.

■ Garlic, dry onions, and potatoes keep best unwrapped in a cool (50° F), dry, dark place with good ventilation (they'll last up to 2 months).

■ Unripe fruit such as avocados or pears ripens best when placed in a loosely closed paper bag at room temperature (turn fruit occasionally). Leave bananas uncovered at room temperature to ripen.

■ Tomatoes can be stored unwashed at room temperature, stem end down, until slightly soft, then refrigerated.

■ Avoid storing overly ripe, bruised, or damaged produce. The bad apple *will* spoil the whole bunch.

Stacking or rolling baskets

Coated-wire or plastic baskets offer ventilated storage for fruits and vegetables that don't require refrigeration—especially those you'll be eating within a couple of days. Storing in cool, dark areas is best.

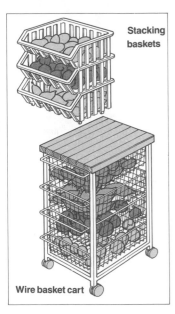

Stacking baskets

Wire basket cart

Drawers and bins

Cabinetmakers can build custom drawers or bins for produce. Tilt-down glass or plastic-front bins are a popular choice for fruits that don't require air circulation, such as citrus. Mesh-bottom or front ventilated drawers or basket inserts can store garlic, dry onions, and potatoes.

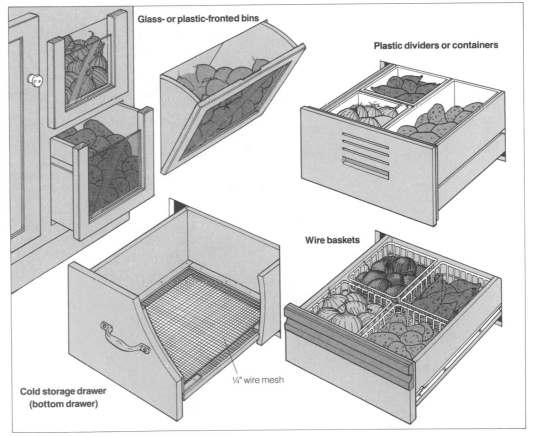

Glass- or plastic-fronted bins

Plastic dividers or containers

Wire baskets

Cold storage drawer (bottom drawer)

¼" wire mesh

Linens for Dining

The ideal storage for table linens keeps them wrinkle-free. With placemats and napkins, this is relatively easy; large tablecloths present more of a challenge. Placemats and napkins can be kept neat in shallow drawers or on short shelves. Tablecloths store best when hung from dowels or slats. If your cabinets can't provide the generous space needed for hanging tablecloths, you can minimize wrinkles by rolling the cloths around large mailing tubes and giving the rolls plenty of room in a shallow drawer.

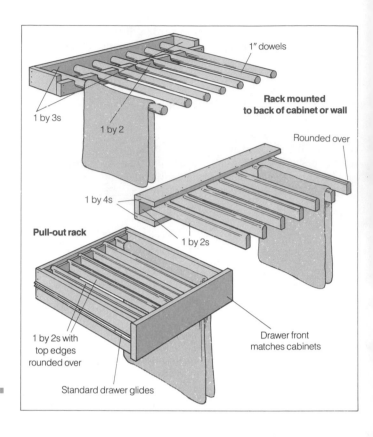

1" dowels

Rack mounted
to back of cabinet or wall

1 by 3s

1 by 2

Rounded over

1 by 4s

Pull-out rack

1 by 2s

1 by 2s with
top edges
rounded over

Standard drawer glides

Drawer front
matches cabinets

Racks for tablecloths

If your cabinets are roomy enough, a wall-mounted or pull-out rack is the best way to store tablecloths. Such racks are easy to make from standard lumber and dowels; pull-out rack mounts on standard drawer glides.

Napkin and placemat placement

Shallow drawers provide convenient, dust-free storage for placemats and napkins. Closely spaced shelves, pull-out baskets, and wire trays that hang from shelves are other good solutions.

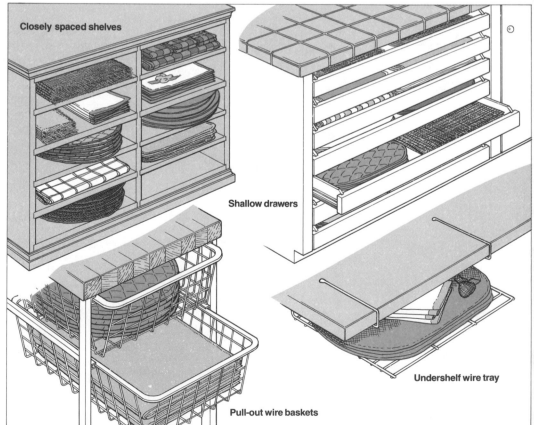

Closely spaced shelves

Shallow drawers

Pull-out wire baskets

Undershelf wire tray

Mixing Bowls

Though large bowls are indispensible for preparing and serving food, they top the list of space-gobblers in cabinets. When designing your kitchen storage system, it's important to provide ample, appropriate storage for large bowls.

Where you put them will depend upon how frequently they're needed. Some you may use daily, while others—a large punch bowl, for example—can stay stashed away for occasional parties. Bowls you use often can be stored in base cabinets on pull-out drawers or corner carousels where they're easy to get to but don't block other supplies. Find space for infrequently needed bowls on top shelves of upper cabinets, or even in another room.

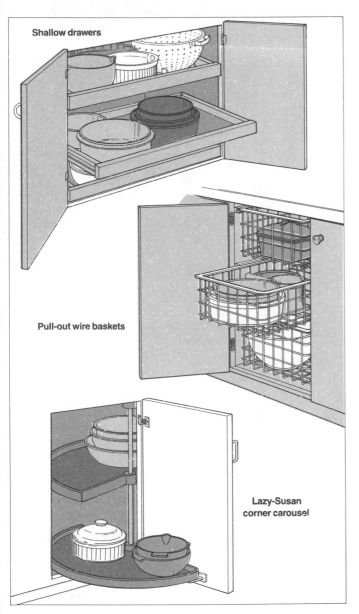

Shallow drawers

Pull-out wire baskets

Lazy-Susan corner carousel

Bowls in base cabinets

Large bowls stay accessible yet out of the way if you place them in shallow drawers behind cabinet doors, in pull-out baskets, or on lazy-Susan carousels in corner cabinets. Base cabinets generally accommodate big bowls best; heavy-duty hardware may be neccessary for drawer glides.

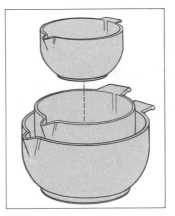

Bowls that nest

When buying bowls, opt for the kind that nest. A set of several won't take up any more space than a single bowl.

Pots & Pans

Whether you need a family-size stockpot for simmering soup or a tiny pan for melting butter, you'll want to have your pots and pans within easy reach of cooktop and oven. Because they are so bulky, pots and pans are often stored in base cabinets. But putting them on standard shelves usually results in a jumbled pile. Use heavy-duty drawers and pull-out trays behind doors for more convenient storage of cookware.

Pots and pans also can be treated as a decorative element. As shown on the facing page, a variety of racks is available for hanging pots and pans from walls or ceilings, keeping them out of the cupboard altogether. One note about racks: because of the weight they will bear, you must be careful to hang them according to manufacturer's directions.

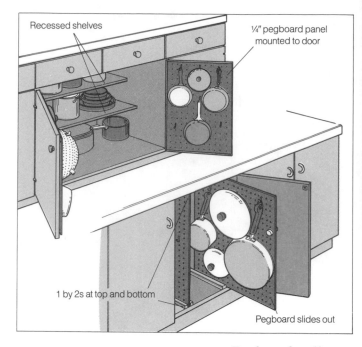

Recessed shelves

¼" pegboard panel mounted to door

1 by 2s at top and bottom

Pegboard slides out

Pegboard pull-outs

Make your own hangers for pots, pans, and lids inside cabinets by using ¼-inch pegboard panels. Use wooden spacers to attach pegboard to cabinet doors in order to give clearance for hooks. For slide-out racks, cut each panel slightly smaller than height and depth of cabinet so it moves freely between pairs of 1 by 2s screwed to top and bottom of cabinet interior.

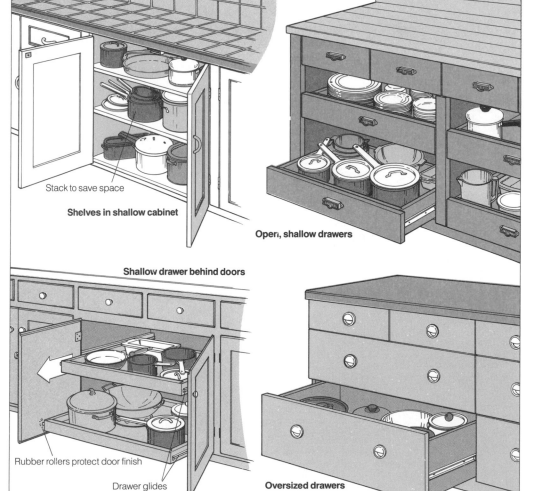

Stack to save space

Shelves in shallow cabinet

Open, shallow drawers

Shallow drawer behind doors

Rubber rollers protect door finish

Drawer glides

Oversized drawers

Shelves and drawers for pots and pans

Pots and pans can be difficult to retrieve from deep shelves in standard base cabinets. Choose shallow cabinets for easier access, or put pots and pans in pull-out shelves or drawers on heavy-duty glides. Small rubber rollers attached to drawer corners protect doors from damage when drawers are pulled open.

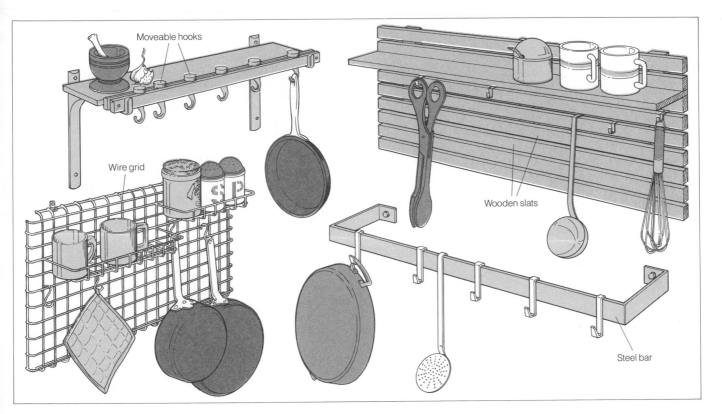

Moveable hooks

Wire grid

Wooden slats

Steel bar

Wall-mounted pan racks

For both decorative and functional storage, you can buy any of a number of pan racks and grids that mount to the wall. Follow manufacturers instructions for installation; often racks must be fastened to wall studs because of the weight they will bear.

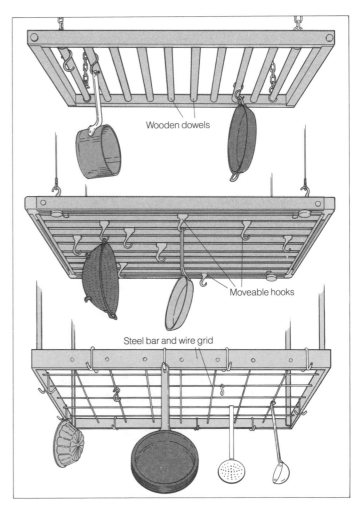

Wooden dowels

Moveable hooks

Steel bar and wire grid

Hanging pan racks

Suspended from ceiling hooks, hanging pan racks can create a dramatic focal point in the kitchen. Best placement is generally above a counter near the cooktop or over a nearby island unit where pots and pans won't be in the way of traffic.

Spices

Almost every kitchen has a healthy collection of jars, tins, shakers, and boxes of spices and herbs. Arranging them is a challenge. There's a wide range of sizes and shapes to contend with, yet many containers look exactly alike except for the name on the label. How can you store seasonings so they're close to where you use them—usually the cooktop or food preparation center—and easy to distinguish from one another?

Here's an illustrated assortment of spice racks to solve the problem, many making use of often-overlooked kitchen space. Whichever arrangement you choose, display spices so they can be recognized at a glance; you don't want to sprinkle cayenne pepper into a dish calling for cinnamon.

Generally, spice and herb containers should be stored away from direct heat, moisture, and light. Keep the tops tightly closed between use to prevent loss of flavor.

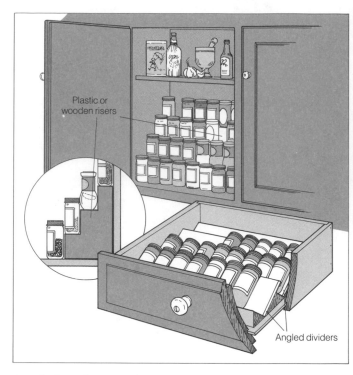

Angled and stepped organizers

Angled dividers tip spices into view and allow bottles to fit in shallow drawers. Stepped organizer at top lines spice bottles up in several tiers on cabinet shelf, keeping each row in view. These kinds of organizers can be purchased premade, or you can make your own from scrap wood.

Swing-out spices

Upper cabinets near the cooktop are convenient places to store spices. Two possibilities are shown here. Coated-wire racks at left hold spices on inside of cabinet door. Hinged, double-sided spice rack, right, holds twice the spice. Both types require recessing interior cabinet shelves to give clearance.

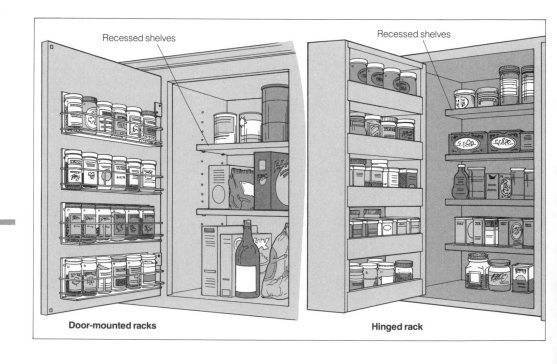

Door-mounted racks

Hinged rack

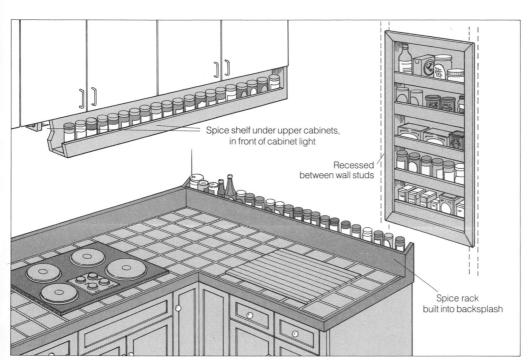

Spice shelf under upper cabinets, in front of cabinet light

Recessed between wall studs

Spice rack built into backsplash

Built-in spice racks

Consider built-in spice racks when remodeling or installing new cabinets. Add a spice shelf beneath upper cabinets, provide a rack along the backsplash, or recess shelves between wall studs.

Pull-out spice storage

In narrow upper or lower cabinet, you can install a tall, two-sided spice cupboard that pulls out on standard full-extension drawer glides.

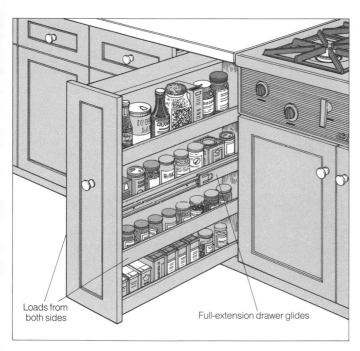

Loads from both sides

Full-extension drawer glides

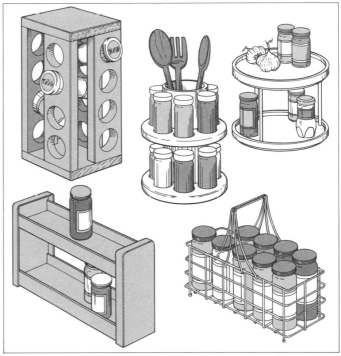

Freestanding spice racks

Cookware, specialty, and department stores sell many types of freestanding racks and turntables to keep spices organized and convenient. Some include bottles—for a uniform look—and labels that help the busy cook locate a particular spice quickly.

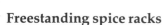

Trash & Items to Recycle

Efficient and orderly ways of dealing with kitchen wastes can put an end to messy, overflowing wastebaskets, unpleasant odors, and some of the drudgery of garbage and recycling duty.

Once you locate all the waste production points in your kitchen—such as the can opener, food preparation counter, and chopping block—you may find that the best place for the kitchen garbage receptacle is under or near the kitchen sink. Always line the wastebasket with a heavy-duty grocery bag or plastic liner; your wastebasket will stay cleaner, and your trash will be more likely to make it outside to the garbage can in one uneventful trip. For the ultimate in trash space-saving, you can install a trash compactor that can compress what would fill three to four 20-gallon garbage cans into one odorless, leakproof, disposable bag.

If you're a gardener, you may want to keep organic wastes in a separate container to add to a compost pile. And if you have room in your kitchen, you can put recyclables in separate receptacles to save sorting time later on. Aluminum and tin cans (flattened), glass bottles and jars, newspapers, and paper bags are all recyclable.

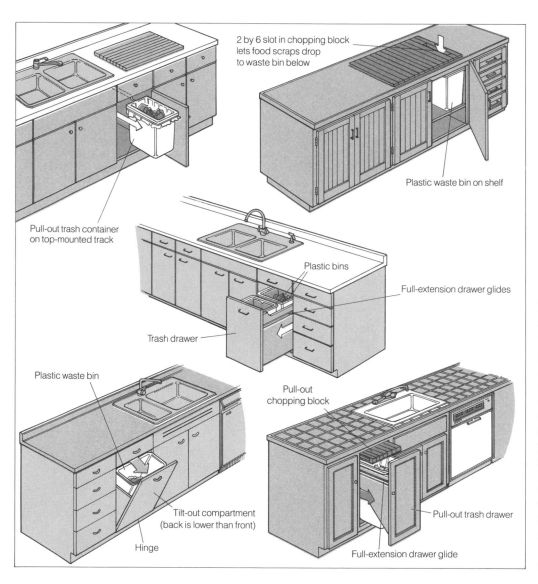

2 by 6 slot in chopping block lets food scraps drop to waste bin below

Plastic waste bin on shelf

Pull-out trash container on top-mounted track

Plastic bins

Full-extension drawer glides

Trash drawer

Plastic waste bin

Pull-out chopping block

Tilt-out compartment (back is lower than front)

Hinge

Pull-out trash drawer

Full-extension drawer glide

Built-in waste receptacles

When planning cabinets, it's easy to give trash and recyclables a place of their own. Cabinet manufacturers make pull-out trash containers, deep trash drawers, and tilt-out compartments. Custom cabinetmakers can duplicate these and offer other solutions as well, such as a slotted chopping block (upper right) to let food scraps drop to a waste bin below.

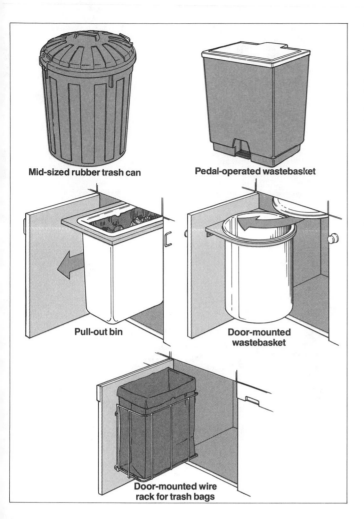

Mid-sized rubber trash can

Pedal-operated wastebasket

Pull-out bin

Door-mounted wastebasket

Door-mounted wire rack for trash bags

Trash containers

Choose a hard-working trash can for your kitchen. A mid-sized rubber one with a lid holds a generous amount of trash; this or a pedal-operated wastebasket can be left out in the kitchen. Containers that pull out or swing out on cabinet's door offer convenience—and stay hidden when not in use.

Recycling solutions

For the serious recycler, a recycling center provides space for newspapers, string, trash bags, tools, and plastic bins for bottles and cans. To crush cans easily, build a smasher from two lengths of 2 by 4 hinged together. Stack newspapers in a store-bought wire rack or a plywood box you make yourself.

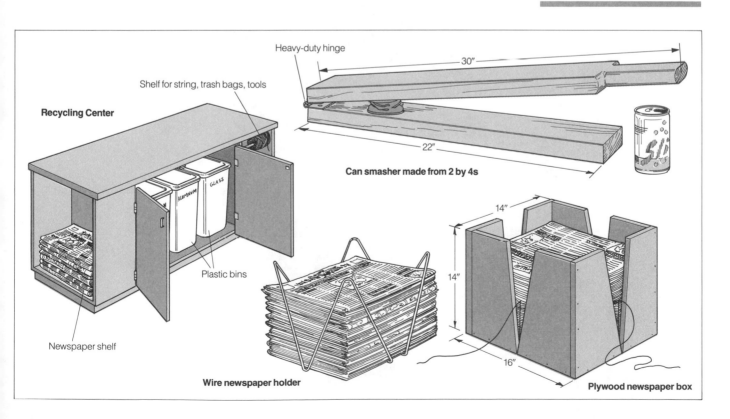

Recycling Center

Shelf for string, trash bags, tools

Heavy-duty hinge

30"

22"

Can smasher made from 2 by 4s

Plastic bins

Newspaper shelf

Wire newspaper holder

14"

14"

16"

Plywood newspaper box

Trays & Serving Equipment

Large cooky sheets, muffin tins, serving trays, baking pans, and similar kitchen equipment demand specialized storage. Most aren't needed on a daily basis, so they can be stored in out-of-the-way cabinets. But because of their large sizes and sometimes unusual shapes, they can consume copious amounts of space if not stored properly.

Deep cabinets above oven or refrigerator or narrow base cabinets are favored for tray storage. Dividers allow tidy, vertical storage so that any tray can be slipped out without disturbing the others.

Vertical cabinet dividers

Several methods can be used to create vertical cabinet dividers. These custom models include dowels inserted into holes in shelves above and below; manufactured wire dividers fitted into holes; short dividers in slotted base; and solid panel dividers.

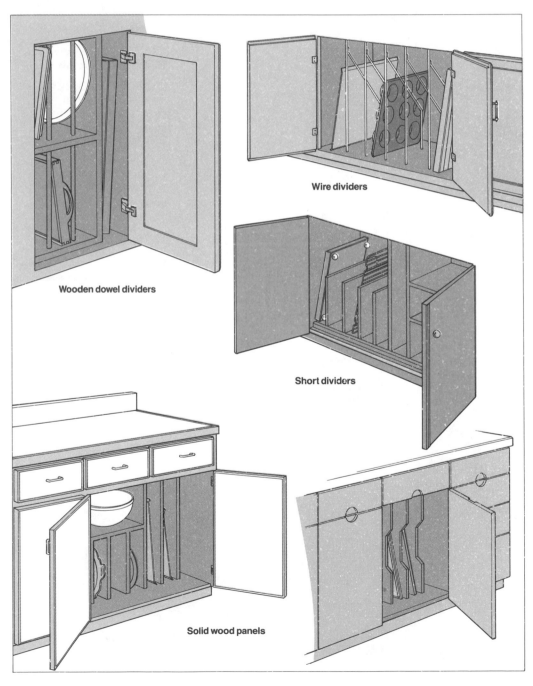

Wire dividers

Wooden dowel dividers

Short dividers

Solid wood panels

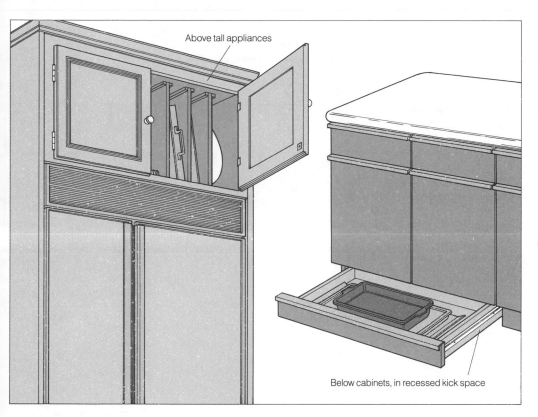

Above tall appliances

Below cabinets, in recessed kick space

Places for seldom-used items

High upper cabinets and deep lower cabinets are good places to keep paraphernalia you use only occasionally. In some European-style cabinet systems, you have the option of a surprise drawer in the recessed kick space.

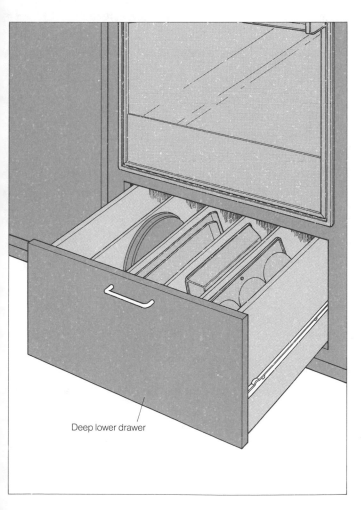

Deep lower drawer

Divided drawer

Just as vertical dividers can organize a cabinet, dividers can turn a deep drawer into efficient storage for awkwardly shaped muffin tins, trays, baking pans, and pot tops. The best dividers can be removed for occasional cleaning and adjusted to accommodate larger items.

Sources

Manufacturers of kitchen cabinets and storage products

When you're transforming an old kitchen into one that's innovative and workable, you'll find a wealth of ideas and information in brochures put out by the various manufacturers of kitchen storage units. Here's a selection of major cabinet and storage product manufacturers who will send you information on request; they can also tell you about local outlets or distributors for their products.

The entries are coded to identify what each company manufactures; importers of European cabinetry are indicated as well. The product codes and addresses in this list are accurate as of press time.

The yellow pages of your telephone directory and the National Kitchen & Bath Association (124 Main Street, Hackettstown, NJ 07840) can help you locate kitchen showrooms, cabinetmakers, designers, architects, and other sources near you.

Codes:	
(C) custom cabinets	(m) metal
(S) stock cabinets	(p) plastic
(SO) special order cabinets	(pv) plastic laminate veneer
(SP) storage products	(w) wood
	(i) imported

Adelphi
P.O. Box 10
Robesonia, PA 19551
(C, SO/w)

Akro-Mils, Inc.
P.O. Box 989
Akron, OH 44309
(SP/m, p)

Allmilmo Corporation
70 Clinton Rd.
Fairfield, NJ 07006
(SO/pv, w, i)

American Cabinet Concepts, Inc.
1021 Columbia Blvd.
Longview, WA 98632
(S, SO/pv, w)

Ampco
P.O. Box 608
Rosedale, MS 38769
(C/m)

Aristokraft Cabinets
P.O. Box 420
Jasper, IN 47546
(S/pv, w)

Art Wire
230 Fifth Ave.
New York, NY 10001
(SP/m)

Bertch Wood Specialties
4747 Crestwood Dr.
Waterloo, IA 50702
(C, SO/pv, w)

Birchcraft Kitchens, Inc.
1612 Thorn St.
Reading, PA 19601
(C/pv, w)

Bosch Corporation
2800 S. 25th Ave.
Broadview, IL 60153
(S/pv, w)

Capri Custom Cabinetry, Inc.
59 Armstrong Rd.
Plymouth, MA 02360
(C, S, SO/pv, w)

City Cabinetmakers
1351 Underwood Ave.
San Francisco, CA 94124
(C/pv, w)

Closet Maid, Clairson Int'l
720 SW 17th St.
Ocala, FL 32674
(SP/p)

Compagnucci USA, Inc.
14 E. 60th St.
New York, NY 10022
(SP/m)

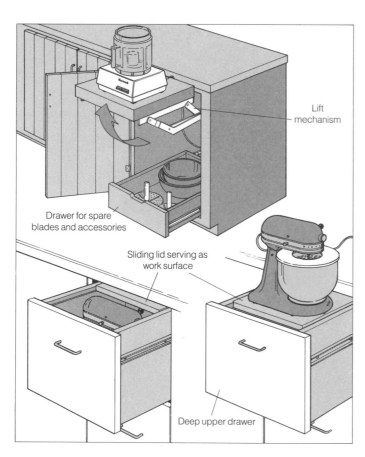

Lift mechanism

Drawer for spare blades and accessories

Sliding lid serving as work surface

Deep upper drawer

Cabinet manufacturers offer specialized fittings for all sorts of kitchen storage needs. Among available options are swing-up shelf for food processor or other appliance (top) and sliding drawer cover to serve as appliance work surface.

Coppes Napanee Kitchens
401 E. Market St.
Nappanee, IN 46550
(C/w)

Cottonwood
12757 S. State Street
Draper, UT 84020
(C, SO/pv, w)

Craft-Maid Custom Kitchens, Inc.
P.O. Box 4026
Reading, PA 19606
(C/pv, w)

Custom Wood Products, Inc.
P.O. Box 4516
Roanoke, VA 24015
(C/pv, w)

Diamond Cabinets
P.O. Box 547
Hillsboro, OR 97123
(S/w)

Elfa/Eurica Marketing, Inc.
14551 Franklin Ave. NW
Tustin, CA 92680
(SP/m, i)

Excel Wood Products Co., Inc.
One Excel Plaza
Lakewood, NJ 08701
(S/w)

Fieldstone Cabinetry, Inc.
P.O. Box 109
Northwood, IA 50459
(S, SO/w)

Grayline Housewares
1616 Berkeley St.
Elgin, IL 60123
(SP/m)

Grovener Industries
938B Clivedon Ave.
Annacis Business Park
Delta, B.C.
Canada V3M-5R5
(C, SO/pv, i)

Haas Cabinet Co., Inc.
625 W. Utica St.
Sellersburg, IN 47172
(S, SO/pv, w)

Hanssem Corp.
68 Veronica Ave.
Somerset, NJ 08873
(S, SO/pv)

Home Crest Corp.
P.O. Box 595
Goshen, IN 46526
(C, S/w)

Imperia Cabinet Corp.
1000 Main St.
Hanson, MA 02341
(C, SO/pv, w)

Imperial Cabinet Co., Inc.
P.O. Box 427
Gaston, IN 47342
(SO/w)

Iron-A-Way, Inc.
220 W. Jackson
Morton, IL 61550
(SP/m)

J Wood
P.O. Box 367
Milroy, PA 17063
(C/pv, w)

Kapri Kitchens
P.O. Box 100
Dallastown, PA 17313
(C/w)

Kemper Division
WCI, Inc.
701 S. N St.
Richmond, IN 47374
(S/pv, w)

Kent Moore Cabinets, Inc.
P.O. Box 3206
College Station, TX 77840
(C, SO/w)

Kitchen Kompact, Inc.
P.O. Box 868
Jeffersonville, IN 47130
(S/w)

Kraftmaid
16052 Industrial Parkway
Middlefield, OH 44062
(C, S, SO/pv, w)

Lager Kitchens
35 Agnes St.
East Providence, RI 02914
(C, S, SO/w)

LesCare Kitchens, Inc.
P.O. Box 3008
Waterbury, CT 06705
(C, SO/pv, w)

Merillat Industries, Inc.
5353 W. US 223
Adrian, MI 49221
(S/w)

Merit Kitchens
12185 86th Ave.
Surrey, B.C.
Canada V3W-3H8
(S/pv, w)

Millbrook
Route 20
Nassau, NY 12123
(S, C, SO/pv, w)

Northwood Products, Inc.
P.O. Box 2008
Coeur d'Alene, ID 83814
(C, S, SO/pv, w)

Pennville Custom Cabinetry
P.O. Box 1266
Portland, IN 47371
(C/w)

Perfection Wood Products
7645 York St.
Denver, CO 80229
(C, SO/pv, w)

Poggenpohl USA Corp.
6 Pearl Court
Allendale, NJ 07401
(C/pv, w, i)

Prestige Cabinet Corp. of America
29 Rider Place
Freeport, NY 11520
(C/pv)

Prestige Products, Inc.
P.O. Box 314
Neodesha, KS 66757
(S/w)

Quaker Maid Division
WCI, Inc.
Route 61
Leesport, PA 19533
(C, S/pv, w)

Ranier Woodworking Co.
16318 S. Meridian
Puyallup, WA 98373
(C/pv, w)

The Refacers, Inc.
1115 Landini Lane
Concord, CA 94520
(C, S, SO, SP, pv, w)

Renee Products
8600 Harrison Rd.
Cleves, OH 45002
(C, S/pv, w)

Rev-A-Shelf, Inc.
2409 Plantside Dr.
Jefferson, KY 40299
(SP/p)

Rubbermaid Inc.
1147 Akron Rd.
Wooster, OH 44691
(SP/p)

Rutt Custom Kitchens
Route 23
Goodville, PA 17528
(C/w)

Ryan Manufacturing Co.
Hager Cabinets
Box 1117
Mankato, MN 56001
(C/w)

Saint Charles Holdings, Inc.
1611 E. Main St.
Saint Charles, IL 60174
(C/pv, w)

Sawyer Cabinet, Inc.
12744 San Fernando Rd.
Sylmar, CA 91342
(C, S, SO/m, pv, w)

H.J. Scheirich Co.
P.O. Box 37120
Louisville, KY 40233
(S/w)

Starmark
P.O. Box 84810
Sioux Falls, SD 57118
(S/pv)

Style-Line Industries, Inc.
2081 S. 56th St.
West Allis, WI 53219
(C, S/pv, i)

Syroco
P.O. Box 4875
Syracuse, NY 13202
(SP/p)

Taylor & Ng
1212B 19th St.
Oakland, CA 94607
(SP/m, w)

Techline
Marshall Erdman and Assoc., Inc.
5117 University Ave.
Madison, WI 53705
(S, SP/pv)

Triangle Pacific Corp.
P.O. Box 220100
Dallas, TX 75222
(C, S, SO/pv, w)

Westech Cabinets
143 Business Center Dr.
Corona, CA 91720
(S, SO/pv, w)

Wilton/Copco Enterprises
2240 W. 75th St.
Woodridge, IL 60517
(SP/p)

Wood-Hu Kitchens, Inc.
343 Manley St.
West Bridgewater, MA 02379
(C, S, SO/w)

Wood-Mode Cabinetry
Wood Metal Industries
Kreamer, PA 17833
(C, S, SO/pv, w)

XA Cabinet Corp.
19063 Valley View
La Mirada, CA 90638
(C, S/pv, w)

Yorktowne
P.O. Box 231
Red Lion, PA 17356
(S/pv, w)

Index

Sunset

Bedroom & Bath Storage

By the Editors of Sunset Books
and Sunset Magazine

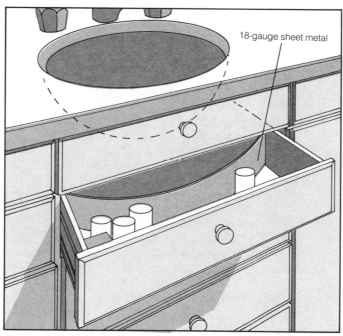

*Drawers with rounded backs make the most of undersink
space (see page 55).*

Lane Publishing Co.
Menlo Park, California

Underbed storage opens up floor space in a child's room (see page 25).

Book Editors
Helen Sweetland
Ginger Smith Bate

Contributing Editors
Scott Atkinson
Fran Feldman

Design
Roger Flanagan
Kathy Avanzino Barone

Photo Stylist
JoAnn Masaoka

Illustrations
Rik Olson

We gratefully acknowledge the following businesses for their help with material for this book: Crate & Barrel, Hold Everything, Just Closets, and Stacks & Stacks.

We also extend special thanks to Marianne Lipanovich for scouting many of the photo locations.

Photographers
Stephen Marley: 9 bottom, 13, 19 top, 23 bottom, 24, 36, 38, 39 top, 47 top, 58, 59 top, 60, 61 bottom, 63 top right, 65 top, 67, 70, 72 top left and bottom. **Jack McDowell:** 11 top, 12, 15, 19 bottom, 20 bottom, 37 bottom, 39 bottom, 43 bottom, 47 bottom, 59 bottom, 62, 63 top left and bottom, 64, 66 right, 72 top right. **Rob Super:** 34 bottom. **Tom Wyatt:** 9 top, 10, 11 bottom, 14, 16, 17, 18, 20 top, 21, 22, 23 top, 33, 34 top, 35 top, 37 top, 40, 41, 42, 43 top, 44, 45, 46, 48, 57, 61 top, 65 bottom, 66 left, 68, 69, 71.

Cover: Dressing area off the master bedroom and adjacent to the master bath offers lots of convenient—and carefully organized—storage. A stack of shallow drawers holds lingerie and accessories. Below is a hamper ready to catch clothing or linens from the bath. Nine pull-out shelves house shoes and sweaters, with room for more above. Long apparel hangs from the single rod at left; shorter items fit on double rods at right. For more on this storage system, turn to page 42. Architect: Mark Hajjar. Photo styling by JoAnn Masaoka. Photographed by Tom Wyatt.

Editor, Sunset Books: Elizabeth L. Hogan

Third printing April 1990

Contents

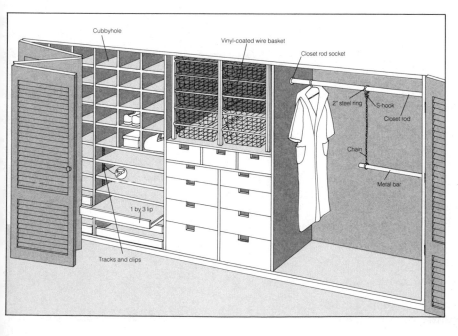

Careful planning turns a simple wall closet into a highly efficient storage system (see page 32).

Bedroom Storage

Because space is at a premium in most homes today, bedrooms must perform more than one role—and still remain restful oases where the cares of the day can be left behind. The challenge is learning how to combine many functions in one space, without ending up with uncontrolled clutter.

The first step is to take an inventory, not only of the items in the room but also of the activities normally carried on there. Is this where you like to read and listen to music? Do you normally do your ironing in this room? Would your home computer be more convenient to use if it were in the bedroom? Is this where your children enjoy playing? Once you have a clear idea of what functions you want the room to serve, you'll be able to organize it to work for you.

Look at your room with fresh eyes, starting with the largest space-gobbler of all—the bed. Make it serve as a major storage spot by surrounding it with a functional and roomy headboard system, by fitting it with underbed storage drawers, or even by adding a storage compartment at the foot. If your ceiling is high, you may want to consider building a sleeping loft, or perhaps raising the bed off the floor. You can even make the bed disappear into the wall, Murphy-bed fashion.

Next, think about the amenities that make the room restful and relaxing—books and magazines for bedside reading, a television and perhaps a stereo system for entertainment, extra pillows and quilts for comfort. Shelves, hollow headboards, linen closets, nightstands, and drawers can put all these items within easy reach.

Finally, you're ready to choose—or design—your own storage units or systems. What you select will depend not only on what you need to store but also on your taste and budget. Perhaps you like the informal look of simple bins or baskets. Or you may prefer antique furniture and closed cabinetry. In any case, efficiency should be your goal.

In this chapter, you'll see how some homeowners organized their rooms, and you'll find some easy projects you can make yourself with basic skills and simple tools. Whatever your requirements and taste, you'll discover a bounty of good ideas to stimulate your creativity.

Storage Chests

Custom designs offer built-in convenience

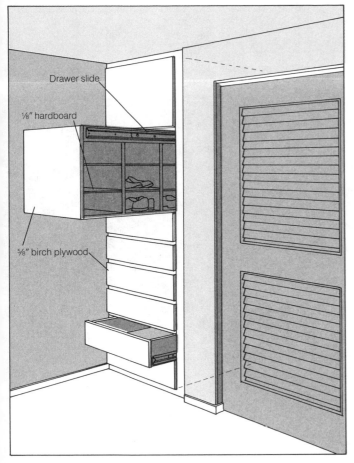

Drawer slide

⅛" hardboard

⅝" birch plywood

Built-in chest saves valuable floor space

A built-in chest that replaces a freestanding bureau can save several feet of floor space in your bedroom. Set into a corner beside a wide closet, this chest leaves room for a larger bed or perhaps a desk and chair. For optimum storage, the drawers are as deep as the closet.

The door and drawer fronts can be cut from one sheet of ⅝-inch birch plywood for a continuous grain pattern. For a finished appearance, band the edges with ⅜-inch alder, walnut, or oak, glued into place.

The vertical supports in the pigeonhole pull-out are made from ⅝-inch plywood; the bases are ⅛-inch hardboard. Use full-extension drawer slides available from cabinet suppliers or well-stocked lumberyards for support and easy access to the compartments. The edges of the drawers are routed for ease in opening. Attach the door for the top cabinet with self-closing concealed hinges. Architect: Rod Terry.

Storage bench

Like a stack of increasingly bigger boxes, this storage bench is deeper at the top for accessibility, shallower at the base for extra toe space.

Horizontal 1 by 4s wrapping the sides and front are glued and nailed to vertical 1 by 8s; these are notched so each of the front 1 by 4s cantilevers about 2 inches over the one below it. For ventilation, leave a 1-inch gap between each 1 by 4. At the wall, the 1 by 4s are glued and nailed to vertical 1 by 2s screwed to wall studs. The bench rests on a recessed 2 by 2 base.

To strengthen the lid, glue 1 by 4s to ⅛-inch tempered hardboard and add tapered 2 by 2s to the underside. Cut the lid's edges at an angle. Designer: John Parsons.

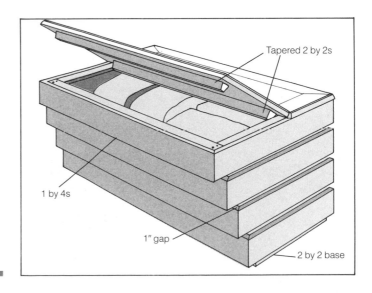

Tapered 2 by 2s

1 by 4s

1" gap

2 by 2 base

Bedside Storage Systems

Four easy-to-build units that you can use separately
—or in various combinations—to boost bedside storage

Build just one component or build them all

A small bedroom, especially one that doubles as a home office or den, is a storage challenge. One way to maximize bedroom space is to make the bed itself as storage-efficient as possible.

The system shown here gives you three units for stowing things—a headboard, a nightstand, and a foot-of-the-bed chest. Just choose the components that fit your storage needs, your room layout, and your taste. Alter the dimensions as you wish. The components are described in detail below and at the top of the facing page. (For drawer-building tips, see page 77.)

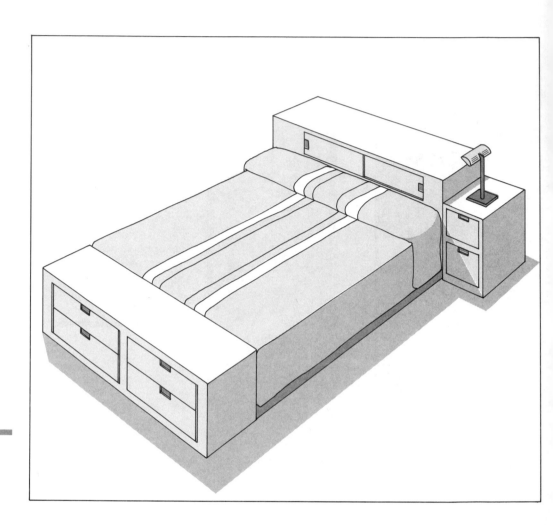

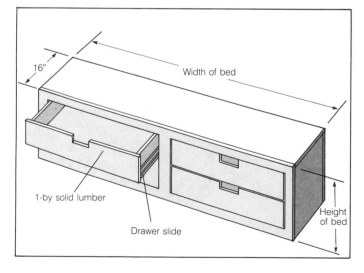

16"

Width of bed

1-by solid lumber

Drawer slide

Height of bed

The foot-of-the-bed chest

A low chest of drawers at the foot of a full-size bed has nearly the same storage capacity as a traditional bedroom bureau, yet it's not nearly as bulky. It can also double as a bench or television shelf.

You can buy a unit built especially for the foot of the bed; or try one designed for a different purpose (such as storing engineers' maps and blueprints).

To put together a chest like the one shown, build a frame from ¾-inch plywood and 1-by solid lumber; then install four custom-made drawers on standard slides. Make the chest the same height and width as your bed and approximately 16 inches deep.

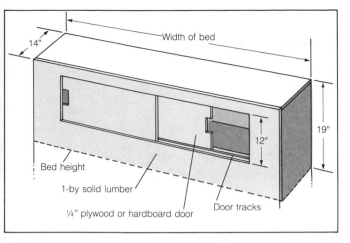

The headboard

The simple unit shown at left has a storage compartment with handy sliding doors to hide clutter. The portion of the headboard above the mattress should be approximately 19 inches high and 14 inches deep; the width and overall height of the headboard will be determined by the size of your bed. Sheets, blankets, pillows, and bedspreads alter measurements, so it's wise to measure when these are in place.

Build the headboard from ¾-inch plywood and 1-by solid lumber. Use ¼-inch plywood or hardboard for the sliding doors, and install plastic, wood, or metal door tracks.

The nightstand

Two storage compartments are stacked inside this compact unit (see at right). The top one is a cubbyhole with a hinged, drop-down door in front; below it is a roomy drawer.

The nightstand shown here is approximately 12 inches wide, 14 inches deep, and 26 inches high; you can adjust these dimensions to suit your own needs.

Build the unit from ¾-inch plywood and 1-by solid lumber. Buy a ready-made drawer—or build your own—and install it on standard drawer slides.

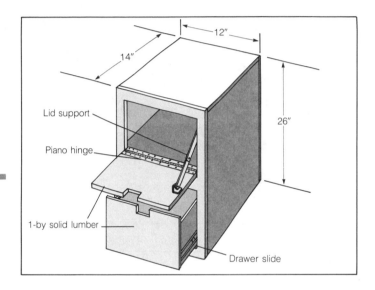

Easy-to-build storage headboard

With two storage levels, this headboard has plenty of room for bulky pillows and comforters, and even hard-to-store sports equipment. What's more, the door of the upper compartment doubles as a slanting backrest.

The depth of the unit is 24 inches. Make the headboard 12 inches higher and a little wider than your bed. The backrest/door slants at a 75° angle.

Build the headboard from ¾-inch plywood. Before assembly, cut a door out of each side piece. Assemble the pieces, nail 1 by 3 cleats to the inside of the headboard to hold the interior shelf, and attach the large door with a piano hinge. Attach the side doors with hinges and add door pulls and magnetic catches.

Underbed Storage

If the area under your bed collects nothing but dust,
add chests or pull-outs—or a custom-designed storage
platform—to utilize that wealth of wasted space

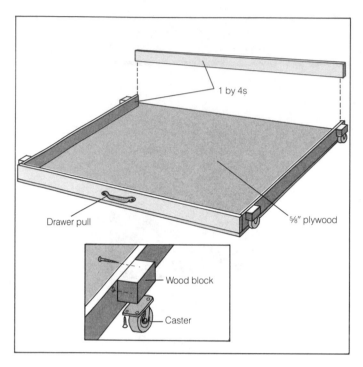

1 by 4s

Drawer pull

⅝" plywood

Wood block

Caster

Make your own roll-out drawers

Even a standard metal bedframe can accommodate under-bed storage. To build a simple drawer, fasten 1 by 4 strips to the edges of a ⅝-inch plywood bottom (as shown). Then add the wood blocks and casters (remember to allow an inch or so for clearance—more for thick carpeting) and attach a drawer pull. A plywood lid will keep items dust-free—but you'll have to pull the drawer out completely for access or hinge the lid in the center.

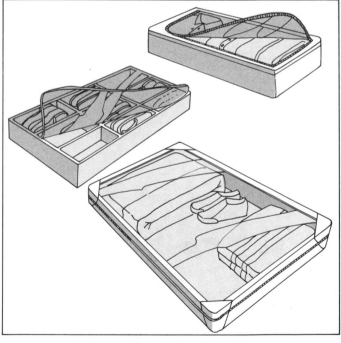

Custom bed holds roll-around cart

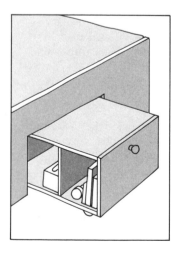

Designing a new bed? Consider leaving space for a handy roll-around cart with storage com-partments, like the one shown here. Tucked away, the unit blends in with the rest of the un-derbed cabinetry. Pulled out, the cart doubles as a nightstand or breakfast-in-bed table.

Ready-made containers slide under standard bedframes

Trays and chests made expressly for underbed storage are commercially available in plastic, wood, or card-board. Many have dividers; most have lids or see-through vinyl covers. These inexpensive storage aids are perfect for shoes, out-of-season clothing, and bed linens. Look for them in the notions sections of department stores or in mail-order catalogs.

Modular pieces that fit your style

Modules that can be arranged under and around your bed can give you plenty of extra stowing space—even in small bedrooms. The drawer under this bed rolls out when you need it. Such drawers are available in various widths and depths. The three-drawer chests on either side of the headboard are separate units, too. Design: The Minimal Space.

Bedframe features double-decker drawers

Two levels of drawers are built into this striking bedframe, which is coated with glossy black lacquer. The upper level is perfect for sweaters and lingerie; the lower level is roomy enough for extra bedding. Heavy-duty metal slides let the drawers open and close smoothly. Architect: Wendell Lovett. Interior design: Suzanne Braddock.

Headboard Systems

Built-in or freestanding, headboard systems
offer bedside convenience

Floral reflections

Mirrors over the bed and
closets open up this very
functional headboard sys-
tem, reflecting light and
enlarging the bedroom.
Just under the bedside
lamps are built-in night-
stands that offer storage
beside the bed. Tall
cupboards—one with
drawers, the other with
shelves—hold clothing
and extra pillows. Interior
design: Patricia Whitt
Designs.

Keeping a low profile

When you need storage
space around your bed but
you don't have room for
an elaborate wall system,
consider this sleek design.
The headboard proper has
two bins for pillows and
extra bedding. The side
sections store books and
other bedside necessities;
doors fold down to func-
tion as nightstands. The
headboard's slanted front
provides gentle support
for television watching or
reading. Design: The
Minimal Space.

Headboard appropriates a whole wall

Commodious and versatile, this headboard wall system provides generous storage for everything from books to clothing to Christmas tree lights, while catering to bedside needs. Tucked into its custom-fitted alcove, the head of the bed has behind-the-pillows storage and a ledge for midnight snacks. For reading, there's ample light from the recessed fixtures above. Design: Eurodesign, Ltd.

Bedside office

Floor-to-ceiling headboard wall system in this bedroom is all business, from the spacious cupboards and drawers for clothes and bedding to the hanging-file drawer beside the bed for papers and records. Recessed downlights above boost the illumination provided by the swing-arm fixtures. Interior design: Ruth Soforenko Associates.

Room-dividing Headboards

A two-faced approach to both spatial and storage needs

Floating island in a tranquil setting

In this pretty, pale bedroom, the bed takes center stage—it's a serene island of comfort as well as hard-working storage. Its massive yet sleek headboard is the focal point, partitioning the room into sleeping and dressing areas. On the sleeping side, almost hidden behind the bed pillows, cabinet doors cover storage crannies for bedside necessities; above them, an airy alcove more than accommodates reading lamps, books, a clock-radio, and a pretty plant. On the opposite side, the headboard serves up a dozen drawers, topped with a mirrored niche for toiletries and a jewelry box. Architect: Phoebe T. Wall.

Extra warmth on one side, extra storage on the other

In a bedroom of generous size, this freestanding fireplace wall separates a cozy sitting area from the sleeping quarters. On the headboard side of the wall, bookshelves surround a center panel that offers swing-arm lamps—and plenty of space to prop pillows—for bedtime reading. Architects: The Bumgardner Architects.

Handsome, clever, and capacious

More than compensating for the bedroom's single small closet, this vast bedframe-headboard-wardrobe unit also creates a private dressing corridor behind the bed. In front, tawny oak shelves climb nearly to the ceiling, framing an upholstered backrest. In back, the same rich oak forms a capacious set of cabinets and drawers. Design: The Butt Joint.

Hideaway Beds

For small bedrooms, guest bedrooms, double-duty bedrooms—
sleeping facilities that literally come out of the woodwork

Sleepy? Just pull down the wall

Mr. Murphy's popular invention of 1905 swung down out of a closet. Today's versions, which operate in a similar fashion, are just as likely to pull down from a recess in a wall, like the one shown here, as from a closet. Gas springs (pneumatic closers) at the head of the bed allow for easy lifting and lowering. Legs at the foot provide needed support and stability.

Other space-saving features of the handsome wall system include a fold-down bedside table on one side and a pull-out work surface on the other. Recessed downlights above the bed are controlled by a switch just above the pillows. To make your own Murphy bed, turn to pages 26–27. Interior design: Legallet-Trinkner Design Associates. Furniture design: Eurodesign, Ltd.

Daytime seating becomes nighttime bedding

Nestled in a nook of a none-too-spacious cedar cabin, the built-in bench pictured above gets in nobody's way during the day. And when it's bedtime, the base and cushion fold out separately, transforming the seating area into the double bed shown on the left. Separate supports for the sleeping platform are kept in a drawer beneath the bench during the day. Architects: Larsen, Lagerquist & Morris.

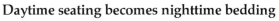

Double-duty Bedrooms

Managing the paraphernalia when sleeping quarters
share space with hobbies or homework

Wraparound cabinetry creates office/guestroom

Built-in cabinets, counters, and shelves convert this small room into an efficient family computer center and office. When the sofa bed is opened up, the room becomes a guest bedroom; there's drawer space for clothing and cleverly concealed pull-out shelves on either side of the sofa for bedside storage. Interior design: Lynn Williams of The French Connection.

Corner cutout for paperwork in privacy

For book-balancing or tax forms, thank-you notes or PTA flyers, epic poems or crossword puzzles, a small home office certainly aids achievement. But where to put it? Most homes nowadays lack spare rooms that aren't already reserved for the television or visiting relatives.

As this situation shows, a bedroom corner may provide the ideal location—out of traffic's way and relatively private. This office is neatly tucked into an alcove originally intended as a closet. The angles of the desk allow for leg room and a bank of drawers, as well as vertical slots large enough for sketch pads and blueprints; the wraparound desktop offers ample work space. Overhead, a small bookcase completes the corner. Architect: David Jeremiah Hurley. Interior design: Jois.

Camera cache in a closet

Most of us connect closets with clothing. Naturalists may think first of moths, psychiatrists and genealogists of skeletons. But to an enthusiastic photographer, the closet in a spare bedroom can serve quite a different purpose: safely storing all the delicate and valuable apparatus of his craft. Here, floor-to-ceiling adjustable shelves behind bifold closet doors keep cameras and gear in tidy, easily accessible order. There's even room on the closet floor for a small refrigerator for film. Closet interior: Just Closets.

Bedroom Wall Systems

Cabinets, drawers, open shelves keep your private world in order

A wall of cabinets and drawers

With a wall system such as this one, nothing need ever be out of place in this bedroom! At the very top are bins that swing down to collect seldom-used blankets and sports equipment. Just below, doors open to reveal vinyl-coated wire baskets, as shown, or adjustable shelves. One unit houses the television. At the bottom are a dozen and a half drawers for sweaters, shirts, and accessories. Track lighting illuminates the scene. Design and construction: Robert Nyden.

A place for everything and . . .

From books to the telephone to towels for an adjoining bath, this headboard system holds it all. There's a pull-out drawer under the bed for bulky sweaters and a roomy bin behind the pillows. The cabinet door even pulls down to become an instant nightstand, as shown at left.

Systems such as this one can be tailored to your own needs, whether you're storing books, bedding, or belts. Design: Eurodesign, Ltd.

That's entertainment!

On display here are some of the essentials of a bedroom entertainment center: stereo components, a library of record albums, and several shelves of books. For stow-away storage, this attractive wooden wall system also offers drawers and more drawers, cabinets and more cabinets. Three cubbyholes along the countertop have the same kind of covering found on rolltop desks. For ideas on storing the bedroom TV—another entertainment essential—turn to pages 20 and 21. Architect: Robert C. Peterson.

In a nutshell—it's natty

Open the big doors in this wall unit, and what do you find but a handy small-scale closet. Crisp shirts on a pull-out rod line up along its center, while neckties hang neatly from racks placed high on either cabinet door. With nary an inch of wall space wasted, cabinets and drawers abound, surrounding the counter and recessed mirror. Design: Euro-design, Ltd.

Television Storage

Keeping the set out of sight when it's out of mind

Rolltop reviewing stand

Early in the morning or late at night, this television, situated in the "adults only" corner of the master bedroom, emerges from behind a rolltop door and slides out of its alcove on a shelf fitted with a swiveling platform. A tiled fireplace, a wet bar with storage, and a small refrigerator concealed behind cabinet doors below the sink complete the scene. Architect: Victor Conforti.

Sharing space with the shirts

The owner of this handsome, custom-built armoire can watch the morning news as he selects a shirt for the day. The television is bolted securely to a swivel-topped pull-out shelf, so it can be turned or brought forward for easier viewing. But when TV time is over and the armoire doors are closed, there's no hint of the screen—or the shirts.

Even in antique storage pieces, there are often nooks and crannies that can be used for television storage; an antique hideaway is shown on page 23. Interior design: Anona Colvin.

Elevated viewing, window seat sound

The owners of this bedroom located their television high above their closet so they could comfortably watch while lying in bed. The controls are, of course, remote. Stereo components and speakers fit in small alcoves on both sides of the window seat; the speakers can be angled toward the seat or turned to project into the bedroom. Interior design: Ruth Soforenko Associates.

One set does double duty

Though located in the sitting room of this two-level master bedroom suite, this television is also visible from the bedroom up the stairs to the right, thanks to a pull-out shelf and swiveling platform. At the end of the wall unit is a linen closet pictured on page 65. Architect: Mark Hajjar. Interior design: Patricia Whitt Designs.

Antique Storage Furniture

Yesterday's chests and dressers still hold their own as storage units

**Treasured chests
for bedroom storage**

This bedroom's storage begins with a closet for clothes that must be hung, then expands storage space with a graceful armoire, a handsome wood-trimmed trunk, and a refurbished tool chest made fresh with paint and stencils.

An antique quilt hangs on a wall hoop, while two others see service on crisp winter evenings.

Victorian hideaway for books, TV

Last century's clothes-keepers can be refurbished to suit contemporary tastes and to hold one of this century's most popular inventions. This richly carved Victorian armoire, American-made of oak, was stripped, bleached, and finally waxed to show off its natural golden color. The interior has been lined, and the doors upholstered, in a fabric that matches the bedroom wallpaper. Finally, a swivel-topped, pull-out plywood tray was added to hold a television set. Interior design: Ruth Soforenko Associates.

For the new generation

Tall wooden wardrobe holds the tiny clothes of the newest entry in the family line. Blankets for the crib fit into the drawer at the bottom. Wicker hampers that may once have served for day trips or afternoon picnics hold little shirts or a few days' supply of diapers.

The rocking horse, wicker rocker, and brass crib echo the traditional theme.

Children's Rooms

Storing toys and clothes so they're easy to reach,
easy to put away, and easy on the eyes

A second level and lots of drawers

This bed-loft system adds several feet of level surface for
games and projects in this child's room. Combine that with
almost a dozen drawers and some shelves, and you have
the potential for order—even in a small bedroom. Design:
Adventures in Space.

Sit and store with handy shelves and drawers

Shelves beside this window seat and drawers underneath
put toys and clothes at arm's reach. Bright pillows and
cuddly buddies invite lingering. Design: Sharon Kasser,
Distinctive Interiors.

Handsome chest bed is a real worker

For tucking away toys, clothing, and consider a chest bed with generous drawer space. In addition to the drawers, there's a deep bin in the back for linens. To get to the bin, you lift up the twin-size mattress and open the lid.

The pieces are cut from good-looking Baltic birch plywood where appearance counts; where it doesn't, less expensive shop-grade plywood is used. Make the rails from solid cherry and use ¼-inch tempered hardboard for the bin and drawer bottoms. The lid under the mattress is attached with a long piano hinge. Design: Robert Zumwalt.

¾″ plywood

2-by cherry

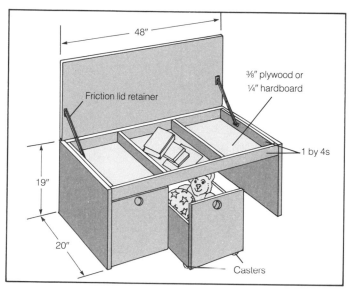

48″

Friction lid retainer

⅜″ plywood or ¼″ hardboard

1 by 4s

19″

20″

Casters

Drawing desk holds a row of rolling toy bins

With the lid down, a toy bin or two pulled out, and a small chair pulled up, this handy unit serves as a drawing desk. But when playtime is over, the toy bins slide under the desktop to form a single, compact storage unit. Desk sides, back, and lid are built from ¾-inch plywood; the bottom of the divided tray is made of ⅜-inch plywood or ¼-inch hardboard; and the tray frame is built from fir 1 by 4s. The unit illustrated is 19 inches high, 20 inches deep, and 48 inches wide, but you can adjust these dimensions to suit your child's needs.

Assemble the desk with glue and woodscrews or finishing nails. Attach the swing-up lid with a piano hinge, and add a lid support (or chain) at each end. Depending on the dimensions of your unit, the drawers of an old file cabinet might furnish ready-to-use bins (just add casters); or make your own bins from plywood. Finish the desk and bins with bright-colored enamel.

Versatility with building blocks

Storage modules do more than organize mountains of playthings. They can be combined to form desks, platform beds, room dividers, and wall systems. You can buy ready-made modules made from wood, particleboard, or plastic—or you can build your own.

Construct your modules from ¾-inch plywood suitable for painting. A convenient size for each module is 16 inches square; for compatibility, make rectangular ones 16 by 16 by 32 inches. Add shelves (they double as vertical dividers when you rearrange the modules), hinged doors, or even simple drawers; use wood molding or veneer tape to hide the plywood edges. Finish with enamel. If you stack several modules, be sure to bolt them to the wall or floor—or to each other—for stability.

Murphy Beds

Fold them up when they're not in use

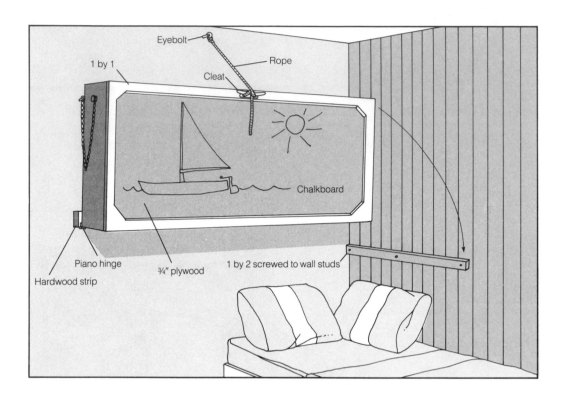

Eyebolt
Rope
Cleat
1 by 1
Chalkboard
Piano hinge
Hardwood strip
¾" plywood
1 by 2 screwed to wall studs

Chalk one up for Murphy

Since 1905, Murphy beds have been folded up or slid into closets, quickly emptying rooms of wrinkled linens and at least 18 square feet of bulk. This simple version of the Murphy, designed for a child's room, is both a top bunk and a chalkboard.

Its base and sides are a shallow box made from ¾-inch plywood. The good face of the base plywood is placed down to form the bed's underside and is painted with chalkboard paint. A 1 by 1, fastened (either nailed and glued, or screwed) to the sides, supports the base, and plywood triangles at the corners add strength. The frame can be designed to hold either a cot- or standard-size mattress.

The bed pivots down on a 6-foot piano hinge, screwed to a hardwood strip anchored to wall studs. A heavy chain, securely fastened at one end to a wall stud or ceiling joist and, at the other, to an end of the bunk, holds the bed level when it's folded down. At the head of the bunk, a 1 by 2 is screwed to the wall studs, further supporting the bed's weight. A rope wraps around a boat cleat to hold the bunk in its raised position.

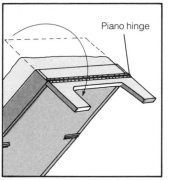
Piano hinge

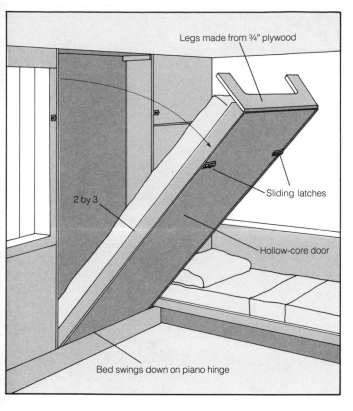
Legs made from ¾" plywood

2 by 3

Sliding latches

Hollow-core door

Bed swings down on piano hinge

Now you see it, now you don't

When guests spend the night, you can create an instant bedroom with a wall bed. Several manufacturers make them and stores that specialize in furnishings for apartments and small spaces carry them.

But if you want to make your own version of a Murphy bed, consider this one. The base is a hollow-core door onto which 2 by 3s are glued to form a shallow box. (You can also use ⅝-inch plywood as a base.) A 6-inch mattress is secured to the frame by woven straps.

The frame swings up on a piano hinge into a 9½-inch-deep well and is held in place by sliding latches. When it's pulled down for use, legs swing down on a piano hinge to support the foot of the bed. The legs, cut from ¾-inch plywood, are curved to allow for kickspace at the foot of the bed.

This version of the Murphy is for one person only, and the mattress is lightweight foam. For a larger bed with a standard mattress, you'll need heavy counter-spring hardware, rather than a piano hinge, to handle the weight.

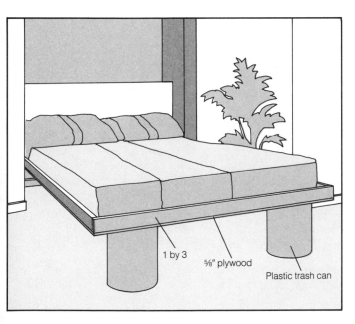
1 by 3

⅝" plywood

Plastic trash can

Queen-size bed stores in closet

The platform of this queen-size bed, fitted with a foam mattress, rests on large cylinders that are actually sturdy plastic trash cans. The platform is made from ⅝-inch plywood and 1 by 3 lumber. A spring-loaded roller catch secures the bed at the top.

Sleeping Lofts & Elevated Beds

If your bedroom has a high ceiling, elevate your sleeping area
to open up storage or living space below

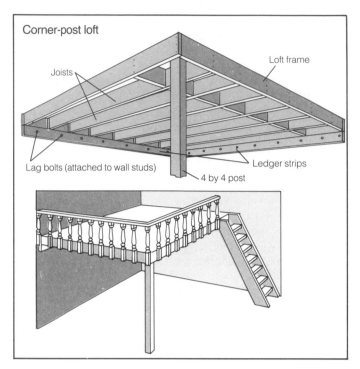

Corner-post loft

Joists

Loft frame

Lag bolts (attached to wall studs)

Ledger strips

4 by 4 post

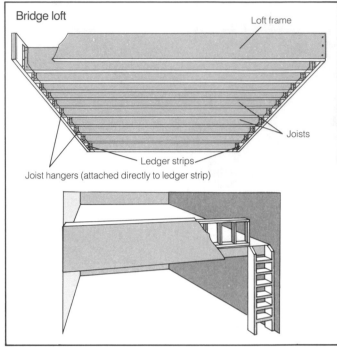

Bridge loft

Loft frame

Joists

Ledger strips

Joist hangers (attached directly to ledger strip)

Lofty ideas

Lofts are simply elevated platforms that add floor space —and visual interest—to a room. They're especially useful in studio apartments (renters should check with the landlord before building, of course) and in bedrooms that double as work or entertainment centers.

Ceiling height, obviously, is a critical factor. As a practical guide, consider $6\frac{1}{2}$ feet the minimum headroom needed for standing below a loft, and $4\frac{1}{2}$ feet the minimum headroom needed for sitting up in the bed above. (But always check your local building codes; the requirements for your area may be different.) Add another foot for the structure of the loft itself, and you'll find that you need a ceiling that's about 12 feet high. If you have the 8-foot ceilings that are standard in so many newer homes, you'll have to remove all or part of the existing ceiling, or be content with the more "down-to-earth" forms of underbed storage (see pages 8–9).

Two basic loft designs are illustrated here. The corner-post loft is supported by a ledger strip on one wall and two corner posts, or by ledger strips on two adjoining walls and one corner post. The bridge loft touches three adjoining walls and is supported by ledger strips on the two opposing ones. A third type (not shown) is a free-standing loft, which requires support posts on all four corners with braces to prevent sway. But the freestanding loft is not as sturdy as the other two, and it's more complicated to build.

Once you've determined your design and dimensions, check them with your local building department.

Use structural fir for the loft frame and wall ledgers. (Essentially, you're building a new floor and supporting it above the existing one, so the size of your structural lumber will depend on the number of feet the loft will span. Check local codes.) You'll also need $\frac{3}{4}$-inch plywood for the loft floor, 4 by 4s of structural fir for any corner support posts, and materials for a ladder and safety rails.

You'll probably want to furnish your loft simply, in keeping with its small scale. And remember that it's a sleeping loft—not designed for heavy storage.

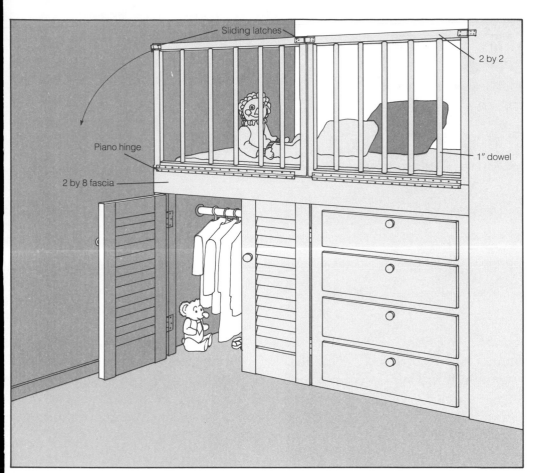

Sliding latches

2 by 2

Piano hinge

1" dowel

2 by 8 fascia

Sleep above, store below

This elevated crib-and-storage unit is just 5½ feet wide, yet handles several functions at once.

A frame of 2 by 6s, hung from the walls with joist hangers, supports a ⅝-inch-thick particleboard platform for a twin-size mattress (cut down to length). Mounted on the 2 by 8 fascia across the front are a pair of safety-rail gates made from 2 by 2s and 1-inch dowels. The gates pivot on piano hinges and fasten with spring-loaded sliding latches.

Drawers and a child-size closet under the crib provide convenient storage for clothing.

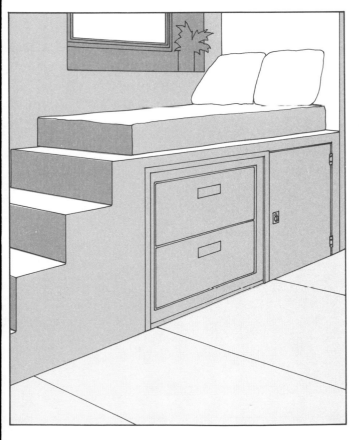

Storage base for twin-size bed

Stepped edge gives a sculptural look to this 4- by 8-foot sleeping platform. It's large enough for a twin-size mattress and high enough to accommodate a 2½-foot double-drawer filing cabinet. A cupboard adds additional storage space; fit it with pull-outs to make the space easily accessible. Architect: Franklin Israel.

Closets & Dressing Areas

Just about everyone would like to have an organized closet—one so well planned and tidy that a desired garment could be easily found, and in sparkling condition, rather than crumpled from crowding. In this chapter, we present many good ideas for turning a cluttered, messy closet into one that easily accommodates your wardrobe.

Most closets are either the roomy, walk-in type or the shallow but lengthy wall type. Both have their advantages. In general, people with large wardrobes prefer the walk-in closet, simply because it holds more. But with good space planning and double-decker closet rods, a wall closet can often accommodate the same-size collection of clothing. Shelves, drawers, pull-out bins, and racks, such as those pictured on the following pages, can make either closet more space-efficient and organized.

Before you purchase any storage aids or design a new closet, take careful stock of what you need to store. Start by eliminating clothing that you don't—or won't—wear. Then put your clothing into categories and take some measurements. Find out just how much room you need to store your shoes, or the height at which dresses should be hung so their hems won't drag on the floor. Then you'll be able to determine if your present closet—with the addition of another rod or two, some shelves, and a few racks and hooks—will give you sufficient space.

If necessary, consider ways to enlarge your present closet, or think about where you can build a new one. On the following pages, we present suggestions for temporary, or movable, closets, as well as instructions for constructing your own built-in or freestanding closet.

If you have a dressing room or a small dressing table or you have the room to add one, you'll find plenty of ideas for organizing and decorating it.

Whether you choose just to add racks and hooks to your present closet or you decide to install a complete closet system with shelves, drawers, and rods, you're sure to be so pleased with the result that you'll wonder why you waited so long to do it.

Planning Closet Space

Specially created spaces can make a measurable difference
in keeping closets free from clutter

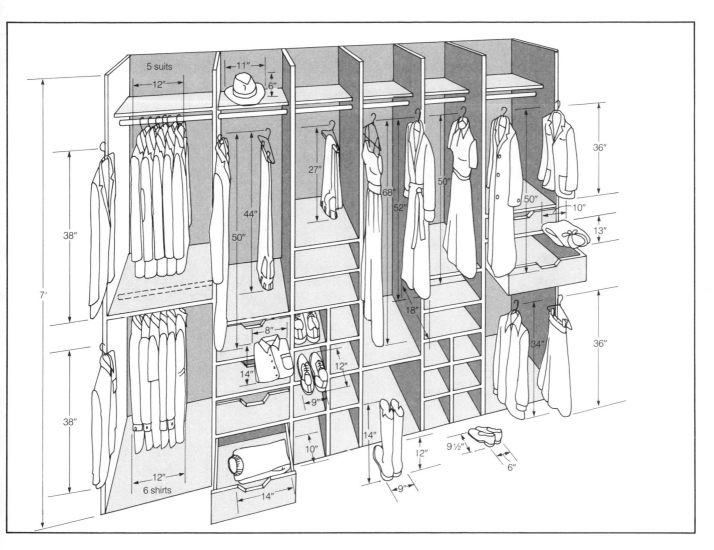

How much space do you need for clothing?

Most of us close our closet doors quickly—either to avoid looking at the clutter or to stop all of those shoes, boxes, coats, and caps in mid-tumble. And even when we take the time to store things where they belong, there's never quite enough space for everything.

Bringing order to a closet may be easier than you think. With some planning, it's possible to have a closet that fits your belongings, one with a variety of spaces for clothing of different shapes and sizes, and one that doesn't crush sweaters, crumple blouses, or wrinkle the hems of dresses. It doesn't waste space and the rods don't sag.

Knowing the general dimensions of items in the basic clothing categories can help you plan just how much room to allow for each article. The drawing above gives measure-ments based on standards established by the American Institute of Architects.

You can assume, for instance, that six men's shirts on hangers will occupy a space at least 12 inches wide, 16 inches deep, and 38 inches high, and that a pair of women's pumps of average size measures 6 by 9½ inches. But check your own clothing against these measurements; you may have bulkier jackets, longer hemlines, or larger shoes.

Wire hangers are usually 16 inches wide, wooden suit hangers up to 21 inches wide, and tubular plastic or metal ones about 17½ inches wide. Again, it's best to measure your own hangers. Plastic, wood, or metal ones give your clothing the best support.

A Closet System

Open shelves, drawers, and multilevel rods
work together to organize your clothes quarters

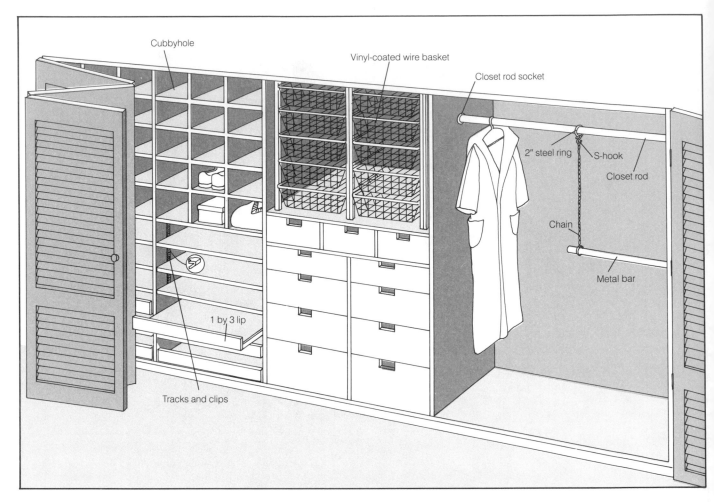

Cubbyhole

Vinyl-coated wire basket

Closet rod socket

2" steel ring

S-hook

Closet rod

Chain

Metal bar

1 by 3 lip

Tracks and clips

Open shelves

Shelves are probably the most versatile components in a
closet system. They accommodate items in a wide variety of shapes and sizes (from ten-gallon hats to hand-
kerchiefs); they keep stored items visible; and they're
easy to install. And if you use an adjustable system of
tracks and clips or tracks and brackets, shelves are also
easy to rearrange.

Fir and pine are good choices for closet shelving; so
are ¾-inch plywood and particleboard, especially if
your shelves will be deeper than 12 inches. If you're
planning a shelf longer than 4 feet (3 feet if it's particleboard), be sure to add a mid-span support.

For added interest—and convenience—use vertical
dividers to form clusters of cubbyholes, or convert some
of your shelves to pull-outs by adding standard drawer
slides and lipped edges made from 1 by 3s.

Drawers, pull-outs, and multilevel rods

Simplify your dressing routine—and gain valuable floor
space in the bedroom—by eliminating your bulky bureau
and adding a new drawer system in the closet. If you want
a built-in unit, construct a frame to accommodate drawers
custom-made to desired dimensions. Or buy a modular set
of drawers. For visible storage, try a system of vinyl-coated
wire bins that glide in and out on their own framework.

In updated closets, the primary space-waster—the traditional single closet rod—has given way to multiple rods
whose heights are determined by the owner's clothing. But
you needn't make any major structural changes to convert
your closet to multilevel rods. Just buy an adjustable sus-
pension bar, or make one of your own from a metal bar or
wood dowel, steel rings, S-hooks, and some lightweight
chain (as shown).

Closet metamorphosis

Before the new storage system was installed (see inset), this all-too-typical closet broke virtually every rule for good closet design and organization. Its one long shelf was crammed with hats and handbags, books and bedding, while the extra foot of space between the shelf items and the ceiling above was totally unused. Clothes were jammed together on the one long closet rod, which was low enough to make long dresses and robes dust the floor, yet high enough to leave several feet of wasted space below jackets, skirts, and blouses. Impossible to vacuum, the closet floor was a dusty jumble of shoes, boots, handbags, and luggage.

With the new organizers in place, the closet holds everything it did before—and more—with room to spare. Five different levels of closet rods make sure that each item gets the space it needs. The closet floor is clear (and dust-free) now that shoes and handbags are lined up on shelves of their own. And, best of all, the owners were able to eliminate their bulky bedroom bureau—thanks to a stack of large-capacity closet drawers and some roomy open shelves for sweaters and other foldables. Closet interior: Just Closets.

Wall Closets

A custom design can double—even triple—
your closet's storage potential

Wardrobe at a glance

Many of us have closets we're only too glad to shut the door on. But this one offers a compartmentalized network so neat that it's actually pleasing to contemplate from the vantage point of one's bed at 6 A.M. (The slide-out tie rack just to the right of the mirrored center panel is shown more closely on page 48.)

When the bifold doors are closed, an expanse of mirrors not only aids grooming but also creates the illusion of doubled room depth. Interior design: Alan Lucas & Associates. Closet interior: The Minimal Space.

Planning ingenuity creates a closet for two

A little engineering carved ample storage for both his wardrobe and hers in a relatively compact space—leaving the rest of this bedroom serenely uncluttered. Baskets of vinyl-coated wire offer several advantages over traditional, and bulky, chests of drawers: they allow ventilation, they make it easier to find your favorite pullover, and they hide neatly behind the closet doors. Architect: N. Kent Linn. Interior design: Joan Simon. Closet interior: The Minimal Space.

Predawn efficiency

For many a commuter, every morning minute counts in the race to catch the train, bus, or carpool, and an efficiently arranged closet like this one can pare down dressing time and ease those important first decisions of the day. Thanks to the bifold doors, even sleep-filled eyes can take in most of the wardrobe at a glance. In the center of the closet, accessible from both sets of doors, are two rods offering double-decker storage for shirts, jackets, and slacks; at the far left, longer coats and robes hang at standard height. Shoe shelves eliminate floor clutter, and a stack of drawers and open shelves keeps folded shirts and other clothing in good order. Closet interior: Just Closets.

Cozy cache in a corner

Like the intricate honeycomb of a hard-working beehive, this remodeled high-and-narrow Victorian closet leaves scarcely a centimeter to chance disorder. New double-decker closet rods carry twice the freight of the original single one, and the newly installed bank of open shelves accommodates volumes of sweaters and other foldables without crush or confusion. Closet interior: Just Closets.

Walk-in Closets

Luxurious spots to shelter a wardrobe—some so spacious
they double as dressing rooms

**Within easy reach
of the bath**

Housing your garments
adjacent to the bathroom can
save flurry and flutter as you
race the clock on weekday
mornings.

Such convenience was
feasible here without threat
of moisture damage to the
wardrobe. The spacious bathroom is well ventilated (a must
for this kind of arrangement),
and a sliding door seals off
the adjoining closet.

Lighting for the closet is
supplied by fluorescent
tubes above the cornices.
Architects: Designbank.

High-rise housing for clothing foldables

Good-looking enough to display books or collectibles, the wall unit at one end of this spacious walk-in is a private cache for quantities of foldable clothing. Cubbyholes at mid-level hold clear acrylic bins full of small items such as socks and lingerie. Double rods along one side of the closet, double shelves and a rod along the other, accommodate two extensive wardrobes neatly and without crowding. Design: Philip Emminger.

For clotheshorses, a spacious livery stable

Most walk-in closets are big enough to comfortably accommodate wardrobes for two people—even when each person makes frequent sartorial acquisitions. In this closet, there's space for floor-to-ceiling shoe shelves, a built-in chest of drawers, and a necktie rack. Double closet rods on either side offer an uncrowded abundance of raiment. And everything is easy to see—thanks to good indirect fluorescent lighting. Architect: Ron Yeo.

Open Closets

Honest, upfront clothes quarters to flaunt your finery

Letting it all hang out

Tucked under an eave, a man's collection of striped, plaid, and tattersall clothing makes an unobtrusive, tidy display that pleases the eye and detracts not a whit from the bedroom's striking design. During the day, skylights illuminate clothing colors; when the sun goes down, that function is performed by wall-mounted fixtures that look like jumbo dressing-table lights.

Above the closet is a compartment with sliding doors; to the left is a tall built-in unit with a white-enameled cabinet topping a dozen black-lacquered drawers. Architect: Wendell Lovett. Interior design: Suzanne Braddock.

Taking the hassle out of the morning

There's no wasted motion here. From the cup of freshly brewed coffee to the morning shave to the selection of the day's clothing, this open closet puts it all within arm's reach.

In addition, there's a built-in bureau to the left of the sink that holds sweaters and accessories, as well as towels for bathroom use. Recessed in the wall beside the door is a pull-down ironing board—right where it's needed. Interior design: Legallet-Trinkner Design Associates.

Two wardrobes separate bed and bath

Curved and compact, this room divider doubles as an open armoire for two people. Reminiscent of the voluptuous furniture styles of the 1930s, the closet curiosity has room for everything from brogues to silk dresses. The curved section offers open shelving, necktie pegs, a pull-out bin for laundry, and deep drawers of clear acrylic for small foldable items. Around the bend, facing the bathroom, there are additional nooks and crannies for towels and toiletries. Architect: Gary Allen.

Children's Closets

Organizing kids' clothes quarters for easy upkeep

Closet revamp encourages tidiness

With all his personal effects piled in a jumble, either on the floor or high up out of reach, it was hard for the eight-year-old owner of this closet to find things or put them away (see inset, right). But built-in shelves and drawers, plus an extra closet rod placed at just the right height for him, brought order out of frustrating chaos. At the same time, as with any well-planned closet remodel, space was cleared for storing at least twice as much. Closet interior: Just Closets.

Small girl's wardrobe makes a fetching display

Her mother's serendipitous shopping trips turned up unusual and elegant organizers for a five-year-old's wardrobe. Pretty hats and colorful dresses hang from an antique coat rack. Below that, a handsome wooden towel rack from a bath accessory boutique holds everyday play clothes. And, most imaginatively, her small-scale footwear lodges in a divided wicker desk tray originally designed to hold stationery. The entire arrangement makes a charming display in a small bedroom that has no built-in closet.

Organized for action

Though his toys may cover the floor most of the time, the right combination of drawers, shelves, and closet rods can make it easier for him to tidy up.

Vinyl-coated wire bins and adjustable shelving in the closet corral his shoes, sweaters, and soccer ball, while the shallow, open shelves in the chest at left keep his games and books visible—but neatly arranged. Two levels of rods in the closet make the most of the space and put the clothes on the lower level within easy reach. Interior design: Helen Kroeger, Interiors by Design.

Dressing Areas

Create a corner—or a luxurious separate room—
where you can retire to attire

Commodious corner closet

Designed for instant accessibility, this corner closet is composed of numerous compartments—glide-out trays for shoes, multiple shallow drawers for sweaters and lingerie, and two separate hanging areas, one for pants and dresses, the other for tops and jackets. There's even a hamper below the drawers.

Louvered doors that allow ventilation slide on tracks. One door is mirrored, which makes this compact area look larger. Architect: Mark Hajjar.

Reflections on the art of dressing

Look beyond the stunning hammered brass sink and brass-trimmed tile counter, and you're aware of something equally impressive reflected in the mirror: a spacious closet on the opposite wall of the dressing room proudly displays its beautifully stacked, stored, and suspended wares. Louvered for both good looks and good ventilation, its trifold doors hinge back to reveal an entire wardrobe. Architect: David Jeremiah Hurley. Interior design: Jois.

Plenty of doors and drawers

Behind the large double doors in this dressing room, you'll find a tidy double-rod clothes closet; behind the smaller doors are individual cubbyholes for as many as thirty pairs of shoes. Below the counter, built-in drawers of varying depths provide streamlined accommodation for folded items. Architect: Charles L. Howell.

Organizing Your Clothing & Footwear

Keep your wardrobe under control with these
closet products and storage aids

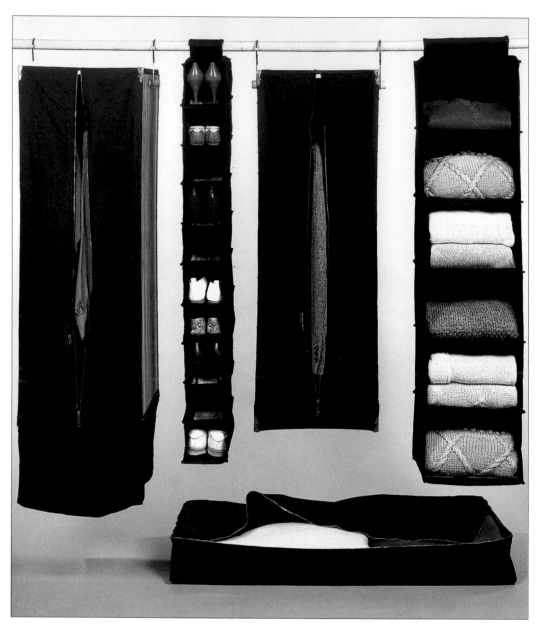

Garment bags give practical protection

Garment bags, like the ones shown at left, not only keep clothes clean and fresh-looking, but also can help organize the contents of your closet. They're especially useful for out-of-season or seldom-used clothing.

Made from fabric or from clear, colored, or patterned vinyl, the bags have front or side zippers for easy access and come in a wide range of sizes. Accessory bags with shelves for shoes, hats, handbags, sweaters, and other bulky items are also available.

You can find garment and accessory bags in the notions section of large department stores or in closet shops.

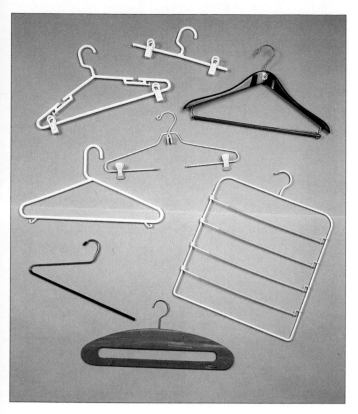

Good-bye to tangled wire hangers

Wire hangers, never meant for longtime use, crease slacks, misshape shoulders, and sag under the weight of heavy clothing. Replace them with sturdy hangers made from plastic, vinyl-coated wire, metal tubing, or wood. Designed specifically to keep garments looking crisp, these hangers come in a myriad of shapes and sizes. Before you shop, take a quick inventory of your closet to determine the types that will best meet your needs.

Footnote on shoe storage

Among the chief contributors to closet clutter are shoes. If you store them on the closet floor, or worse, under your bed, pulling out a matched pair can often be a challenge.

Ready-made shoe racks or boxes can provide an instant solution. Or, with some inexpensive materials, you can put together a custom rack of your own. Measure your closet space and count the pairs of shoes you need to store; then you'll know the size and shape rack to use.

Dressing Tables

Sitting down to all the accouterments of good grooming

Neatness counts

No tangle of cords and plugs mars the artful beauty of this carefully designed grooming area. Instead, holes drilled in the sides of the roomy drawers allow the hair blowers, curling irons, and other small appliances stored there to be plugged directly into a power strip under the counter. Only the cord emerges through the drawer's corner cut, which also serves as a drawer pull. A hole drilled in the corner of the counter carries the cords for the television and make-up mirror to the power strip.

Note how the accent stripes on the cabinetry echo those on the tile floor. Neon design: Wylie Mertz. Design and construction: Robert Nyden.

The romantic allure of wicker

An appealing beginning—and end—to each day are practically guaranteed at this charming little wicker vanity. Its simple, arched design catches the eye and may even divert attention from the clutter that all dressing tables inevitably collect. The unobtrusive glass shelves are easy to wipe clean. Furniture courtesy of de Benedictis Showrooms.

For today's fair lady, antique beauty

"The Fair each moment rises in her Charms/Repairs her Smiles, awakens ev'ry Grace/And calls forth all the Wonders of her Face." So wrote Alexander Pope early in the 18th century, addressing himself to the mysteries of a lady's toilette. For many of us, such marvelous transformations would be aided by an inspirational setting. Here's the very thing—an elegant Louis Philippe vanity with upholstered bench, both crafted of walnut. Lighting—essential to any dressing table—is stylishly supplied by smartly draped windows and a pair of lamps.

Organizing Your Accessories

Use baskets and barrels, hangers and holders
to arrange those all-important extras

Fold-up, slide-away tie ladder

The sides of this ladder rack swing up for easy access
to more than four dozen ties on six dowels. Once the tie
selection is made, the sides swing back down for compact storage. The entire unit slips in and out of the
closet on standard drawer slides. Design: The Minimal
Space.

Hidden jewelry storage

Tucked away in the back of a closet and concealed behind hanging garments is this clever hideaway for
jewelry. Built between the wall studs, the cabinet houses
eight fabric-lined, shallow drawers. For camouflage, the
outside of the cabinet door is painted the same color
as the rest of the closet wall, and the door opens by
means of a touch-latch. Design: Philip Emminger.

Put baskets and barrels to work as handy holders

Use baskets—wire or woven—to organize socks, lingerie, gloves, and scarves. Place them on closet shelves, tuck them into drawers, or suspend them from the closet ceiling.

Try a fiber drum, a small wine barrel, or an enameled metal drum to hold those tall, skinny items that are propped up precariously in the back corners of your closet: umbrellas, walking sticks, and sports equipment such as fishing rods, skis, baseball bats, and hockey sticks.

Hangers that major in accessories

Some smart-looking accessory holders, like the ones shown here, are designed to slip right over the closet rod. Available in the notions sections of most department stores or through mail-order catalogs, these specialty hangers hold belts, ties, scarves, handbags, or various combinations of accessories.

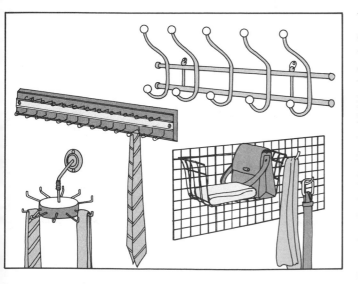

Wall hang-ups

One or more wall hang-ups in or near your closet can organize and display a variety of clothing accessories. Some simple plastic holders have an adhesive backing; others—fancy brass hooks, plastic or metal racks, and high-tech grid systems, for example—are screwed into the wall. For ties, there are collapsible racks or, if you prefer, revolving racks that bring favorites around at a touch.

Temporary & Portable Closets

Versatile storage pieces on hand when you need them—
and out of the way when you don't

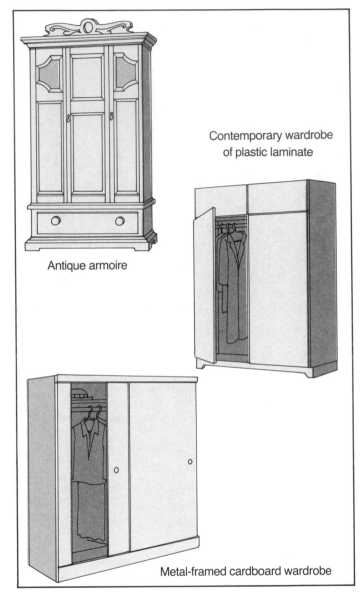

Contemporary wardrobe
of plastic laminate

Antique armoire

Metal-framed cardboard wardrobe

Freestanding wardrobes
go where they're needed

Whether they're carved and mirrored antiques, sleek
contemporary pieces of glossy plastic laminate, or inexpensive metal-framed cardboard units, freestanding
wardrobes are as practical as ever. The original portable
closets, they're a solution for bedrooms with little or
no built-in closet space.

"Flying" closet

"Off-the-wall" closet

Suspended storage

Here are two commercially available hanging closets
that are easy to carry and quick to install.

The "flying" closet is suspended on cotton webbing
from two mounting hooks screwed into the ceiling joists.
Garments hanging on the wooden closet rod are protected
from dust by an attractive natural-color canvas awning.

The "off-the-wall" closet has a shelf built from
natural-finish hardwood dowels with another dowel
suspended below as a closet rod. The whole assembly
hangs from natural-color cotton webbing straps that are
attached to the wall studs. Closet designs: Richard Pathman.

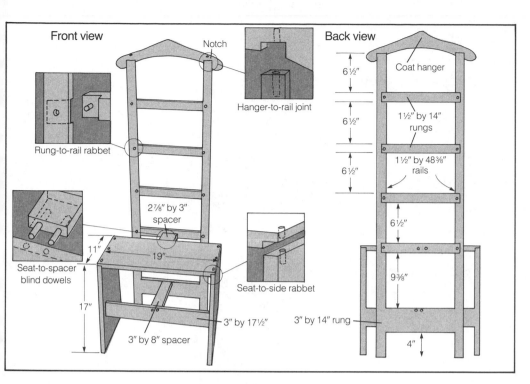

Front view

Notch

Hanger-to-rail joint

Back view

Rung-to-rail rabbet

2⅞" by 3" spacer

Coat hanger

6½"

6½"

1½" by 14" rungs

6½"

1½" by 48⅜" rails

Seat-to-spacer blind dowels

11"

19"

6½"

17"

9⅜"

Seat-to-side rabbet

3" by 17½"

3" by 8" spacer

3" by 14" rung

4"

A valet for clothes

This valet can help you lay out your clothes the night before or hold them for you after a hard day. Dowels and wood glue join parts. Equally spaced rabbeted rungs fit into dadoes in the back rails; the wider rung at the bottom is held with four dowels for stability. The seat is rabbeted.

Make the valet from hardwood except for the contoured hanger; buy a round-shouldered hardwood coat hanger at least ¾ inch thick; remove the hook and manufacturer's finish. Notch the hanger and glue it into place. Design: C. Stuart Welch.

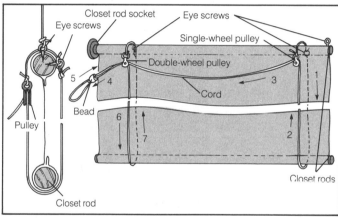

Closet rod socket

Eye screws

Eye screws

Single-wheel pulley

Double-wheel pulley

5

4

3

Cord

1

Bead

6

2

Pulley

7

Closet rods

Closet rod

Quick muslin closet on pulleys

Hung from the ceiling, this lightweight corner closet provides temporary storage in a minimum of space. Materials are simple: heavy muslin or duck canvas, thread, two wooden closet rods, closet rod sockets, #12 eye screws, ⅛-inch cotton shade cord, 3-penny finishing nails, a single- and a double-wheel ¾-inch pulley, a 3-inch cleat, and a large bead with a ¼-inch hole.

Cut the muslin into two pieces the desired height and width of the closet. The closet rods, cut into four pieces, slip into hems sewn at the top and bottom of each muslin piece. Drill holes in the upper rods for eye screws. Use cord and eye screws to fasten the fabric panels to ceiling joists; one end of each upper rod fits into a socket screwed or bolted to the wall (secure the rods with finishing nails). You can also fasten the panels to the floor to keep them taut. The drawing above shows how to rig the pull cord. Secure it to a cleat. Design: Diane McKenzie and Victor Budnik.

Adding a Built-in Closet

Constructing a closet where none existed before

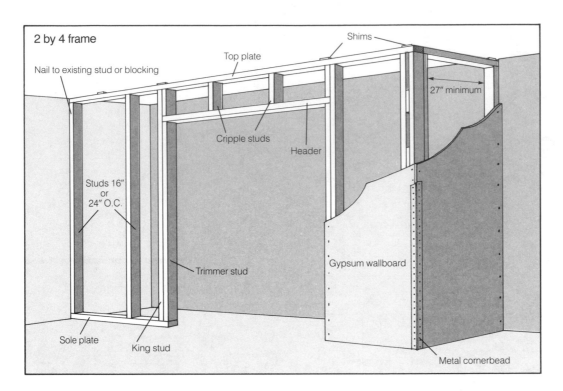

2 by 4 frame

Nail to existing stud or blocking

Top plate

Shims

27" minimum

Cripple studs

Header

Studs 16" or 24" O.C.

Trimmer stud

Gypsum wallboard

Sole plate

King stud

Metal cornerbead

Two types of built-in closets

If you have the floor space and some basic skills, you can construct a built-in closet that looks as if it's been there since the beginning.

You can make the closet either with standard 2 by 4 framing and the wall covering of your choice, or by installing floor-to-ceiling plywood cabinets. For either, allow an inside depth of at least 27 inches.

To build a 2 by 4 frame, space the studs 16 or 24 inches on center. To frame the doorway, add the header and trimmer studs (be sure to have your doors—and the correct dimensions for the rough opening—on hand before you begin). Size the walls about ¼ inch less than ceiling height.

Once they're built, swing them into place, shim between the top plate and the ceiling joists, and nail the sole plate to the subfloor (but *not* inside the doorway). Cut out the sole plate between the trimmers. Anchor the end studs to existing wall studs or to blocking inserted between the studs. Next, add wallboard or another wall covering to match existing walls. Finally, hang the doors (see facing page).

Build plywood cabinets as multiple units (4 feet wide or less), carefully level and plumb them, and screw them to wall studs. Though not required, a kickbase at the bottom adds a custom touch.

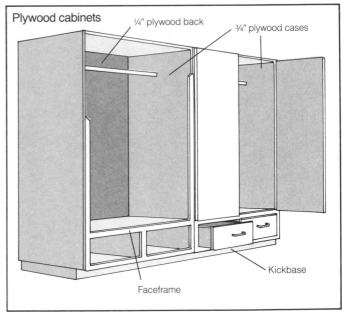

Plywood cabinets

¼" plywood back

¾" plywood cases

Kickbase

Faceframe

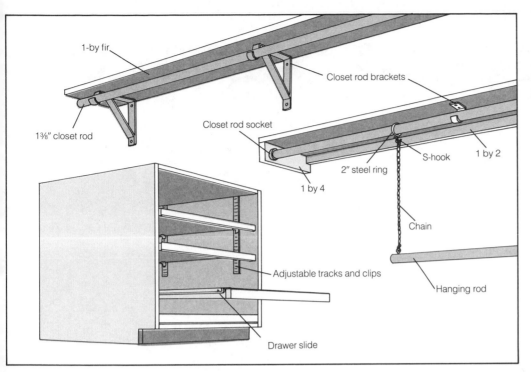

1-by fir

Closet rod brackets

1⅜" closet rod

Closet rod socket

S-hook

1 by 2

2" steel ring

1 by 4

Chain

Adjustable tracks and clips

Hanging rod

Drawer slide

A variety of closet rods and shelving

Closets with only one rod and one shelf often don't meet today's storage needs. With easy-to-install brackets, you can add a rod and shelf on an unused wall. A simple hanging rod allows you to take advantage of the wasted space below short garments. Pull-out shelves in the corner of a closet can augment bureau space and keep your sweaters and other knits in shape.

Your local hardware store or closet shop can offer additional ideas for increasing your closet's storage capacity.

Closet door close-ups

If you're building a small closet that has ample clearance in front, a standard interior door may be all you need. But you may want to use one or two sets of either bifold or sliding doors. Both types are simple to install, as long as your rough opening is square.

A standard 2 by 4 closet frame requires some prep work before you can hang the doors. Add standard head and side jambs and trim the opening as you would any standard doorway.

Bifold doors move in metal tracks mounted to the bottom of the head jamb; pivots turn in top and bottom brackets, and a center guide at the top runs in the track.

Sliding doors run on rollers inside metal tracks; floor guides keep the doors in line below. Tracks are available to fit either ¾-inch plywood or standard 1⅜-inch interior doors.

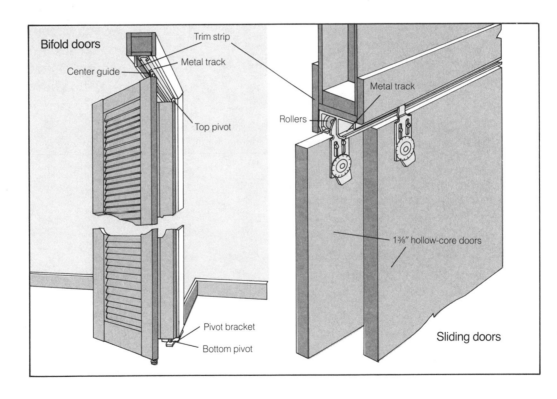

Bifold doors

Trim strip

Center guide

Metal track

Top pivot

Metal track

Rollers

1⅜" hollow-core doors

Pivot bracket

Bottom pivot

Sliding doors

Bathroom Storage

Of all the rooms in the house, the bathroom is usually the smallest—and the least seriously considered in terms of effective space planning. Yet today's bathrooms collect all kinds of paraphernalia, from hair blowers to hampers and from exercise equipment to magazines and books. Often, it all ends up in one big jumble.

To help you find your way, we've assembled a collection of photographs and drawings showing successful storage solutions tailored to the bathroom. Foremost among them is the bathroom vanity. Usually made from wood, vanities organize everything from cosmetics to cleaning supplies. Racks and hooks attached to the inside of doors can make the space even more efficient. In this section, we give instructions on how to build your own bathroom vanity. All you need are a few simple tools and some basic woodworking knowledge.

Medicine cabinets can do the work of several drawers or shelves. Some sit right above the sink; others fit between wall studs beside the sink.

Open shelving for towels, books, or even plants can take advantage of now-wasted space—above toilets, between the studs, or in corners. If moisture isn't a problem and you have the floor space, consider moving in a small piece of furniture, such as a bookcase or an attractive wood chest.

Small appliance caddies or a grid system that's attached to the wall can organize your vanity top in a jiffy, as can a soap dish and toothbrush holder. And a shower caddy can place soap and shampoo just where you need them—in the shower.

Think carefully about what you use frequently in the bathroom as you're planning your storage needs. Whether you build your own units or buy them ready-made, your best resources are your imagination and a clear understanding of your needs.

Space-makers

Maximizing storage around the sink

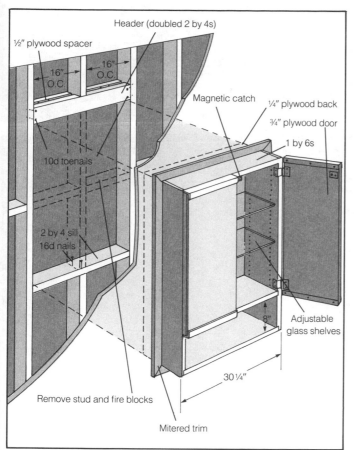

Header (doubled 2 by 4s)

½" plywood spacer

16" O.C.

16" O.C.

Magnetic catch

¼" plywood back

¾" plywood door

1 by 6s

10d toenails

2 by 4 sill
16d nails

8"

Adjustable
glass shelves

Remove stud and fire blocks

30¼"

Mitered trim

Built-in bathroom cabinet

A built-in cabinet recessed between wall studs can provide needed storage without taking over the room. Though you could fit a very narrow cabinet between studs, in most cases you'll have to remove part of one middle stud and reframe the opening.

First, locate the studs in the area and check for any wiring or plumbing. If all is clear, mark the inside edges of the studs you'll keep; also mark top and bottom lines at the height you want the cabinet, adding 3½ inches at the top and 1½ inches at the bottom for the new header and sill.

Cut an opening through the wall covering along the lines. Knock off any fire blocks. With a handsaw, cut the middle stud squarely and carefully pry it away from the wall covering on the other side. Make the header as shown and toenail it inside the opening. Cut a 2 by 4 sill to the same length and nail it in place.

Build the cabinet frame from 1 by 6 lumber, making it ¼ inch less in height and width than the size of the opening. Nail on a ¼-inch plywood back. Drill holes for shelf pegs or pins, add doors, and finish.

Position the cabinet in the opening, shimming it level and plumb, and nail it to the framing. Attach the trim, mitering the corners, and then add shelves.

No wasted space under this sink

Most bathroom cabinets have one large space under the sink, often stuffed with layers of bottles, sponges, bath toys, and packages of toilet tissue—none of which is easy to reach or see.

One simple solution is to build drawers that wrap around the sink and its plumbing. Each drawer has a curving rear, cut from 18-gauge sheet metal and fastened to the sides and bottom with sheet-metal screws. Design: Bill Ridenour.

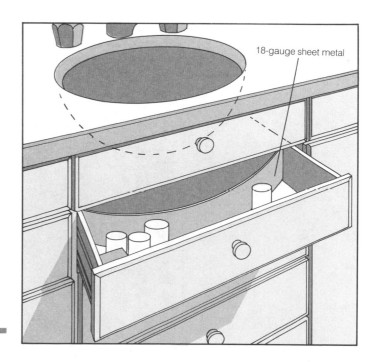

18-gauge sheet metal

Cabinetry: The "Inside" Story

Clutter-swallowing helpers that hide behind closed cabinet doors

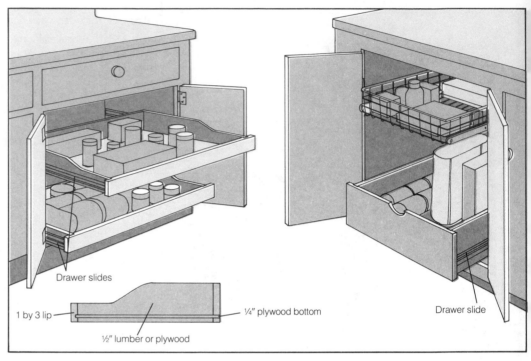

Drawer slides

1 by 3 lip   ¼" plywood bottom

½" lumber or plywood   Drawer slide

Back-of-the-door bonanza

A wood or vinyl-coated wire storage rack mounted to the inside of a cabinet door can help you organize soaps, shampoos, and other cosmetics, as well as bathroom cleaning supplies.

Problem-solving pull-outs

There's no need to grope around in your bathroom cabinets in search of that extra tube of toothpaste or the bubble bath you got last Christmas. With pull-outs like the ones shown here, bath supplies glide right out for easy access. Available in plastic, wood, and regular or vinyl-coated wire, pull-outs can be installed on full-extension drawer slides or on their own special framework.

Not-so-lazy Susans

These hard-working storage-go-rounds help keep bathroom paraphernalia from finding its way into the far reaches of your cabinetry. Single-level or tiered, a lazy Susan rotates so that everything you store is visible and accessible. Be sure to measure your cabinet carefully—allowing for drainpipe clearance, if necessary—before you buy or build one of these organizers.

These cabinets put away plenty

Imported from Germany, this plastic laminate bath cabinetry carries all the soaps, cleansers, lotions, creams, and scents you'll need for some time to come. The gleaming chrome towel rack swings out of the way to allow easy access to the spacious undersink compartment; the cabinet on the left features swivel-out trays in various sizes. Cabinetry courtesy of European Kitchens & Baths.

Mirror magic

Concealed behind a mirrored door, these under-the-counter pull-outs glide into view when you need them. Two shallow and two deep drawers hold cosmetics, towels, and cleaning products. Doors operate with touch-latches. Interior design: Helen Kroeger, Interiors by Design.

Cabinetry of Wood

The traditional raw material of the cabinetmaker's art,
shown here in designs that are far from ordinary

**Old wood adds
warmth to a new bath**

Antique cabinet, fitted
with modern basins, takes
on a new life in this older
home's remodeled master
bathroom. Capacious
drawers in the center section hold towels and toilet
articles. There's also plenty
of undersink storage at
either end. Architect:
William B. Remick.

Hollywood glamour, right at home

Curving cabinetry and theatrical make-up lights add star quality to this sleek sink and storage area. The mirrored panels at either end of the unit are actually mirror-faced doors for twin medicine cabinets. And below the sink, a cupboard and bank of drawers offer roomy recesses for tucking away towels, lotions, and other accouterments of glamorous grooming. Architects: Olsen/Walker. Cabinet design: The Butt Joint.

Orderly without, organized within

There's nothing trendy about this bathroom storage wall and sink counter. The attractive traditional-style wood cabinetry and a mirrored medicine cabinet just look great and do their job—keeping bath necessities and even clothing in their proper place—while giving the whole room a pleasing sense of order. Who could ask for more? When open to view, the drawers and doors disclose a wealth of storage organization, including a roomy set of wooden pull-outs. Design: Dennis O'Connor.

Cabinetry of Plastic Laminate

The sleek, chic European imports
are a bold new bath-storage option

**Plastic pizzazz,
Italian-style**

From the ultra-modern
approach of northern Italian
design comes this factory-
molded sculptural elegance
for the bathroom. The clever
countertop towel rack whim-
sically plays with terrycloth
tones, creating vertical stripes
that balance the horizontal
strokes of navy blue on the
wall above. Drawers and
cabinets are anything but
boring—they're concave or
convex; they can be pulled
or swiveled. And even the
vanity stool stands for more
than just plain seating—it
stores things, too. Cabinetry
courtesy of Dahl Designs.

Wall-covering cabinetry

This German cabinetry puts every square inch of a bathroom wall to work— with precision. The fine-lined pattern on drawers and cabinet doors provides an interesting texture that's resistant to fingerprints, as well. Behind the beautiful façade are cleverly designed interiors to accommodate everything from cosmetics to laundry. (You can peek behind the doors on pages 57 and 71.) Cabinetry courtesy of European Kitchens & Baths.

Not corners, but curves

This sand and charcoal-colored cabinetry presents a rounded look that's a refreshing contrast to the harsher, predominantly angular environment of many bathrooms. So there are no handles to interrupt the smooth façade, all cabinets open with touch-latches. The bottom cabinet on the far side (shown open) features a swing-out towel rack. Cabinetry courtesy of Dahl Designs.

Open Shelves

Out-in-the-open storage puts towels
and other bright bath supplies on display

Tubside art enhances the bath

Surely one of the most sumptuous of life's simple pleasures is a good, hot soak in a bubbly bath. To enrich the experience, this bathroom provides a colorful gallery of miniature folk art for bathtime viewing. Besides display space, the handsome cedar shelves offer storage for bright towels, and even for a few books. Architect: William Abbott.

Towels sit high up in brassy splendor

In days gone by, this vintage piece held luggage overhead in a cramped train compartment. Today, in a crowded bathroom, it keeps extra towels out of the way, yet within reach. Its brass mesh shelf and filigree framing are a treat to view from underneath. Design: Rand Hughes.

Greenhouse windows offer shelf space

Greenhouse popouts, available from building-supply and home-improvement centers, can provide extra space and daylight, as well as wide views of the leafy world outside. At the same time, they offer attractive shelf space for both practical and decorative items. Since the room faces a shady corner of the garden, there's no worry that sunlight might fade the towels. Design: Woody Dike.

Mini-library for private browsing

Many people appreciate the privacy bathrooms afford for reading in undistracted solitude. Here, a colorful collection of paperbacks offers not only food for thought, but hospitality and decorative cheer as well. You'll find more ideas for bathroom libraries on pages 72–73. Design: Jeanne Kleyn.

Graceful niche for bath necessities

An arched alcove, traversed by a single glass shelf, creates open wall storage with a clean and airy feeling. The rectangular opening just below houses a fluorescent light behind a frosted glass panel; more glass functions as sliding doors for the base cabinet.

Under the window, a laundry hamper disguises itself as a simple ledge when its lid is closed. Architects: Ted Tanaka and Frank Purtill.

Linen Closets

Orderly accommodation for the bulk of your bed and bath needs

Closet chic

Clean-as-a-whistle white shelving etches a crisp border around stacked sheets and towels in this walk-in linen closet.

Derived from an industrial design, these vinyl-coated wire shelves are available for the home through specialty shops, interior designers, and home centers. Besides their look of high-tech sophistication, they offer other advantages: good air circulation, light weight, quick installation, and easy access to their contents. Architect: John Galbraith.

Sleek exterior, hard-working interior

One basic aim of good storage design is an everything-in-place look that's gentle on the eyes. When all its doors and drawers are closed, this floor-to-ceiling storage wall blends unobtrusively into its all-white bathroom surroundings—only the glistening brass hardware calls attention to its function. Behind the cabinet doors, colorful linens are neatly arranged on lipped, pull-out shelves. Architects: Fisher/Friedman Associates.

Storing linens for just one room

Often, each bedroom has its own linens—sheets and blankets that coordinate with the decor and fit the bed in the room. What better place to store them than in the bedroom itself? Here, a narrow cabinet at the end of a wall system (see page 21 for another view) is fitted with shelves deep enough to accommodate pillows, sheets, and a quilt. Interior design: Patricia Whitt Designs.

Medicine Cabinets

Handy, high-style housing for home remedies
and prescriptions, first-aid supplies and cosmetics

Pops open at a touch

Just give this medicine cabinet door a little push and it'll pop right open— thanks to the convenient touch-latch. Since the door opens upward, you'll want to position the cabinet low enough for adults' convenience, but high enough to prevent bumped foreheads. Cabinet courtesy of Plus Kitchens.

Low-lying cabinets leave room for a view

For many of us, the first sight of the day, as we splash cold water on our faces, is somewhat less inspiring than a gentle garden view. But as this thoughtful arrangement makes clear, the traditional over-the-sink mirror is not compulsory. Here, you can have it both ways: twin medicine cabinets with mirrored sliding doors are recessed into the back-splash area, leaving space for a window above one sink and for a mirror above the other. Architects: Ted Tanaka and Frank Purtill.

Prescription for storage

Built in between the wall studs, this wooden medicine chest is compact yet roomy, with storage space on the inside of the cabinet door as well as on the interior shelves. Small-diameter wooden dowels keep door-stored items in place. Design: Jeanne Kleyn.

Cabinet puts corner to work

Tucked into a corner between the sink and bathtub, this jumbo medicine cabinet holds cosmetics, remedies, and bath supplies for the whole family. Below it is a tip-out laundry hamper (you see it open on page 70). Architect: William B. Remick.

Bathroom Organizers

Caddies, soap dishes, and hampers keep
bathroom counters and shelves clean and orderly

Shower heads have hang-ups, too

No longer do you have to perch your shower supplies precariously on a windowsill or tub ledge. These shower caddies, which hang from a shower head, hold shampoo, soap, and washcloths. Open shelves allow articles to drain and dry between showers.

Catchalls for containers and appliances

Slanted compartments of the clear acrylic appliance caddy hold hair dryers and curling irons; its straight section puts combs and brushes within easy reach. The caddy can sit on a countertop or hang on a wall.

Vinyl-coated wire or plastic baskets, like the one shown, corral items of different shapes and sizes, reducing bathroom clutter and eliminating last-minute hassles.

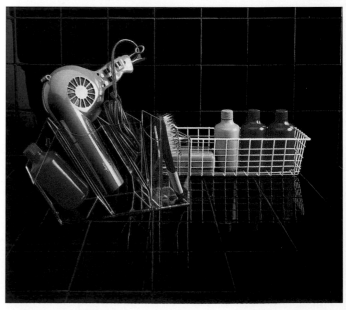

An array of soap dish designs

Even the lowly bar of soap rises to new heights in today's distinctive soap dishes. Whether your decor is starkly modern or traditional, your choices range from clear acrylic to colorful plastic to clear-finished wood. If your dish doesn't have drainage holes or slats, you can add a ribbed or spiked plastic insert specially designed for this purpose.

Movable hampers— and they're washable, too

These two alternatives to the traditional bulky bathroom hamper are made from fast-drying nylon. The hanging hamper can collect clothing for a few days on a wall hook or at the end of a shower bar. It's available in a range of colors to complement almost any bathroom decor. The larger laundry bag slips onto a lightweight metal-tubing frame.

Hampers

A fresh, new look at those bathroom basics

Hatch lifts up to catch clothing

The sturdy fir deck around this bathtub provides more than just good-looking surroundings for a sudsy soak. It also makes efficient use of the space between the tub and a wall by offering a roomy built-in laundry hamper. When the lid is closed, the spot doubles as a dressing bench. Design: James Fey.

Tip-out bin for a tight spot

In this bathroom, a tip-out laundry bin takes clever advantage of the corner between the sink and bathtub. It serves its purpose smoothly in a tight-cornered room where a conventional freestanding hamper would only be in the way. Architect: William B. Remick.

For towel-tossing

Flip open this sleek tilt-down cabinet door and you find a laundry hamper just waiting for you to play doff-and-toss. The vinyl-coated wire basket lifts out so that after you've flung your clothing and towels into it, you can carry the whole works over to the washer. Cabinetry courtesy of European Kitchens & Baths.

Laundry collection point

With a hamper between these double sinks, dirty towels need never clutter the towel bars or floor. A finger reveal in the drawer top lets you pull the bin out and tilt it slightly. It's deep enough to hold a load of wash. Interior design: Teri Rickel, Dovetail Interior Design.

A Very Private Library

Racks to display your current collection
of periodicals and paperbacks

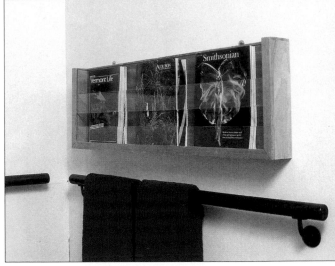

Three-in-one wall unit

With a small bathroom, you can't afford to waste even the awkward space between the toilet and the adjacent wall. The handy redwood unit shown here offers a lot in a limited area: a shallow yet roomy cabinet for extra soap and paper products, a tissue holder, and a very simple magazine rack. (Magazines stand on top of the supply cabinet and are held in place by two redwood trim strips.) Design: Marshall Design-Built.

See-through strips let magazine covers brighten bath

In this wall rack, magazines are held in place by two strips, as in the rack shown on the left. But instead of redwood, the strips here are made of clear acrylic to give a sleek, contemporary look—and to let colorful magazine covers show through. The rest of the unit is simply a shallow, three-sided wooden box. Design: John Matthias.

Cabinet creates a paperback perch

Spanning a toilet alcove, the top of this wooden medicine cabinet is home to a collection of paperback books. Open shelves are an appealing—though often overlooked—option for bathroom storage; pages 62–63 show several other ways in which creative homeowners and designers have put them to work. Design: The Butt Joint.

72 Bathroom Storage

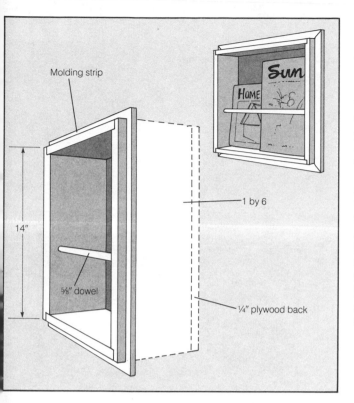

Between-the-studs box library

This recessed rack for reading matter is a simple box that fits snugly between two wall studs. Since wall studs are usually 16 or 24 inches apart (center to center), your box library will probably need to be 14½ or 22½ inches wide; 14 inches is a convenient height for it. Locate the studs, measure and mark your wall carefully, then remove only enough wallboard to accommodate the box. (Pick a location for your box library where you won't run into electrical wiring and plumbing lines inside the wall.)

Use fir 1 by 4s or 1 by 6s for the box frame (1 by 6s will add extra depth, but they'll stick out slightly from the wall). Before assembling the frame drill shallow holes in the side pieces to hold a ⅝-inch dowel (see illustration). Assemble the frame and add a ¼-inch plywood back. Slide the unit into the wall cutout, and side-nail the box to one or both wall studs. Add molding strips or wood trim around the box to hide the rough edges and give a built-in look. Finally, finish the unit with enamel, varnish, or polyurethane. Design: John Schmid.

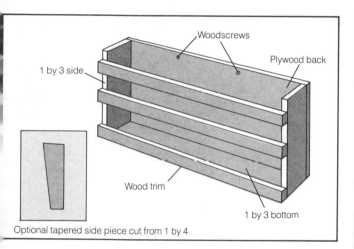

No-frills wall rack

This simple wall rack is remarkably easy to build. Cut two side pieces and a bottom piece from pine or fir 1 by 3s, and cut a back from ¼-inch or ⅜-inch plywood. Assemble the rack, then nail ¼-inch-thick strips of wood trim across the front to keep magazines and books in place. Finally, drive two woodscrews through the back of the rack and into the wall studs and apply a paint, varnish, or polyurethane finish. The unit illustrated is approximately 12 inches high and 20 inches wide, but these dimensions can be adjusted to suit your needs and wall space.

If you must get fancy, build the rack with tapered side pieces (cut from 1 by 4s) so your reading matter tilts forward for easier access.

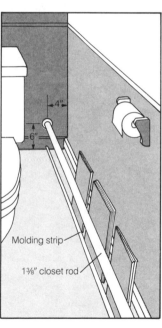

Closet rod corrals magazines

A 1⅜-inch wooden closet rod, mounted 4 inches out from the wall and 6 inches above the floor, can keep magazines rounded up in what would otherwise be wasted space. A molding strip attached to the floor (as shown) will keep magazines from sliding forward. If your bathroom floor tends to collect water, add a narrow wooden platform (with the molding strip on top) to keep your reading matter high and dry.

Towel Hang-ups

A whole raft of racks, rails, rods, and rings
that you can buy or build

Redwood and towels—two ways to go

Here's a pair of easy-to-make variations on the basic towel
bar theme. One is a no-nonsense rail; the other is a fancier,
and slightly more challenging, two-rung rack.

The rustic rail is made from a long redwood 2 by 2 held
out from the wall by 4½-inch-long end blocks made of 2
by 3s. Lag screws 3½ inches long attach the rail to the end
blocks; the end blocks are attached to wall studs with 5½-
inch-long lag screws. (Be sure to find the wall studs before
you decide on a length for your rail.) If lag screw heads
seem too rustic, you can countersink them and cover them
with dowel plugs.

For the two-rung rack, use 1½-inch wooden rods and
redwood, fir, or pine 2 by 12s. From the 2 by 12s, cut two
curved wall mounts like the one shown; smooth them with
a rasp and sandpaper. Drill shallow holes in the mounts to
support the rods, positioning the lower rod in front of the
upper one, as shown. Two screws fasten each mount to the
wall studs. (Again, determine the length of your rack after
you've located the wall studs.)

A bathroom's humid climate can be tough on unfinished
wood, so be sure to protect your new towel bars with several coats of polyurethane finish or penetrating resin.

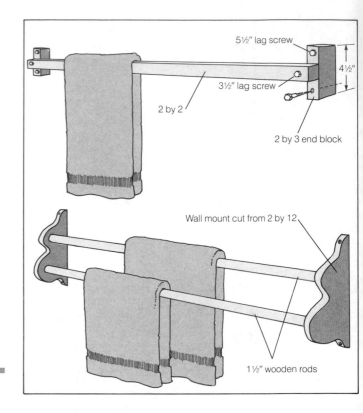

Recessed towel bar

Located just below and
slightly to the side of your
bathroom sink, this 1 by 2
bar allows you to grab a
towel without having to
grope for it. Make the
pocket 2½ inches deep
and line its surfaces to
match the cabinet facing.
The bar itself is inset ½
inch from the cabinet
front. Architect: Henry
Wood.

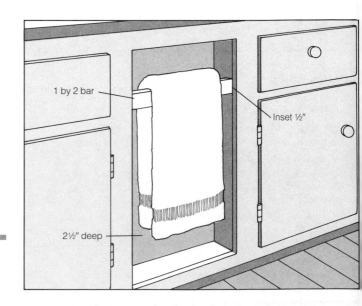

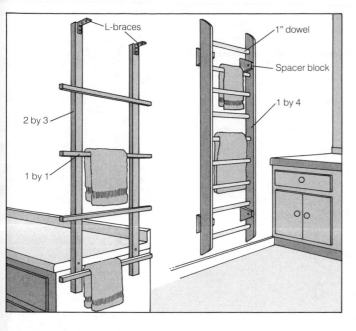

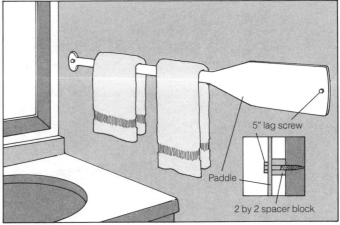

The lowdown on ladders

Floor-to-ceiling towel ladders make the most of narrow spaces. They're also very easy to build.

Simply nail 1 by 1 strips to the front edges of two parallel 2 by 3 uprights. Or recess 1-inch dowels into matching holes in two parallel 1 by 4 uprights; glue the dowels in place and clamp them securely until dry. Fasten your ladder to the floor and/or ceiling with L-braces (be sure to allow at least ¼ inch between the top of the ladder and the ceiling for clearance) or attach it to spacer blocks that you've screwed into wall studs.

Redwood is an excellent material for towel holders because it's moisture-resistant. Hardwoods are also good but are somewhat more expensive. Protect the wood with a polyurethane finish or penetrating resin.

This paddle stays high and dry

This sleek 5-foot towel bar is actually a canoe paddle that was purchased for under $10 at a marine supply store. It's attached to the wall studs with two 5-inch-long lag screws that run through holes drilled in the paddle and in two spacer blocks cut from a 2 by 2. Several coats of clear marine varnish make this unusual towel bar "weatherproof."

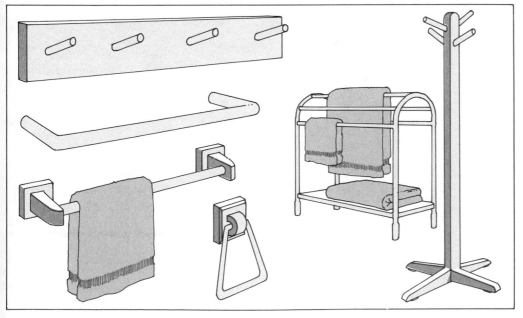

Ready-made racks

If you'd rather buy a towel rack than build one, you'll find a large selection of ready-mades. Standard bars and rings, sold individually or as components in matching accessory sets, are available in a wide variety of materials—from brass to chrome, from oak to plastic. Another option is a wall rack with wooden pegs or brass hooks.

If you have floor space to spare, consider a free-standing rack, such as a towel tree or a floor stand with room for both hanging and folded towels.

Building a Bathroom Cabinet

In remodeled bathrooms and in new ones,
cabinets add both style and efficiency

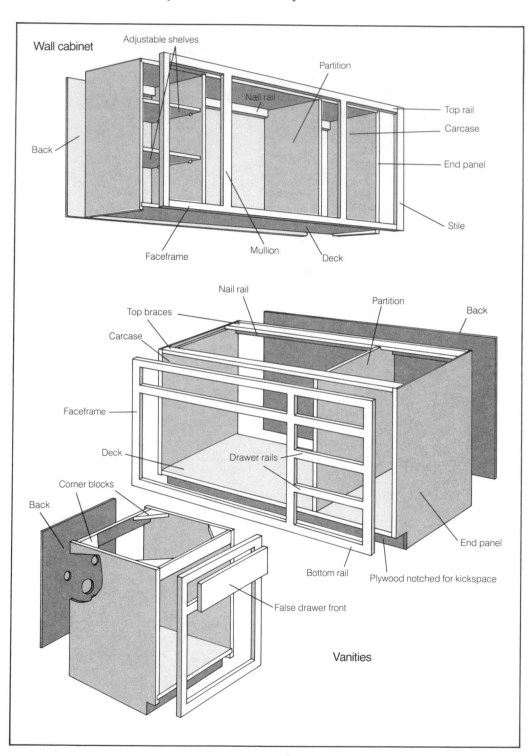

Wall cabinet — Adjustable shelves, Partition, Nail rail, Top rail, Carcase, End panel, Back, Stile, Faceframe, Mullion, Deck

Vanities — Nail rail, Top braces, Partition, Back, Carcase, Faceframe, Deck, Drawer rails, Corner blocks, Back, Bottom rail, End panel, Plywood notched for kickspace, False drawer front

Building the basic box

Basically, cabinets are boxes fitted with drawers, doors, and shelves. Called carcases, the boxes, usually made from plywood, are then fitted with solid-lumber faceframes that hide the plywood edges.

The carcases of both vanities and wall cabinets are composed of end panels, a bottom (called a deck), a back, and, often, interior partitions. Ends, partitions, and decks are usually made from ¾-inch plywood and the back from ¼-inch plywood. Typically, vanities are 32 inches high (including the countertop) and 21 inches deep.

Wall cabinets have plywood top panels; vanities are fitted with top braces, which both square up the case and serve as nailers for the countertop. Small vanities sometimes have flat, triangular corner blocks for the same purpose. Nail rails aid in attaching the cabinet to the wall.

Rabbets and dadoes make strong connections for carcase parts, but basic butt joints work well, too. Use glue and nails or screws to secure the joints.

Usually, faceframes are made from 1-by hardwood joined with glue and dowels. Attach the faceframe with finishing nails.

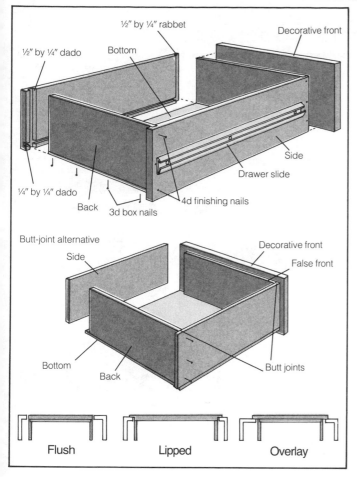

½" by ¼" rabbet
Decorative front
½" by ¼" dado
Bottom
Side
Drawer slide
¼" by ¼" dado
4d finishing nails
Back
3d box nails

Butt-joint alternative
Side
Decorative front
False front
Bottom
Back
Butt joints

Flush   Lipped   Overlay

Designing drawers

Drawers come in three basic styles: flush, lipped, or overlay (see drawing at left). A *flush* drawer lines up even with the front of the cabinet; on a *lipped* drawer, part of the front projects slightly past; the entire front of an *overlay* drawer sits outside the faceframe. It's easiest to build drawers with a false front, which allows you to build a basic box, hang it, and then align the decorative front exactly.

Make the drawers from ½-inch plywood or pine; the fronts are made from either ¾-inch plywood or solid lumber. Drawer bottoms are typically ¼-inch plywood or hardboard.

Drawers are stronger if the pieces are joined with dadoes and rabbets, but simple butt joints will work, too. Make the box height the same as the opening minus ¼ inch. Drawer width is also nominally the opening minus ¼ inch—subtract extra for any side-mounted drawer slides. Generally, box depth is ¼ inch less than the depth of the recess, unless your drawer slides require additional space in back.

Be sure when you're measuring box depth to allow for your front style: measure flush drawers from the back edge of the faceframe, add ⅜ inch for lipped drawers, and measure from the cabinet front for overlay drawers.

For trouble-free drawer action, metal ball-bearing drawer slides are the best choice. Be sure to leave sufficient clearance for them.

Building doors

Study any cabinet door and you'll most likely find it's either a flat plywood door or a frame-and-panel style.

A *flat* door is the simplest to make, whether it's flush, lipped, or overlay. For best results, cut the door from ¾-inch lumber-core plywood.

The rails and stiles of *frame-and-panel* doors are made from 1-by or 4/4 lumber; panels can be ¼-inch plywood or edge-joined ½-inch lumber. The easiest type to make is a plywood panel that fits into a rabbet in the back of the frame. Raised-bevel (see at right) and square-shoulder panels are made from ½-inch plywood or ½-inch solid stock.

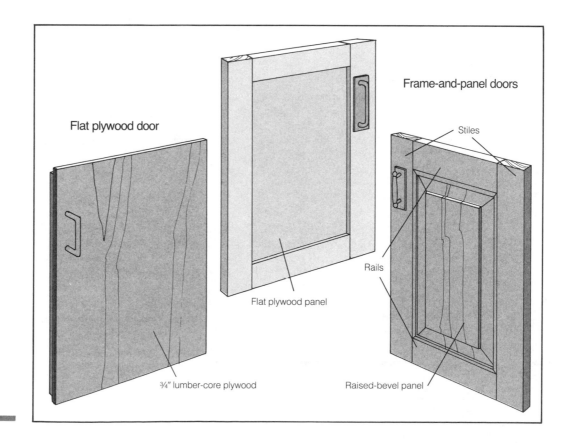

Flat plywood door

Flat plywood panel

¾" lumber-core plywood

Frame-and-panel doors

Stiles

Rails

Raised-bevel panel

Small Appliances & Accessories

Here are several solutions to the problem of where to stash your grooming gadgets, plus some holders for tissue and toothbrushes

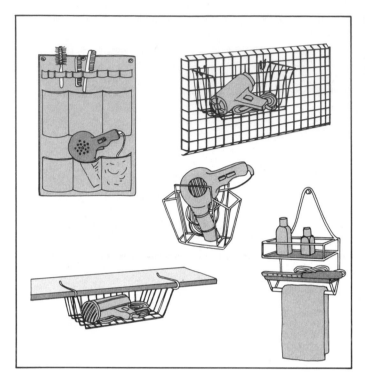

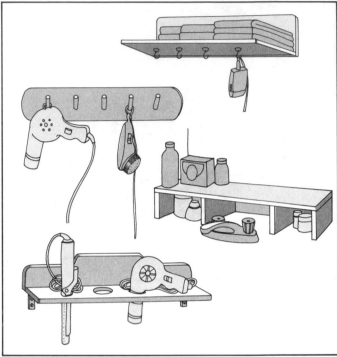

Ready-made solutions to appliance storage problems

The popularity and proliferation of personal-grooming gadgets have put bathroom storage at an even greater premium. We have electric toothbrushes and water jets; blow dryers, curling irons, and electric rollers; shavers, tweezers, complexion brushes, and manicure machines—but how can we keep them all organized and within reach?

Storage aids not designed specifically for small appliances can be easily pressed into service: consider shower caddies (remember that they can be hung on an open wall as well as over a shower head), wall-mounted vinyl pouches (often sold as closet organizers), and under-shelf baskets of vinyl-coated wire.

Perhaps the most flexible approach to small appliance storage is a vinyl-coated wire grid system. Appliances with hanging loops can be suspended on hooks; those without loops can be stored in the bins and baskets that are available as components of such systems.

Some improvised solutions

If your small grooming appliances have hanging loops, then simple hooks or pegs are all you'll need for storage. Put together a taproom rack from a redwood backing strip and some brass hooks or hardwood-dowel pegs; or simply screw cuphooks to the underside of a bathroom shelf.

If you'd rather not hang your appliances, consider a narrow shelf with carefully measured holes drilled through it to form holsters for your curling iron, your shaver, or the nozzle of your blow dryer. For several large or heavy appliances, try a wider shelf running the length of the sink counter and 6 to 8 inches above it; support the shelf with wood blocks spaced to form counter-level cubbyholes for cosmetics and grooming aids. For moisture protection, finish wood shelves with enamel or two coats of clear polyurethane.

Tissue holders to buy or build

Tissue holders are available in a wide variety of styles and materials—from traditional steel or ceramic holders with spring-loaded inserts, to high-tech plastic models in bright colors, to costly antique reproductions in solid brass. But tissue holders are also very easy to make, and the handsome wooden ones shown here are fine examples.

The two ends of a teak ship's rail (from a marine supply store) make a very stylish holder. Just drill a small hole in the inside edge of each piece to accommodate a spring-loaded insert (available at most hardware stores), and add shims, if necessary, to increase wall clearance. (Remember that a new roll of tissue is about 5 inches in diameter, so the insert's center must be at least 2¾ inches from the wall.)

The horizontal-dowel holder substitutes a 1-inch dowel for the spring-loaded insert. Cut two end pieces (in any shape you like) from a fir 2 by 6. Then drill a 1-inch-diameter hole halfway through one end piece and a corresponding hole completely through the other end piece (so the dowel can be removed). Allow at least 4½ inches clearance between end pieces (that's the width of a standard roll).

With the vertical-dowel holder, the tissue roll stands on end. Use scrap blocks of fir, oak, or redwood and a 5-inch-long 1¼-inch dowel. Assemble the pieces (as shown) with woodscrews and glue.

Mounting tissue holders may require some patience. Some end pieces are easier to mount if they are first bridged by a backing piece which is then attached directly to the wall. Try to anchor a holder to a wall stud; if that's not feasible, use expanding anchors or toggle bolts.

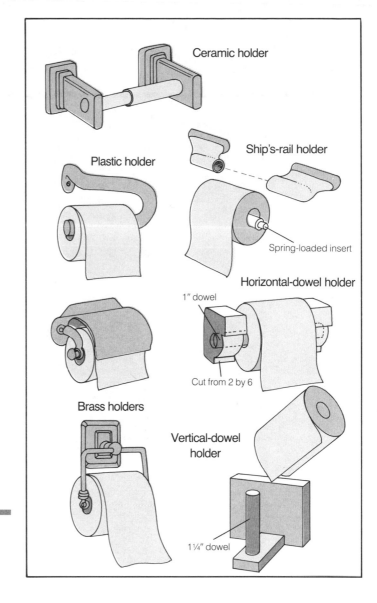

Ceramic holder

Plastic holder

Ship's-rail holder

Spring-loaded insert

Horizontal-dowel holder

1" dowel

Cut from 2 by 6

Brass holders

Vertical-dowel holder

1¼" dowel

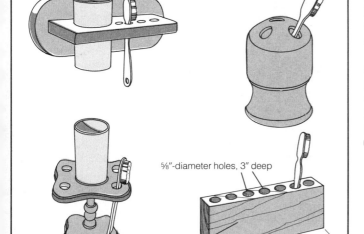

⅝"-diameter holes, 3" deep

2 by 4

9"

Dental details: a brush-up course

Choose one of the many commercially available toothbrush holders—freestanding or wall-mounted, with tumbler or without—or make one of your own from a scrap block of oak.

Begin with a 9-inch-long 2 by 4. Into one edge, drill eight ⅝-inch-diameter holes, each 3 inches deep (see illustration). Smooth the entire holder with fine sandpaper. Finish the wood with two coats of clear polyurethane to protect it from the humid bathroom climate—and from dripping toothbrushes.

Sunset
Proof-of-Purchase
ISBN 0-376-01122-X

Index

Sunset
Garage, Attic
& Basement
Storage

By the Editors of Sunset Books and Sunset Magazine

LANE PUBLISHING CO. • Menlo Park, California

We wish to thank the architects, designers, and homeowners whose innovative ideas for storage are included in this book. A special thank-you goes to Kirsten Fedderke for her assistance in assembling the color section.

Cover: Boxes, baskets, bins, shelves . . . these are tools of the storage trade. Labels and see-through panels make them especially convenient; pegboard, hooks, and brackets make them adaptable. Photographed by Jack McDowell. Cover design by Zan Fox.

Photographers

Gerald Fredrick: 28 left. **Gene Hamilton:** 36, 60 left, 62. **Jack McDowell:** 3, 4, 5 bottom left, 11, 12, 13 bottom, 19, 20, 21 left, 22, 29 left, 35, 37, 38, 43, 44, 45 top, 46 left, 53, 59, 60 right, 61. **Steve W. Marley:** 5 bottom right, 27 left. **Ells Marugg:** 29 right. **Rob Super:** 45 bottom left. **Tom Wyatt:** 5 top, 6, 13 top, 14, 21 right, 27 right, 28 right, 30, 46 right, 51, 52, 54.

Editor, Sunset Books:
Elizabeth L. Hogan

Seventh printing March 1990

 Library of Congress Catalog Card Number: 82-81369. ISBN 0-376-01200-5. Lithographed in the United States.

Supervising Editor:
Maureen Williams Zimmerman

Staff Editors: **Susan E. Schlangen**
Susan Warton

Contributing Editor: **Scott Atkinson**

Design: **Roger Flanagan**

Photo Editor: **JoAnn Masaoka**

Illustrations: **Rik Olson**

Contents

Behind sturdy blonde doors, *this custom storage wall works hard at organizing a garage-load of goods. Architect: Glenn D. Brewer.*

About This Book...

Some of life's greatest pleasures are associated with the possessions we own and must store—garden tools that help ensure fragrant blossoms in spring, sleek new skis that sink into fresh powdery snow, sturdy old suitcases that wear the scars of travel as surely as we carry the memories. It seems that the more we enjoy life, the more we have to store.

What's *your* storage situation? Do you know where you'll stack the firewood to stoke the new wood stove you've been thinking about? How will you put to use the knowledge gained at that great wine class, if you don't have a proper place to store wine? What do you do with your multiplying financial records, mystery novels, family photos?

We think it's best to start simply. That's why our first section (pages 6–11) is devoted to storage units and accessories. You'll be pleased at how much even a few hooks, racks, and bins can do. For specific belongings, we've included an item-by-item storage section (pages 12–59). Filled with ideas, it's an alphabetical showcase that tells you what to do with items—outdoor furniture, sports equipment, and workshop supplies—that may be stumbling blocks in your storage path. The section also contains special features about auxiliary storage areas—the patio, deck, and garden shed—and a feature on storage safety.

Crowded garages, stuffy attics, and wet basements receive in-depth treatment in the back of the book (pages 60–79). Here, we explain ways to remedy some of the more complicated but common problems of garage, attic, and basement storage.

A place for everything *and everything in its place. Pine boards and vertical plywood spacers form cubbyholes—large ones for basketballs and ice skates, small ones for wine and miscellany. See pages 8–9 for more shelving ideas.*
Design: Richard and Sandra Pollock

Triangular cupboard *with folding door exploits vacant storage space in stairwell on one side of basement wall. Roomy drawers and wall shelves also put space to work that would otherwise go to waste.*

Loft frees floor space *below for table saw, freezer, extra refrigerator. Commercial fold-down stairs offer easy access to lightweight storables. For more on lofts, see page 65.*

"Tools" of the Storage Trade

Pegs, hooks & racks • shelving • boxes & bins • cabinets & closets

Simple storage aids *can handle complex storage needs. Here, a modest shelving unit corrals camping gear and gardening equipment, nails grip tennis rackets, and a bin brims with sports gear. The bike dangles from ceiling hooks.*

It's the hottest day of the year, and you still haven't stored your winter woollies, holiday decorations, and snow tires. Don't worry; you're suffering from a common ailment. And here you'll find some tested remedies—the most basic storage units and accessories.

This section is like a catalogue, with some tips to help you select the kinds of storage units and accessories best suited to your needs. The emphasis is on simple, utilitarian storage aids that are easy to build or install: pegs, hooks, racks, shelves, boxes, bins, cabinets, and closets. Many of these items can be purchased in a variety of colors, materials, and designs.

You'll probably want to choose a combination of open and closed storage. Open storage—for example, heavy-duty hooks securely fastened to garage wall studs—may be ideal for hanging up your snow tires. Fragile holiday decorations, on the other hand, require closed storage— say, cardboard boxes on track and bracket shelves —for protection from dust, moisture, and accidents.

By adding a few storage aids, you'll open up more floor space and gain better clearance—important benefits in full garages, attics with steep walls, and basements. You may even discover new space for work or play.

Consult *Sunset's* companion volumes, *Wall Systems & Shelving* and *How to Make Bookshelves & Cabinets*, for more details on tools, techniques, and materials.

Pegs, hooks and racks

Pegs and hooks are the simplest storage aids, great for items that you want immediately accessible. Use them to hang objects from walls, ceiling joists, rafters, shelf undersides, and cabinet interiors. Rack systems, which make use of pegs and hooks, provide great storage diversity and capacity.

Pegs and hooks are particularly easy to install. For pegs, you can use large carpenters' nails hammered into wall studs or rafters, dowels recessed into drilled holes, spring clips, and even cabinet pull knobs hung on the wall. The range of hooks available includes coat hooks in many sizes, shapes, and materials; cup hooks screwed into shelf undersides; and large hooks for hanging such heavy items as bicycles (see page 15).

Wall racks are great for organizing garden tools, outdoor clothing, folding lawn chairs, hand tools, sports equipment, and many other items. The classic rack system for garages is a pegboard equipped with various hooks and hangers. Pegboard, or perforated hardboard, is made in ⅛ and ¼-inch thicknesses; install ¼-inch board for heavy-duty use. When you install pegboard, use spacers to hold it slightly away from the wall, allowing clearance for hooks.

Racks made of steel and vinyl-coated steel have either horizontal or vertical metal tracks or grids that attach to the wall. Both kinds can be equipped with a range of accessories—from hooks to shelf brackets to hanging bins—to handle specific storables.

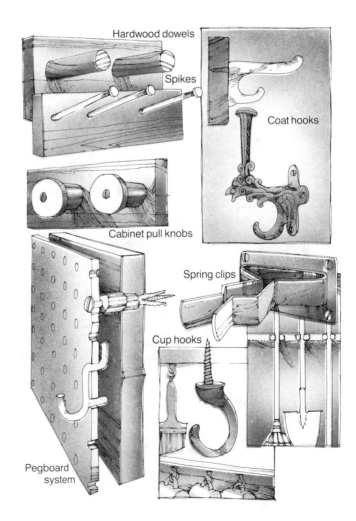
Hardwood dowels

Spikes

Coat hooks

Cabinet pull knobs

Spring clips

Cup hooks

Pegboard system

Shelves

Shelves and storage go hand in hand...the two words are almost synonymous. Shelves can be hung from the wall, suspended from the ceiling or rafters, or used to span an enclosed frame or opposing walls. Adjustable shelves and freestanding shelf units give you more flexibility, but are less stable for heavy loads.

Formal shelving units are unnecessary in storage areas. Instead, consider the following simple, less expensive ways to assemble basic units or fasten individual shelves to walls or ceilings.

Materials. What materials make good shelves for storage? Sturdy utilitarian shelves can be made from solid fir or pine, plywood, or particle board. Fir is stronger than pine, but pine is less expensive. Plywood is best for shelves more than 12 inches deep. Larger platforms can be fashioned from hollow-core doors or plywood and supported by a solid lumber frame (see page 65). You can cut your own shelves, ask lumberyard personnel to cut them for you, or purchase precut or preassembled units. Easy-to-clean plastic laminate shelves are handy for laundry or crafts areas.

Shelf spans. When planning your shelving, follow this rule: no shelf should have a span of more than 48 inches. For light loads, 1-inch thick lumber spanning 32 inches is ideal; for medium to heavy loads, shorten the span to 24 or even 16 inches, or use 2-inch-thick lumber. For very strong shelves, sandwich together two layers of ¾-inch plywood with glue, and reinforce with 1 by 2-inch strips around the edges (see drawing below). Heavy particle board shelves tend to sag, regardless of the load; if you use particle board, keep the spans very short.

Blocks and boards. Stack bricks or cinder blocks to support solid lumber or plywood shelves, preferably against a wall. If your stack is higher than 5 feet, anchor the top shelf to the wall.

Brackets. Common shelf brackets (with or without gusset supporters), continuous Z-brackets, or L-braces are easiest for fastening individual shelves or a small series of shelves to the wall.

Cleats and ledgers. Made from 1 by 2 trim or L-shaped aluminum molding, cleats and ledgers can be used to support shelves that span opposing walls and rafters or the insides of closets and cabinets. Cleats hold up the shelf ends, and a ledger runs along the back edge (see drawing below). For extra support, use 2 by 4s.

Ropes and chains. Suspended from eyescrews attached to ceiling joists or rafters, ropes and chains provide sturdy shelf support. Rope is knotted—or clamped with electrical cable clamps (see drawing below)—to secure shelves. Chain-supported shelves

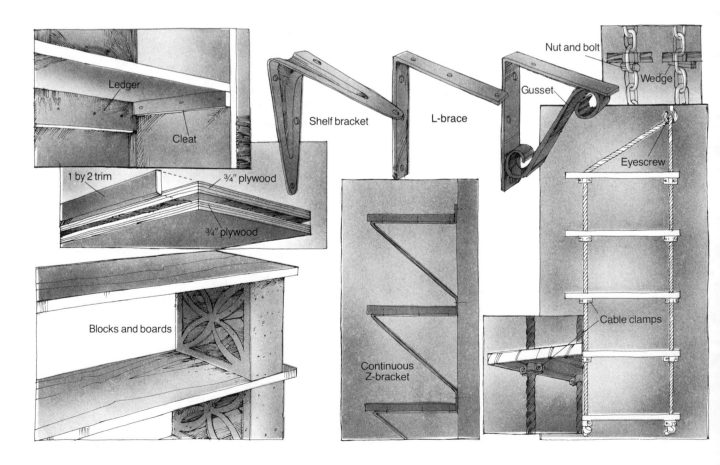

Ledger

Cleat

1 by 2 trim

¾" plywood

¾" plywood

Blocks and boards

Shelf bracket

L-brace

Continuous Z-bracket

Nut and bolt

Wedge

Gusset

Eyescrew

Cable clamps

must be wedged in place with wood scraps or secured with nuts, bolts, and washers below each shelf. Attach chains to the eyescrews with S-hooks. For added stability, also attach the ends of the ropes or chains to the wall behind.

Ladder supports. Use old ladders or build them from 2 by 2 or larger lumber. Suspend them from ceiling joists or rafters, or tie them together with cross braces for a freestanding unit. Nailing shelves in place will help stabilize the unit.

Adjustable shelving hardware. Track systems—tracks and brackets, or tracks and clips—have become the most popular way to hang a series of adjustable shelves. Generally, bracket systems are hung on a wall, and clips are used within a cabinet frame or other enclosed area. Brackets are available in several styles and finishes; the most common sizes accommodate 8, 10, or 12-inch-deep shelves, but some systems will support shelves up to 24 inches deep. For heavy loads, use industrial systems. Adjustable clips are made in two designs: gusseted and flush (see drawing below). The gusseted type holds more weight.

Tracks should be fastened to wall studs if possible, especially if your shelves will bear a lot of weight. If you must fasten tracks to wall coverings alone, you'll need spreading anchors or toggle bolts for the job. If your walls are block, brick, or solid concrete, you'll have to use masonry fasteners (see pages 78–79).

Boxes and bins

Midway between shelving and more formal cabinetry are boxes and bins—containers more casual than cabinets, more protective than shelves.

Bins: tilt-outs and roll-outs. The most useful storage bins tilt or roll out from beneath a counter, from inside a cabinet or closet, or from along a room's perimeter. They're excellent space savers. Roll-out bins are good for moving items to and from a congested work area; tilt-outs angle down for quick top access.

Boxes: build, buy, or recycle. When stacked with some kind of support, cardboard boxes and wood crates don't clutter up the floor or fall apart. Try organizing them on wide shelves, or on a frame made as shown below.

Wood boxes can be hung from wall studs with nails or screws, or attached to a piece of plywood.

Box modules. A set of box modules consists of plywood boxes that you construct. They fit together well because they're all alike or have complementary dimensions. Rectangular units (see drawing below) should be exactly twice as long as square modules.

Build modules from ¾-inch exterior plywood, then finish them with enamel or polyurethane. Bolt high stacks together or bolt them to the wall. Add simple doors or pull-out drawers for a fancy system.

"Ladder" supports

Tracks and clips

Flush

Gusseted

Tracks and brackets

Standard

Heavy-duty

Adjustable

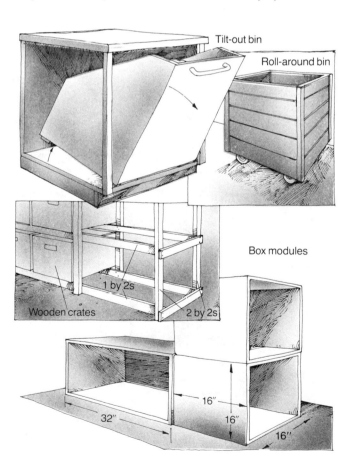

Tilt-out bin

Roll-around bin

1 by 2s

Wooden crates

2 by 2s

Box modules

32"

16"

16"

16"

Cabinets, closets, or both?

Cabinets and closets rank above other kinds of storage units in usefulness, complexity, organization, and cost. Efficient cabinets and closets—whether freestanding, framed in, or hung from a wall or ceiling—often include other storage components such as shelves, drawers, rods, and hooks. For ultimate flexibility, an integrated storage wall of both cabinets and closets is ideal. Consider the following features when shopping for premade units or when building or refurbishing closets and cabinets for the garage or basement.

Doors. You have several choices: hinged, sliding, folding, and roll-up. A hinged door—whether of the flush, lip, or overhanging type—gives you quick access to what's inside; it's also the most secure and weathertight kind of door. However, hinged doors on large units may be heavy and unwieldy, and hinged doors require more clearance than other kinds of doors. Sliding doors—with wood, metal, or plastic tracks—demand no clearance, but allow access to only half of a closet or cabinet at any one time. Bifold doors are a good compromise for large units; they're usually louvered, which allows for ventilation. Roll-ups of plastic or canvas are economical choices, but not as durable or protective.

Drawers. Odds and ends that have a way of getting lost need drawers. Ideally, drawers should be no deeper than 30 inches and no taller than 12 inches.

You can build your own drawers—a sticky task for the uninitiated—or choose from a large selection of manufactured drawers or "drawer frames" (drawers, hardware, and the support frame). Before building or buying, select your drawer guides. Commercially made guides are usually the smoothest. However, simpler systems of wooden strips or plastic channels work adequately for most loads. Lightweight drawers that won't carry much weight can slide in and out without guides.

The case for closets. Large, open closets are effective for storing seasonal clothing, garden and house maintenance goods, cleaning supplies, firewood—even roll-out bins and power tools on casters. Design your closet for many uses: add clothes rods, hooks, or pegboard walls inside; shelves or cabinets above; and a bank of drawers. This kind of unit is especially useful if security is a problem; the outer doors can be locked.

Security and safety. Depending on the contents and location of your cabinet or closet, you may want to make it secure. To foil burglars, use a heavy-duty padlock with a steel or solid brass case and a hardened steel shackle attached to an integral bolt and security hasp. When closed, the hasp should cover the screws that attach it to the unit. If you're worried about keeping your children out, a simpler, less expensive lock and hasp should do. Purchase rust-resistant locks, bolts, and hasps. Standard hinged doors, especially with hinges mounted to the inside of the unit, offer the most protection.

Hinged door

Sliding door

Roll-up door

Commercial drawer runners

Bifold door

To 30"

To 12"

Security hasp

Padlock

Storage bays. *To gain storage space without crowding cars, bays were built in three walls of this new garage. Each projection hangs from the rafters and features narrow side windows. Two include plywood shelves on a frame built of 1 by 4s; the third has a workbench instead of shelves. The projection in the side wall shown at right takes advantage of an underused side yard. A similar bay can be added to an existing garage as part of a remodeling project. Architect: William Patrick.*

Item-by-Item
Storage Ideas

From bicycles and books to workshop tools and wines

Reels on redwood door. *Fishing reels and fishing line hang on the inside of a redwood door. Items are placed so the door closes without disturbing tackle boxes and other gear on shelves. Design: Jean Chappell.*

All in a line. *Everything has its place on this brightly painted garage wall. Tools, some of which dangle from cords looped through holes drilled in the handles, hang on nails. Fuel is stored in safety cans.*

Sideways rungs: a storage switch. *Simple wooden racks, securely attached to the garage beams and positioned for convenience and clearance, support an extra-long ladder. Cars are removed when ladder is being loaded and unloaded. Design: Emil Marent.*

Bicycle Bulk

Space-saving ways to keep bikes off the floor, out of harm's way

If your family has caught the cycling bug, you've no doubt discovered that those bikes take up a lot of space. To accommodate bicycles, you can add an extension to your garage (see below), make do with available parking space, or look for another likely storage spot around the house or yard.

In the garage, get lightweight 10-speed bikes off the ground if possible. You'll save floor space and probably boost the life of your tires, which tend to crack and go flat when left sitting on the floor over long periods of time. A solid bike rack or hook can be especially handy at repair time: while the rack holds the bike in place, your hands are free to do the work. Heavier bikes should be stored on floor stands such as the ones shown in the drawing on the facing page.

No garage? If you have to store bikes in a carport, security can be a problem. Lockable, walk-in closet units are one way to guard against both theft and weather. A patio or garden shed can also provide shelter for your bikes.

Easier lifting
Large, heavy hooks slip between the spokes of the front and rear tires, raising these lightweight bikes off the garage floor. The owner fitted the hooks together from sections of ¾-inch PVC pipe and finished them with red spray paint.

Clever hang-ups

Brightly colored screw hooks from the cycling shop, driven into wall studs or ceiling joists, support bicycles with ease. More elegant braced wall brackets—originally intended for a closet rod—give better clearance from the wall (secure them solidly with ¼ by 3-inch screws). Stagger single hooks to hang several bikes close together; two brackets secure both wheels of a bike high above the floor.

Hoist them high

This handsome, easy-to-build rack made from fir 2 by 4s and 1 by 3s keeps bicycles off the floor and out of the way. Notches in each upright board slip over a ceiling joist and are secured with 4-inch carriage bolts; lap joint notches at the opposite ends cradle the 1 by 3 racks. Adjust the diagram dimensions to fit your bikes, the garage height, and the height of cars beneath.

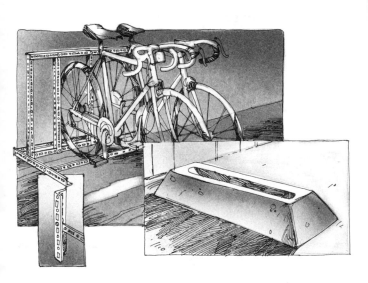

Stand them, school-style

Bicycle floor stands—like those from the school playground —are very convenient at home. Buy commercial racks or build your own from L-shaped slotted metal channel and nuts and bolts from hardware stores. Or check with local building suppliers for cement bike blocks that have slots for front bicycle wheels. Though heavy enough to stay put when you want, bike blocks can still be moved as needs and seasons change.

Books, Documents & Photographs

Pamper paper—it damages easily

Books, magazines, personal documents, financial records, photographs, and correspondence: no collection grows faster, is more difficult to keep organized, and requires such stable storage conditions. Light, moisture, heat, insects, and poor ventilation are all enemies of stored paper products.

What conditions are ideal? Librarians recommend temperatures between 60 and 75° and humidity between 50 and 60 percent for storing most papers. If you use good quality storage units that permit air circulation, a dry and insulated attic or basement should be fine. For photographs and papers that need to be perfectly preserved, hot attics and damp basements are out (see pages 68–73 and 74–79 for more details and solutions).

If you store paper items in cardboard boxes, the lids or flaps should be loose enough to allow a free flow of air. Pack books and magazines loosely, and check occasionally for signs of dampness or mold. Metal units or units lined with metal (see drawing on page 75) will protect paper from insects and rodents. Boxes—whether of cardboard or metal—block out light, as well.

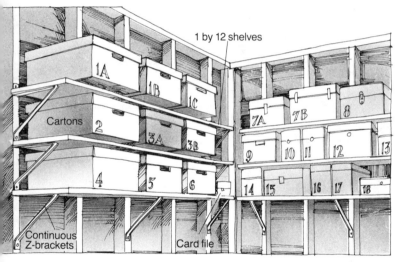

1 by 12 shelves

Cartons

Continuous Z-brackets

Card file

Orderly filing for easier finding

An organized collection of cardboard or metal containers for household records, receipts, documents, and correspondence will meet the storage needs of most homeowners.

Individual filing boxes or cartons handle large items. Also available are canceled check organizers with filing inserts, slipcover letter files, and binding cases for documents. Metal and cardboard card files—manufactured in many sizes—make compact containers for lots of bits and pieces of paper.

Arrange your box system on 1 by 12-inch shelves supported by continuous Z-brackets or individual shelf brackets. To keep track of what's where, number each box to match a corresponding index card listing the contents of the box.

Space-saving file cabinets:
Safe as houses, almost as strong

A metal office file cabinet, with one to five stacked drawers, is a very efficient and safe way to store important documents and photo negatives. If appearance and neatness count, recess the file cabinet into a knee wall or under stairs, for example, so that only the drawer fronts are exposed. For maps, oversize documents, and art paper, use wood or steel flat files. File cabinets are expensive, but you can reduce the cost by purchasing used equipment; look up "Office Furniture and Equipment—Used" in the Yellow Pages.

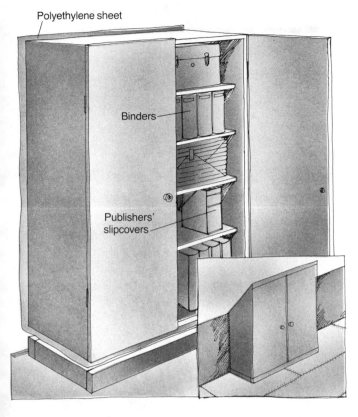

Polyethylene sheet

Binders

Publishers' slipcovers

Catching library overflow

Lovers of the printed word are always running out of shelf space for their collections of mysteries, reference texts, or favorite magazines. Inevitably, part of the library is "off to storage."

Even in the attic or basement, books and magazines should be stored on standard shelves. Set up shelves in a dry area that has a stable temperature. It's all right to store books in a cold area as long as it's dry. Don't place shelves against a wall that hasn't been insulated; fur out the wall (see page 78) or at least place polyethylene sheeting between the wall and shelves. If your books will be exposed to a lot of light, especially direct daylight or fluorescent light, the shelves should be equipped with doors or curtains. Magazines can be stored in slipcover cases or binders sold by publishers or office suppliers.

Protecting photos & film

Fortunately, photographic films and papers are more stable and long-lasting today than they were in the past, but your photo memories can still fade or discolor if exposed to excessive light, heat, or moisture. Keep them in covered boxes, cupboards, or flat file drawers. Place a small amount of silica gel in each container to help absorb moisture. Storage conditions for photo materials must be temperate and dry.

Store color transparencies in boxed projector trays or special clear plastic 8½ by 11-inch sheets. Black and white and color negatives are best kept in negative file sheets inside a binder and drawer. Separate prints with pieces of paper or enclose them in individual rag paper envelopes, and lay them in flat file drawers or boxes.

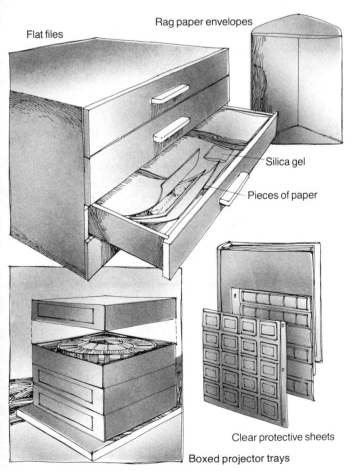

Flat files

Rag paper envelopes

Silica gel

Pieces of paper

Clear protective sheets

Boxed projector trays

Cans, Glass, Newspapers & Discards

Simple sorting systems for home recycling and disposal

Taking out the garbage is a familiar chore, but recycling is a newer responsibility for most of us—and easy enough when you're organized. You'll need up to four adjacent bins for presorting and storing tin, aluminum, glass, and newspaper. An easy-to-carry container located in or near the kitchen will save you extra steps until you have a full load. Bins should be lightweight and made of plastic, metal, or plywood treated for moisture.

Place both garbage cans and recycling bins in any well-ventilated area protected from the elements: a corner just inside the garage door, a carport enclosure, or a small outdoor shelter in the side or back yard (check local building codes before constructing). For convenience, cans and bins shouldn't be too far from either the kitchen or the driveway or street. Prefabricated metal garbage can shelters, whether separate or part of a large garden shed (see pages 42–43), are handy.

Stackable slide-outs save space

Neatly separated recyclables await pickup within a stack of lipped plastic laundry baskets. On recycling days, the baskets easily slide forward and out. A welder assembled the iron brackets shown, but you can attach wooden drawer guides or cleats inside an open cabinet frame to hold each basket. Or for a more finished look, try one of the commercial bin systems that roll on their own frames.

Plastic laundry basket

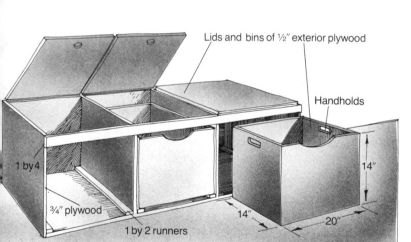

Lids and bins of ½" exterior plywood

Handholds

1 by 4

¾" plywood

1 by 2 runners

14"

14"

20"

Sorting bins swallow plenty

Here's a basic enclosed three-bin recycling system; you can modify it for special needs. Side-by-side bins house recyclable aluminum, tin, and glass. (You might install an extra large newspaper bin, too—papers pile up quickly.) You can leave the hinged tops up for easy access, or flip them down to double as counter space. On recycling days, slide each bin out by gripping the cutout on the front, then carry by using the two side handholds.

Don't lug it. Roll it.

Do you dread the weekly chore of lugging heavy overflowing garbage cans out to the curb and back? A simple remedy is to mobilize those cans. A crisscross dolly on wheels, sized to fit, is the answer for one can; two cans can ride in style on the rolling wagon shown. Pull the wagon up and down the driveway with a thick rope or chain handle.

Outdoor storage wall

Open doors reveal a tightly organized space: shelves for garden and automotive supplies, room below for several garbage cans, and a deep woodbin with a pass-through to the house in its back wall. To hide the contents from view, just close three doors. Architects: The Hastings Group.

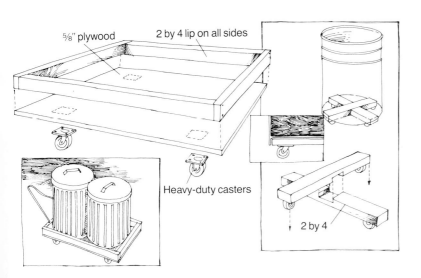

⅝" plywood

2 by 4 lip on all sides

Heavy-duty casters

2 by 4

Coping with All-weather Wear

How to contain the mess and let outdoor clothing dry

Whether you must deal with snow-caked boots, sandy sneakers, or rain-soaked jackets, a "mudroom" can save both your temper and the garments themselves. In this spot close to an exterior door, clothing can be shed and left to dry.

A mudroom ideally is furnished with a long bench for removing wet boots and rain pants, and pegs or hooks and a long shelf for parkas, gloves, and hats. Equip the area beneath the bench with drawers or a storage chest for dry socks and shoes. Deep, open cubbyhole shelves or a clothes closet and bureau turn

an enclosed mudroom into a changing area.

A complete mudroom might include some source of heat—an adjacent water heater or heating duct—to help clothes dry quickly (for a heated shelf idea, see page 47). A louver or pegboard closet door and a ventilating fan inside the closet help check moisture and odor buildup. A floor cover of removable wooden slats or a galvanized metal grate allows water to drip down to a waterproof floor; the grates and slats also allow air circulation. In truly muddy climates, install a faucet and drain for rinsing boots and rain gear.

Concealed pull-down
The space between the joists in this basement makes room for an overhead pull-down compartment, an easily accessible hiding place for ski boots or other gear. Outdoor clothing for rain and cold weather hangs on a metal closet rod just below the pull-down. Architect: Karlis Rekevics.

Heel toe, heel toe

Shoes and boots hang on dowels recessed at an upward slant into a thick board. The board is bolted to a wall stud. Easy-care flooring makes cleanup simple. A tension closet rod fits neatly below the sloped ceiling. Architect: James Elliott Bryant.

Corner cache catches all

Before entering the house, family members shed their out-door wear in a storage corner in the garage. The clothes rack, built of 1 by 2s that rest on triangular supports, holds slickers and jackets. Boots, shoes, and roller skates tuck into bottom compartments. Shelves above organize less frequently used items, including camping supplies and sports equipment.

Clothing in Hibernation

Simple shelters sequester out-of-season wardrobes

The key to storing clothes is protection—from moisture, dust, and insects. Moisture, in the form of condensation or actual seepage, is best controlled within the entire storage area; see pages 75 and 76–77 for details and remedies. Closed units are best where dust or insects are major concerns. Built-ins are the most functional, but steel wardrobes—even the cardboard wardrobes used by movers—provide serviceable closets. To prevent mildew, closed units should be vented with finely screened openings or, for problem cases, an exhaust fan.

A traditional cedar closet or chest will help deter moths. Remember, though, that while cedar repels moths it does not kill them. Cedar-scented moth-controlling substances—spray and solid—can be used inside garment bags, chests, or closets.

Make sure that clothes are thoroughly cleaned before storing them.

A closet for off-season clothes
Make room in bedroom closets by storing out-of-season and seldom-worn clothing in their own portable closet in the garage. When closed, the door protects clothes from dust and light. There's even room for stowing bulky bags and luggage inside and on top.

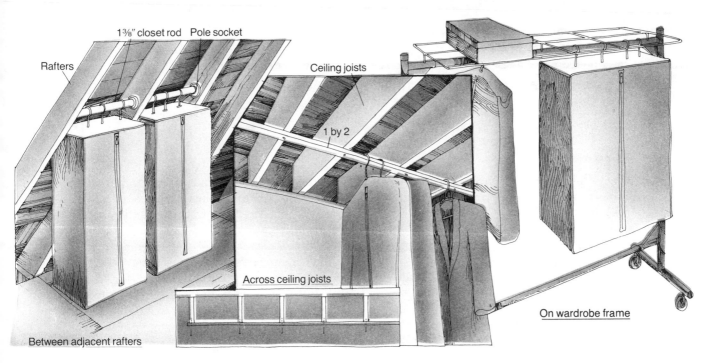

Rafters

1⅜" closet rod   Pole socket

Ceiling joists

1 by 2

Across ceiling joists

On wardrobe frame

Between adjacent rafters

Makeshift closets: quick, easy, safe

Open units are the simplest, though least protected, means to out-of-season clothes storage. Lengths of 1⅜-inch closet rod, adjustable metal rods, or 1 by 2s can be strung between opposing or adjacent attic rafters, fastened to the bottom of ceiling joists, or suspended from chains or ropes. A mobile wardrobe frame is both adjustable and collapsible.

Protect clothes and shoes stored in the open with vinyl or fabric garment bags—available in several types and sizes.

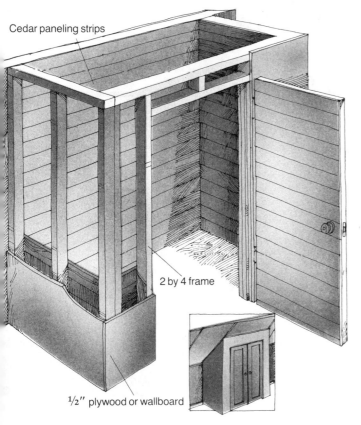

Cedar paneling strips

2 by 4 frame

½" plywood or wallboard

Cedar—for extra care

To fashion your own cedar closet—or to convert an existing closet—line the closet frame inside with tongue-and-groove cedar paneling strips, available in kits from home improvement centers. Just cut the strips to length and lay them in horizontally, one wall at a time, with paneling adhesive and finishing nails. For maximum protection, line the ceiling, floor, and door too. Weatherstrip the door edges tightly.

Don't finish or seal your cedar with varnish—you'll lock the fragrance inside the wood. To revive the fragrance, sand lightly with fine sandpaper.

Stashing Firewood

Protecting wood, seasoning it, getting at it with ease

To an increasing number of people, firewood has become an important supplement or primary alternative to other energy sources which are expensive and sometimes in short supply.

These are basic rules for storing firewood: 1) split the wood before stacking; 2) raise the wood off the ground; and 3) don't pile wood against a house wall—leave some space between the wall and firewood stack.

Wood can be stacked in parallel or perpendicular (crisscross) rows. For safety and neatness, brace tall woodpiles. If you're seasoning wood outside, don't seal it off completely because you'll trap moisture and condensation inside. Instead, store wood under a shed roof in an area sheltered from the elements.

Should you store firewood inside? If you have the space, by all means yes. Wood stored inside dries faster and contains less residual moisture. But before you bring your split wood inside, check it for insects. Don't store infested wood inside. Metal or masonry surfaces below and behind your indoor woodpile will help prevent insects from homesteading in your walls and baseboards.

Snoop around for nooks & crannies

Survey the garage, basement, or carport for likely places to store your firewood. Here are two good places to look: under the basement stairs and below hanging garage or carport cabinets.

Farmhouse idea: the lean-to

This kind of woodshed can be a simple lean-to bin or a full-scale add-on with pass-through access or a door to the house. Keep a simple lean-to open on the sides, and make sure that firewood is raised off the ground. A good roof overhang ensures adequate air circulation and protection from the weather.

Raised off ground

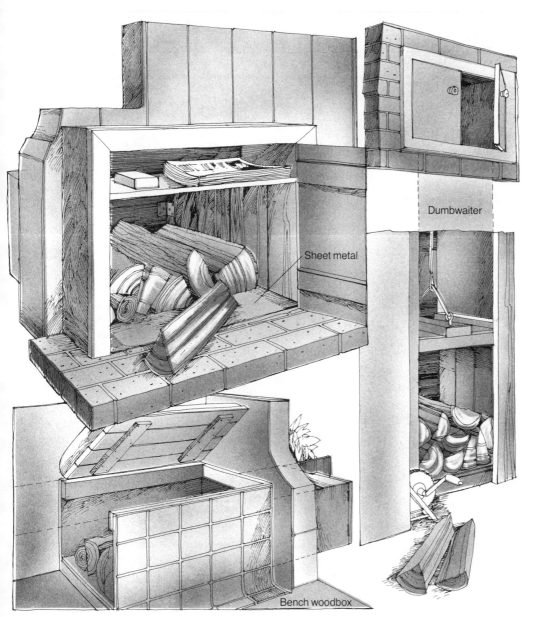

Dumbwaiter

Sheet metal

Bench woodbox

Save toil with pass-through

With a woodpile and a fireplace, the shortest distance between two points is a straight line—that's the idea behind pass-through access doors. If your storage area or add-on woodshed is adjacent to a wall near the fireplace or woodstove, a simple wood box with an interior access door can save you from stepping into the teeth of a gale to stoke the fire on a stormy night. Building codes require that a wood box opening into a garage or carport have a solid-core, self-closing door. To keep insects out of living quarters, line the wood box with sheet metal.

For a stylish variation, store your wood under a fireside bench seat that can be loaded from the outside; when you need a log, just lift the hinged seat. Have a mechanical bent? A basement-to-fireplace dumbwaiter, operated by cables and a hand winch, is a helpful friend to the fire tender.

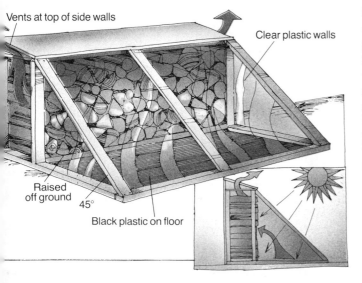

Vents at top of side walls

Clear plastic walls

Raised off ground

45°

Black plastic on floor

Solar seasoning

With this unit, green wood is seasoned in far less time than in the open air. The design can be modified to suit your budget, available space, and architecture. However, you'll want to make sure that the woodshed's positioning, materials, and ventilation are appropriate. The unit's front wall should face south and slope at close to a 45-degree angle. Use clear walls to let the sun in and black plastic or painted plywood inside to absorb heat. Side vents at the top pull warm air up past the wood, carrying moisture out the top.

Food...for Next Winter, Next Week

"Putting by" plenty in pantries, larders, root cellars

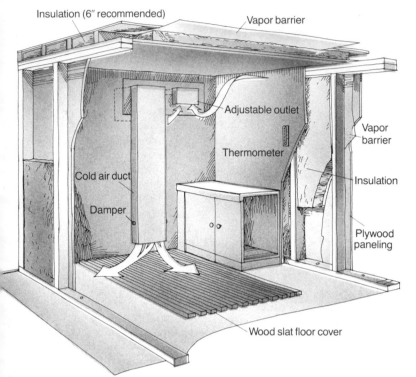

Insulation (6" recommended)
Vapor barrier
Adjustable outlet
Vapor barrier
Thermometer
Cold air duct
Insulation
Damper
Plywood paneling
Wood slat floor cover

Home cornucopia: a food cellar

To build a food cellar in your basement, partition off an area adjacent to a shaded north or east wall and away from heating ducts and pipes. Then insulate the ceiling, new interior walls, door, and (unless the climate is cool year-round) the exterior wall above ground level. Cool ground temperatures and, when the weather is cool, the outside air will keep cellar temperatures low; the insulation will keep out heated air from the living quarters. If possible, choose a site for your cellar with an outside opening—a window is convenient—to provide air flow. Install a cold air duct with a damper, and sliding outlet vent in the opening. A power fan and an automatic thermostat may be useful additions. A floor of sawdust sprinkled with water, with a platform of wood slats laid over it, will maintain humidity at the high level necessary for some food crops.

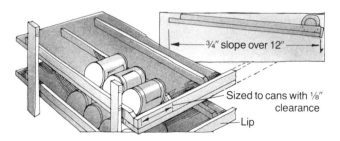

¾" slope over 12"
Sized to cans with ⅛" clearance
Lip

Cans roll right into reach

Food shelves that hold only bulk canned goods can be sloped forward so that cans will roll to the front. No more digging for buried cans—and the shelves can be as deep as you like. Molding strips laid across the front and along each shelf keep cans aligned.

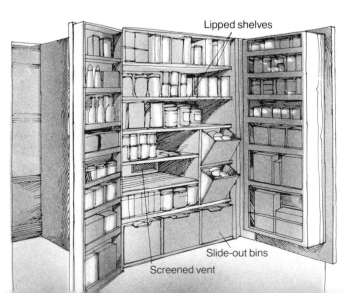

Lipped shelves
Slide-out bins
Screened vent

Granny's larder, revisited

If you'd like a multipurpose food storage area for canned goods, grains, cheeses, and bulk produce, revive an old tradition: the built-in larder. Lipped shelves hold canned goods, jars, and packaged foods securely; the double doors are lined with narrow shelves that provide additional—and highly accessible—storage. Down below, slide-out bins—a commercial system or homemade—hold fruits and vegetables. Screened vents to the outside or to a cool crawl space act as an old-time cooling device, keeping larder temperatures low.

Household food storage can be divided into two categories: pantry or room-temperature storage for canned goods and nonperishables; and root cellar cold storage for fruits, vegetables, staples, and preserves.

You can place cans and jars just about anywhere that's convenient (except near a furnace or water heater) in the garage or basement: on orderly shelves, inside an unused utility closet, or behind cabinet doors. However, most basements are too warm for root cellar storage. One way to bypass the temperature problem in a basement is to insulate a small area for food storage along a cool basement wall (see details shown at left and on page 78).

To cool the food storage area, you can use natural or mechanical methods (see page 77).

An old-fashioned root cellar with a cool dirt floor is another food storage option. Traditionally, root cellars were dug below the house, into the ground outside, or into a hillside. A modern-day crawl space may be just the place to locate your root cellar (see page 79 for ideas).

Most root crops require moist, cool storage conditions. Other crops, including winter squash and pumpkins, like warmer, drier surroundings. Consult an agricultural extension service for more detailed information about proper food storage. In addition, see the *Sunset* book *How to Grow Vegetables & Berries*.

Harvest headquarters
Metal utility shelves, durable and warp-resistant, are a practical choice for food storage. Lipped edges on the shelves hold jars safely. Adjustable—and available in many sizes—the shelves can be bolted to studs for added stability.

Contoured shelves offer simple-to-see storage
For maximum visibility, cans, jars, and bottles fit one or two-deep on narrow ends of contoured track-and-clip shelves above the counter. Bulkier items are stowed below. The counter is handy for unloading groceries—food goes right onto the shelves or into the freezer or extra refrigerator. The pantry floor is kept clear for the drop-down ladder. Architect: Bo-Ivar Nyquist.

Patio Paraphernalia

Bags of charcoal, comfortable cushions, sun umbrellas, hammocks, badminton and croquet sets, inner tubes and inflatable rafts — sometimes it seems we have as much furniture and equipment for the patio, deck, and pool as for the house. It's most convenient to store such things close to where you need them — wheeling the portable grill just a few feet makes spur-of-the-moment barbecues easier.

Most outdoor equipment does require shelter from an occasional summer shower. Closed storage units and roof or deck overhangs provide needed protection. Units should be built according to durable, waterproof designs, and from good materials: redwood, exterior plywood, and masonry are standards.

Patio, deck, and poolside storage should blend with or complement a house's architecture and landscaping.

Barbecues in dividers or against the house. The most durable barbecue is set into a freestanding unit built from brick, stone, or concrete blocks. Below the barbecue or to the side, you can build in cabinets for starter fluid, charcoal briquettes (in metal or plastic cans with tight-fitting lids to keep out moisture), utensils, and accessories. A barbecue-plus-storage unit often doubles as a divider wall, separating the patio area from the garden or yard.

Portable barbecues rust quickly when exposed to dampness and precipitation. A deep cabinet to house a portable barbecue can be built against the house wall, protected beneath the eaves. Barbecue storage cabinetry could include shelves, hanging pegs, and possibly drawers for tongs, mitts, and rotisseries; a fold-down door could double as a serving counter.

Using space beneath a deck. Even the space beneath a deck is often useful for storage. If yours is a low deck, consider a trap door with a built-in box below for hoses and gardening supplies. The trap door should match the decking materials; it can be set in place or attached with leaf-type hinges set flush with the deck. You might provide access to a larger below-deck space from the side; store lawn furniture or other large items there, protected from the weather.

Corner cabinets for outdoor entertaining

Barbecuing is a joy when the essentials are close at hand. Double-door cabinets and a well-lighted countertop, as shown above, make it as convenient as cooking in the kitchen. Design: Armstrong & Sharfman.

Bring on the barbecue

When it's time to light the fire, the barbecue kettle pictured at right swings out from its storage space under a wooden porch. The kettle pivots on an adjustable welded-steel arm.

For storage, sunning, sitting

Hinged deck bench holds a cargo of gardening supplies. Solid to keep out the rain, the bench invites snoozing and sunbathing. Design: Ed Hoiland.

Disappearing act

Collapsible director's chairs tuck neatly and conveniently into an outside deck locker. The storage spot is actually space stolen from a corner cabinet in the kitchen. The well-camouflaged door was cut from the deck's wall paneling. Architects: Larsen, Lagerquist & Morris.

Furnishings & Other Bulky Items

Here's how to handle those hard-to-fit objects

How can you make bulky belongings like dining room tables, overstuffed chairs, or china cabinets disappear? Unfortunately, there's no magical solution.

Most furniture is much too heavy or awkward to fit into standard storage units. You may be able to get lighter furnishings up onto overhead platforms (see page 65) or tuck them into "backwater" spots; but the best basic procedure for storing furniture is to keep it out of the traffic flow—in attic or basement corners and against walls—and arrange the pieces as compactly as possible.

Protect furniture by covering it with old mattress pads or blankets. Polyethylene sheeting, canvas, or even newspaper can also help keep the dust off. Lamps, decorations, and breakables should be stored on heavy-duty shelves.

See "Outdoor Furniture" (pages 32–33) and "Luggage & Game Tables" (pages 40–41) for more ideas.

Storage space that opens wide

A large, gabled dollhouse, a collection of baskets, and other seldom-used belongings call for special problem-solving. This custom-built closet has three sliding doors that open two at a time, accommodating large items. Sturdy shelves are raised or lowered on easily adjustable dowels.

Rugs require rolling

To store a rug or carpet for any length of time, roll it—never fold it—around a pole or cardboard tube. Wrap the carpet in paper or plastic, but leave some room for air to circulate. For rugs and carpets, the storage environment shouldn't be damp or overly warm: excessive drying is as bad as mildew. Moth balls or crystals will help keep insects away, but some fibers react adversely to these repellents. Consult a carpet expert before storing a prized carpet.

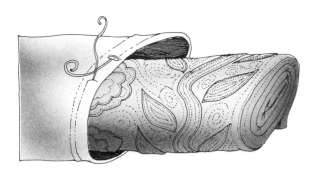

Quality quilt care

Ideally, heirloom quilts or fine blankets should be rolled or loosely folded, then inserted into a clean, all-cotton pillow-case or a larger covering made from a sheet. Never store a quilt in a plastic bag (the fibers need to breathe), and keep quilts from direct contact with wood. Take your quilts out of their cases occasionally and refold a different way.

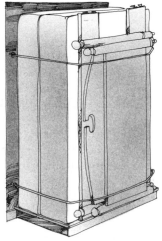

Managing bed bulk

Keep your mattresses and box springs off the floor, and don't let them sag. Stand them upright against a wall. Prop them up with a large sheet of plywood or hardboard, or the bed's own headboard and slats; and secure the whole assembly against the wall, if necessary, with loops of wire, light chain, or rope attached to the wall behind.

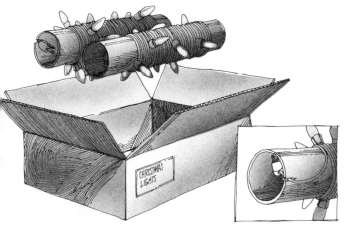

Tangle-free Christmas tip

Here's a way to save aggravation next year when you un-pack the Christmas tree lights. This year, save the cardboard tubes from rolls of gift wrapping paper and a few small-to-medium cardboard boxes. Cut the tubes to box length; then push each light strand's plug inside a tube end and secure with masking tape. Coil the lights firmly around the tube, as shown, by rotating the tube; tape the end in place. Tubes then slip snugly inside the box.

A 12-inch-long box and tube will handle a strand of 35 to 50 small twinkle lights. Use a larger box for a big-bulb strand.

Outdoor Furniture

Fair-weather forecast for longer-lasting beauty, service

When the weather prediction is "weekend showers," do you hope for sunny skies because you don't want to move your patio furniture? Whether the weather takes you by surprise or it's time to prepare for a change in season, you need convenient ways and protective places to store your outdoor furniture.

Hang lightweight objects on garage or basement walls, or place them on a loft platform or overhead rack, or inside carport storage units. If necessary, store bulky items in a garden shed (see pages 42–43), patio storage unit (see pages 28–29) or garage extension (see page 67).

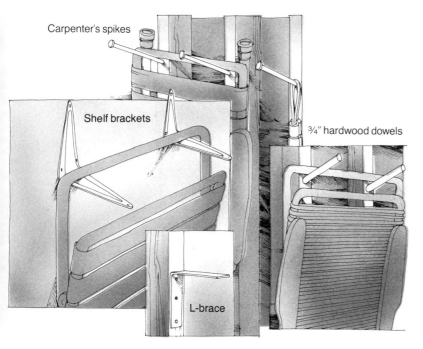

For fold-ups, easy hang-ups

Save precious floor space by hanging lightweight folding lawn chairs and recliners from wall studs, on ceiling joists, or even high on the rafters. For simple supports, use carpenter's spikes (oversized nails) driven into framing members, or ¾-inch dowels glued and inserted into predrilled holes; common shelf brackets or L-braces are other possibilities. Arrange supports in pairs that fit each piece.

A simple track-and-bracket system, intended for shelving, can also be used for storing furniture on the walls.

High-rise storage for window sections

Storm sashes, screens, and window shades are safely out of the way when placed on parallel wood racks suspended from ceiling joists or rafters. Racks for heavy storm windows should be assembled with bolts; racks for lightweight screens can be built with nails or screws. The hardware on sashes prohibits flat stacking; offset every other sash an inch or two. A similar rack is shown in the photo at the bottom of page 13.

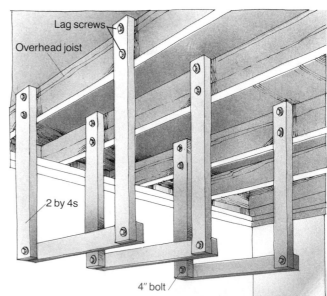

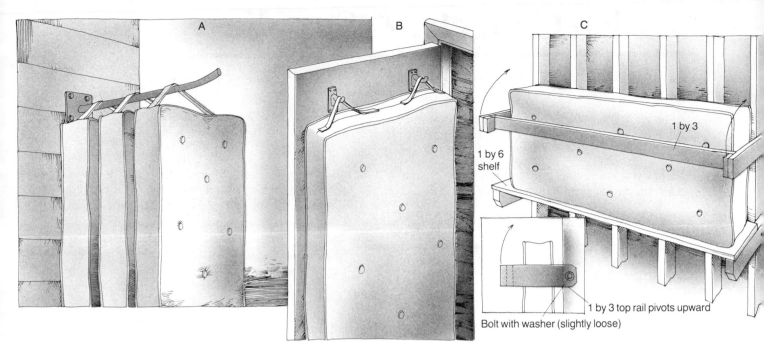

A

B

C

1 by 3

1 by 6
shelf

1 by 3 top rail pivots upward

Bolt with washer (slightly loose)

Airy care for outdoor cushions

Those colorful and comfy cushions deserve some attention when it comes to storage. With a heavy summer storm or the first fall freeze, it's time to bring outdoor furniture cushions inside.

Cushions should be stored off the ground to provide good air circulation, promote quick drying, and prevent mildew problems. A wrought iron rod (A) attached to a wall stud is a handy device for hanging several cushions from their hand loops or from loops you've sewn in place. Metal coat hooks (B) hold individual cushions. Build horizontal racks from fir or pine (C) for long chaise lounge pads; attach the racks to open studs. The upper rail pivots.

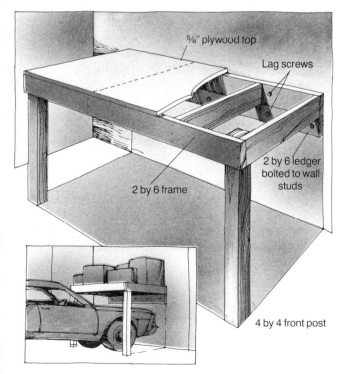

⅝" plywood top

Lag screws

2 by 6 ledger bolted to wall studs

2 by 6 frame

4 by 4 front post

Up and away in a loft

Get on top of the storage situation by placing patio tables and pool furniture under the garage roof—or better yet, over the car. If you and a helper can lift the furniture, store it on this loft platform. The back of the platform sits on a ledger strip, which is attached to wall studs or to a masonry wall. The front of the platform is supported by sturdy posts that straddle the car hood. For more information and ideas about loft storage, see page 65.

Garden Gadgetry & Supplies

Pruning shears to potting soil ... a place for everything

Whether you keep small garden tools in the garage or garden shed, you need handy and safe storage.

A pegboard and hanger system is ideal for organizing light to medium-weight tools and supplies. Closed cabinets are best for garden poisons, sprayers, and extra-sharp tools—keep your cabinets locked if small children are afoot.

If you're putting your garden center to bed for the winter, tools need an environment where they won't rust. If rust-producing dampness is a problem, treat tools with liquid rust cleaner, emery paper, or a wire brush; then oil any working parts and apply a light coating of grease to surfaces likely to rust again. Fertilizers, potting soils, and chemicals should be sealed from moisture inside bins or cabinets; metal containers help keep rodents and insects out of grass seed and bird feed.

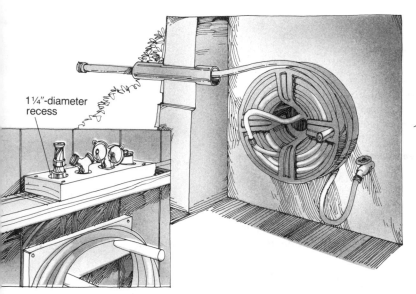

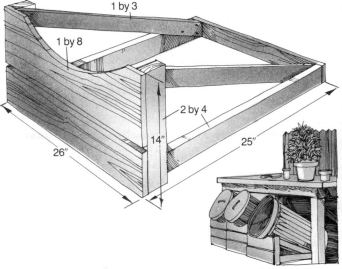

Keeping hoses unsnarled

Wrestling with the garden hose can often be a muddy, tangled proposition. One solution is a reel, mounted next to a water outlet inside a garden shed, garage, or basement. A 20-inch length of 2-inch PVC pipe runs through the wall leading to the garden; you just reel in the hose when it's not in use.

To organize hose nozzles and accessories, drill recesses with a 1¼-inch Foerstner bit into a length of 2 by 4; you could fit the board between wall studs near the hose, or mount it to a wall or fence with L-braces.

Storing soil additives

Tucked beneath a potting table or workbench, these containers make a handy, space-saving addition to any gardening center. Use them to store peat moss, potting soil, sand, and fertilizers. Lay garbage cans atop a slanting wooden rack, as shown; from there, your materials can be transferred directly to pot or wheelbarrow. This rack could be built with a third board across the front to increase the angle.

Sunlit shelving for potted plants

Plywood shelving under the large greenhouse window
provides storage space for empty pots and saucers below,
and a convenient counter on top. Attached to wall studs, the
sturdy potting shelf at left is at comfortable working height;
there's room below for large bags of lawn fertilizer. The high
shelves hold miscellaneous supplies. The window in this
garden storage area bathes plants with light; the plastic roof
and swinging plastic panel overhead keep the corner warm.
Architects: Sortun • Vos Partnership.

Heavy Garden Gear

Big and ungainly machines and tools need space, easy access

Large and bulky garden equipment—power mowers, mini-tractors, rototillers, sprayers, and snowblowers —usually requires a spacious, sheltered floor area (dry to prevent rust) and a clear path to the access door. On the subject of doors: they must be wide enough for your biggest piece of machinery, and the sills must be low, or you'll have to build a ramp or two.

If your equipment inventory is growing steadily, consider building a garden shed (see pages 42–43) or a garage extension (see page 67).

Easy wheeling into the back yard

Gardening equipment rolls conveniently onto a brick walkway through a large sliding door at the back of the garage. Architect: Thomas Jon Rosengren, Inc.

Dowels prop long-handled tools

Brooms, shovels, cultivators, and other garden tools stay vertical, thanks to dowel dividers in this roomy carport closet, just a short walk away from flower and vegetable gardens. The remaining floor space accommodates a garden sprayer and sacks of charcoal. When closed, the sliding doors blend with the wall of the carport. Architect: Buzz Bryan.

Wall space, floor space, even shelf space

Nails in wooden walls do the work of brackets, holding garden equipment. A single shelf stores garden supplies that otherwise might clutter up valuable floor space, reserved here for a mower and bags of potting soil and manure. Architects: Moyer Associates Architects.

Laundry Needs

Tips to save you time, fuss, and mismatched socks

Storage units and accessories above and around your washer and dryer make an efficient work area. Place a long, deep shelf—or shelves—directly above the machines for frequently used supplies. Above the shelf is a perfect spot to install ceiling-high cabinets for cleaning supplies, linens, and overflow storage.

Every laundry area needs counter space for folding, sorting, sprinkling, and mending clothes. Plastic laminate counters are easy to clean. In cramped quarters, a fold-down counter is convenient. You may also want a sink for washing delicate garments or soaking out stains. Hang clothes for drip-drying on a simple metal or wooden closet rod over the sink. A ceiling fan directly above promotes quick drying.

Install more cabinets or a set of large-capacity storage bins below the counter. On the wall attach a narrow cabinet for your ironing board. Close off the area with louvered double doors: they hide clutter and muffle the noise of machines while providing adequate ventilation.

Laundry layover

Custom-fitted to an odd-shaped area in the basement laundry room, these wide-open shelves are a vital link in the laundry assembly line. The cubicles, made of particle board and faced with fir, hold washing supplies and folded laundry; blouses go right on hangers. Architects: Sortun • Vos Partnership.

Out-of-sight ironing board

A full-size ironing board can be stored inside a storage closet near the laundry or in a shallow cabinet of its own. In a storage closet, secure the board with a chain or strap. For greater convenience, build a special slot for the board. A cabinet built to house an ironing board alone should allow several inches around the board for access. The average board would fit in a space 65 inches tall, 21 inches wide, and 5 inches deep; but dimensions vary, so be sure to measure your board.

Built-in ironing boards commonly fold down from behind a door, or pivot or slide out from a slot below the counter top.

Add an electrical outlet inside your board compartment or nearby for your iron.

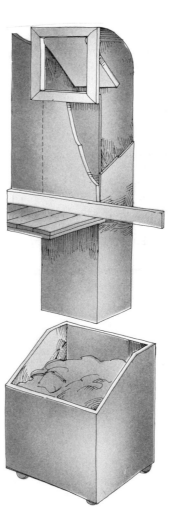

More fun than bother ...a laundry chute

A laundry chute effortlessly directs dirty clothes from your home's main or second floor to a laundry center in the basement or garage below. You can locate the chute opening in an inconspicuous but handy spot—inside a clothes closet in the master bedroom; in a wall, with a hinged or flap door; or inside a bathroom cabinet. If you have curious youngsters on the loose, be sure that the opening is raised high above the floor or measures no more than 12 inches across.

The best time to think "laundry chute," of course, is when you're designing or remodeling your house. Materials? Plywood, sheet aluminum, or 18-inch-diameter furnace heating duct (look in the Yellow pages under "Furnaces," "Sheet Metal Work," or "Plumbing Contractors").

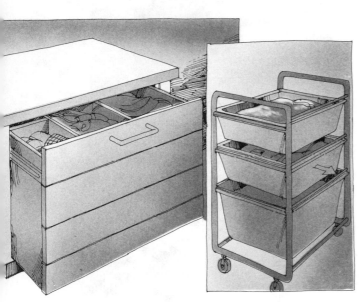

Order out of clothing chaos

Whether below a counter, inside a freestanding island, or stacked floor to ceiling, sorting bins keep clothes ready to go when laundry day arrives. Have at least three large bins for sorting whites, colors, and permanent press items; a fourth bin might hold towels or work clothes.

Below the counter, try wooden tilt-out bins or one large pull-out drawer with internal compartments. Against the wall, you could use a commercial system with bins that slide out of their own frames, or improvise with plastic dish bins on wooden drawer guides (see page 55). A roll-around hamper, or removable bins, can go right with you wherever they're needed.

Luggage & Game Tables

Often awkward to fit anywhere—but here are solutions

Whether you spend your free time traveling to faraway places or enjoying ping-pong or poker at home, you'll face pretty much the same storage problem: because of their special sizes and shapes, neither luggage nor game tables fit neatly into regular cabinets and closets. All too often, these items are stacked clumsily against a wall or take up space in the wrong place.

To store card or ping-pong tables, train or game boards, and suitcases during the off season, you might look for out-of-the-way ledges; or build enclosures specially tailored to their dimensions; or construct a high-up platform. With a pulley system, you can even pull an unwieldy table or trunk up out of the way without having to build a platform.

Tailor-built hideaways

Card tables and folding chairs—for morning bridge parties, late-night poker games, and Sunday afternoon barbecues —always pose a storage problem. It's wise to find them a spot of their own. Some convenient places are (A) inside a cubbyhole cabinet below a staircase; (B) in a narrow, deep slot at the back of a garage storage wall; and (C) in a tilt-out bin built into a cabinet. These places work well for luggage, too.

Before building a cabinet or otherwise modifying a storage area, measure your tables, chairs and luggage. Collapsible tables and chairs require very little depth; luggage needs a little more. Most square tables come in sizes up to 36 inches square, and round tables are usually 30 to 36 inches in diameter. A folded chair is usually 20 to 22 inches wide and up to 38 inches high. Make your hideaway snug enough for tables to stand upright, but allow several spare inches of clearance in width and height for access.

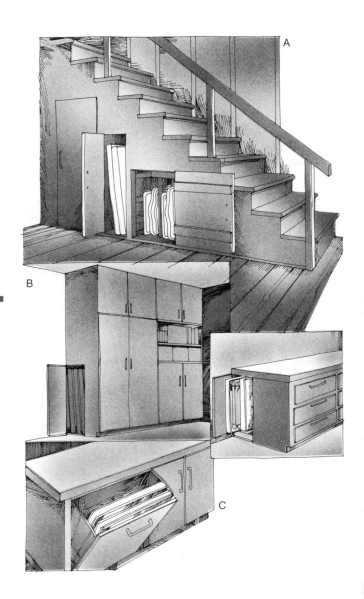

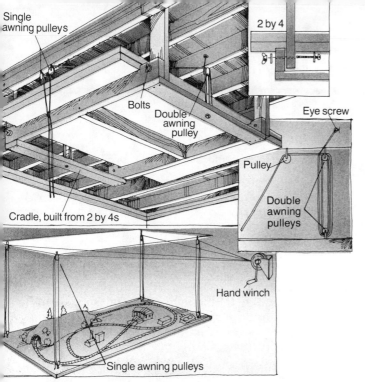

Single awning pulleys

2 by 4

Bolts

Double awning pulley

Eye screw

Pulley

Double awning pulleys

Cradle, built from 2 by 4s

Hand winch

Single awning pulleys

Winch-and-pulley hoist-ups

Nothing eats up basement or garage space like a ping-pong table or model train board. A hand pulley system, or a hand winch and pulleys, can give such storables a big lift. At top, a folded ping-pong table is set onto a wood cradle, then hoisted to the ceiling and secured there with bolts. The train board shown below has matching single awning pulleys above and below, and is raised with a small hand winch. It's always best to have two people around when it's time to hoist your table or board.

3" lag screw

6" lag screws

1 by 2

2 by 4s

3" lag screw and washer

1 by 2

Put a wall to work

If you have spare wall space inside or a roof-protected space outdoors on the leeward side of the house, here's a basic rack that will hold your ping-pong or card table securely. Nail parallel rails of doubled 2 by 4s across wall studs. Make the space between the rails equal to your table's width plus ¼ inch for clearance. Eight-inch lengths of fir 1 by 2 pivot on lag screws and washers to hold the table in place. To store tables more than 3 inches thick, consider adapting the rack shown in drawing C on page 33.

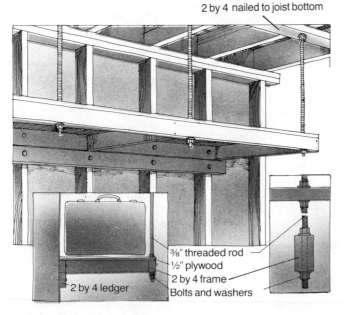

2 by 4 nailed to joist bottom

⅜" threaded rod
½" plywood
2 by 4 frame
Bolts and washers

2 by 4 ledger

Luggage line-up

Luggage and other bulky storage odds and ends line up along this secure ledge, which takes advantage of high wall space in garages or basements. The 38-inch-wide shelf sits atop a 2 by 4 ledger strip fastened to wall studs. It's supported in front by threaded rods tied into a 2 by 4 nailed across ceiling joists or rafters. Line the ledge with carpet scraps to avoid scraping luggage.

Sheds for Storage Overflow

A separate shed serves two storage purposes: garden and yard gear can be near to where you use them, and more space is available in the garage, attic, and basement.

Simple or elaborate, a shed can be a model of efficiency and convenience, actually making it easy to transplant petunias or put away the tricycle.

Check local building codes

Before setting your sights on a certain kind of shed, visit the building inspector in your area. You'll need to find out whether to apply for a building permit and what codes affect your project. Detached buildings are often subject to requirements regarding minimum setbacks from property lines. You may also face limits on installing water and electrical lines or be required to build your shed with fire-retardant materials. Codes vary: sheds aren't allowed in some communities; in others, you can locate a shed almost anywhere on your property, as long as it isn't anchored to the ground or set on a concrete slab.

Should you buy or build?

Depending on how industrious you are, you can erect a metal shed frame from a kit, assemble the parts of a prefab unit, or build your shed from scratch.

If you choose the metal frame, you'll play the roles of a mechanic and carpenter. You can also select what kind of siding and roofing to use: wood, aluminum, fiberglass, or heavy translucent plastic. The heavy plastic can be used to create a greenhouse effect.

Convenient to install, prefab metal sheds come in standard designs; some can be assembled in an afternoon. However, they tend to rust, and it's difficult to attach storage units and accessories to their thin walls. So before buying a prefab kit, find out whether the manufacturer provides a line of shelves, racks, and other accessories especially designed for the metal shed. If accessories aren't available for the design you want, you can always build a wood frame inside the shed.

Wood frame sheds allow you to create an attractive custom design that meets your exact needs and suits your available space. You can easily attach storage units to wall studs or overhead rafters. Unlike a metal shed, a wood shed is flammable; and you'll have to devote considerable time to planning and building.

Shed specifications

A shed should be at least 6 feet wide and a minimum of 4 to 6 feet deep, depending on your needs. If you're building it, plan your access wisely. Install a wide door —4 to 5 feet.

If allowed by code, a shed should be on some kind of foundation to secure it from wind and frost heave. The foundation also prevents wood floors from rotting. Metal sheds often come without floors; a concrete slab is an ideal foundation for these. Some prefab sheds come with special ground anchors or floor supports. Concrete piers and wood beams make a simple, efficient foundation for a wood frame shed.

If your shed floor is above ground level or if the door has a high sill, you'll probably want to use some kind of ramp. A ramp makes access more convenient for wheeling in a wheelbarrow or driving in a mini-tractor. If the floor of the shed is on the ground, elevate equipment on concrete blocks in the winter.

Planning your shed's interior

The rule for storage in tight spaces like sheds is to keep small objects off the floor. Floor space is valuable, and you'll want to use it for access and heavy equipment. You can fasten cabinets, shelves, tool racks, and workbenches to the framing members in a wood shed. If you don't use the manufacturer's storage accessories for a metal shed, consider building a wood frame inside it.

To help you plan your shed's innards, review the following storage ideas:
- Old kitchen cabinets or a counter with built-in drawers are great for a mid-size shed.
- Garden poisons should be locked in a cabinet out of children's reach.
- If you have a hinged door that swings out, install narrow shelves on the back of the door.
- Industrial metal shelves can be used in a shed; they won't warp from dampness, but they may rust.

If your lawn chairs and other outdoor items won't take up all of your shed space, incorporate a garden work center into the shed. Set up a potting counter, and provide garbage cans or tilt-out bins for fertilizer and potting materials; a sink; racks for tools and pots; and small shelves for seeds and bottles. Hang a chalkboard on the wall to record planting timetables and schedule weekly garden duties. See pages 34–37 for specific ideas on storing garden tools and supplies.

Tree-side potting nest

Set against a backdrop of towering redwoods, this potting shed repeats the design and materials of the adjacent structures. The doorway, partial walls, and slatted roof contribute to the open feeling and let light into the shed, making it ideal for growing plants from seeds. Potting supplies fit on shelves that run the length of one shed wall. Along the other walls are a work counter, a utility sink, and below-counter bins. Landscape Architect: G. E. Talbot.

Summer Sports Gear

Ready when you are: boats, bats, balls, rackets, fins, tackle

Summer sports equipment ranges in size from the compact softball to the 16-foot canoe. You'll have to vary your storage methods accordingly. You may want to rotate summer sports equipment by season: keep baseballs and swim fins in less accessible spots during winter months and within easy reach during the height of summer activities.

Some sporting goods, such as baseball bats, tennis rackets, and water-skis, can be stored on organized racks or pegboards. Equestrians might hang bridles and bits on hooks and pegs, and saddles on horizontal "saddleback" rails made with 2 by 4s. For organizing a variety of items of various sizes and shapes—such as

camping and fishing gear—shelves, closets, and storage chests are the most convenient. A stack of deep cubbyhole shelves by the garage door keeps gear immediately accessible. For the dedicated athlete, metal school lockers—either new or recycled—make familiar storage units. A simple nylon hammock strung overhead can keep basketballs, footballs, and sleeping bags from disappearing.

Very light boats can be hung on ropes or racks attached to inside or outside walls; canoes and rowboats are often suspended from overhead joists or collar beams—providing they can handle the weight. For storing heavy or large boats, see pages 50–51.

Angled walls for rifles and poles

Racks mounted on angular corner walls offer out-of-the-way places to store rifles and fishing poles, keeping these items accessible, yet removed from the rest of the garage. Because only fishing nets and boots are on the floor, the storeroom door can swing open without banging into any equipment. Architect: Glenn D. Brewer.

Chains and frame cradle canoe

Attached to the rafters with chains, a strong wood frame supports this heavy canoe and keeps it out of the way of cars. Neatly stacked firewood functions as a windbreak at the back of the carport. Architect: James Van Drimmelen.

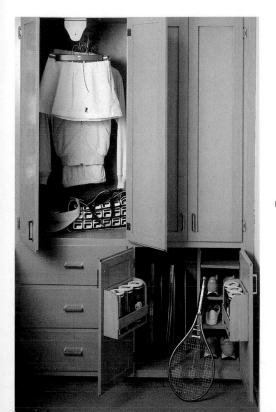

An ace of a storage place

Custom cabinetry keeps tennis equipment and running gear neatly packed away. Sets of double doors open into mini-clothes lockers with room for bags at the bottom. The lower unit is fitted with cubbies for shoes, dividers for rackets, and racks for cans of tennis balls. Design: Betsie Corwin and William G. Florence.

Winter Sports Equipment

Safe stashing of skis, skates, saucers, sleds

During the winter, you might want to keep your seasonal sports gear where it's ready for a quick weekend trip to the mountains or a morning visit to the slopes. In the spring, winter equipment can trade places with golf clubs, baseball bats, or camping equipment, and go into less accessible areas—up into attic corners, against the ridge line or rafters, or into a crawl space.

The rule for most winter storables, in and out of season, is to hang them up. Skis are easily hung by the pair or grouped in a rack. Snowshoes, saucers, skates, and small sleds are best hung on nails, spikes, pegs, or hooks (see page 7). Toboggans and bigger sleds can rest atop raised platforms, ceiling joists, or collar beams.

Easy access to car

Packing up for skiing is simple when the ski equipment is behind double doors in the carport. Skis, poles, and a ski rack rest on dowels in this long, shallow closet. Boots go on the floor. Architects: The Hastings Group.

Family line-up

Boots and skis for a family of seven could easily get mixed up. But these neat compartments, built into a stairway landing, keep good order. As each child outgrows a ski item, it's saved for the next youngest brother or sister to grow into.

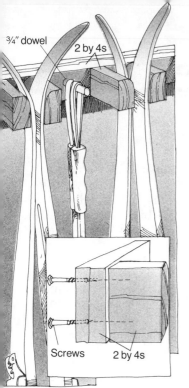

¾" dowel

2 by 4s

Screws   2 by 4s

Block-and-peg ski rack

Because skis conveniently curve at the tips, they'll hang from many kinds of blocks or runners spaced 1¼ inches or so apart. This simple and effective ski rack uses short blocks cut from a 2 by 4 of oak, pine, fir, or redwood. The blocks are glued and screwed to a longer 2 by 4 backing piece. Ski poles hang on adjacent recessed dowels. To add a finishing touch, and to protect skis from scratches, round off and sand smooth the inside top corner of each block. Finish the rack with penetrating resin or polyurethane varnish.

Overhead joist

Making the most of joists and beams

Open ceiling joists or collar beams supply a ready-to-use storage spot for sleds, saucers, and other outdoor equipment: simply rest the runners across a couple of joists. Another idea is to hang snowshoes and skates from nails, spikes, pegs, or hooks sunk into the joists.

Wire screen

1 by 3s

Drying out that soggy gear

When you get home from the slopes or the pond, you head for the warmth of the fire . . . but where do you put your cold, damp ski boots, skates, snowshoes, gloves, and socks?

These drying and storage shelves, adjacent to the water heater for extra drying power, are built from wire screen sandwiched by two 1 by 3 frames; the screens allow air to circulate and moisture to drip. For even quicker drying, run copper tubing—heated by the water heater—underneath each shelf.

Guard Against Storage Hazards

Open boxes spilling over with useless papers, a rickety ladder propped in a corner, carelessly placed sharp tools — these hazards deserve attention. If you're setting your storage in order, make room for safety, too.

Garages, attics, and basements are very susceptible to accident and fire. To prevent storage disasters, your first jobs are to sort, organize, and clean. Discard old paint cans, broken toys, and other unneeded items.

Following are some specific pointers and suggestions to help you with your task. For more safety guidelines, contact fire, health, and other appropriate officials.

Organize your workshop

A clean workshop is a safe workshop. Make it a habit to frequently discard wood scraps and vacuum up sawdust, especially behind panels, boxes, and equipment where highly flammable sawdust collects.

Power tools present a host of dangers. Power tools and lighting should be on separate circuits; a tool circuit should be at least 20 amps to prevent overload. Grounded (three-prong) outlets are a necessity. Also, don't use power tools in damp conditions. A master switch controlled by a key is a wise precaution. To guard against shock, purchase double-insulated power tools.

Make sure that your workshop has sufficient lighting (see page 66) and that the floor is clear of items that could cause a fall.

Guard garden supplies

Your garage or garden shed makes a perfect secret place for little ones playing hide-and-seek. Children—yours or your neighbor's — can easily get into toxic garden

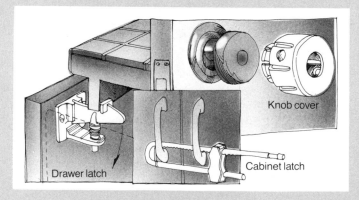

Knob cover

Drawer latch

Cabinet latch

supplies or play with sharp tools if these items aren't properly stored.

Place dangerous tools and poisons well out of children's reach. Hang sharp tools high on walls with strong hooks; make sure they won't fall. Tools can also be stored, along with toxic substances, in drawers and cabinets that have plastic "childproof" latches (see drawing below left) or metal locks. Do not store poisons under utility sinks, on the ground between wall studs, or near bulk food supplies. Remember, pets should be protected from these dangers, too.

Ladders and staircases: watch your step

Ladders and staircases should be adequate for the loads you'll be carrying up and down them, and should always be in good condition. Never block a ladder or staircase with boxes or overflow storage.

Position a ladder so that its base is offset from the perpendicular by ¼ of its length (the foot of a 20-foot ladder, for example, should be 5 feet from the point directly beneath the top of the ladder). Fold-down ladders usually aren't intended for heavy use; buy one with minimum bounce.

Handrails on staircases should be solidly secured, and the steps clear and well lighted, with light switches at the top and bottom. A minimum of 6½ feet of headroom all the way up is often required by code.

Be cautious with heating equipment

Make sure that combustibles are not positioned near heating equipment such as a furnace, water heater, heating ducts, or a chimney.

Store ashes in a metal container; don't place ashes in cardboard boxes or in a place where a breeze can stir up embers.

It's wise to have a professional inspect and clean your heating equipment every year. Do not leave portable heaters unattended, or place them where they can be tipped over.

Avoid electrical problems

Plugging too many tools or appliances into an extension cord is hazardous because the cord's insulation can ignite. Generally, do not rely heavily on extension cords. You can start a fire by stringing extension cords under rugs, tying them to nails, or using extra-long cords of insufficient gauge. Periodically inspect extension cords for cracks, fraying, and broken plugs.

Check with an electrician to make sure that your circuits aren't overloaded; you may need to install additional circuits in your basement or garage workshop, or in your attic for lighting.

Isolate flammable liquids

Storing flammable liquids is a risky practice. Gasoline for lawnmowers and other equipment should be stored in a safety can (see drawing below) with a spring closure valve, vapor vent, pouring spout, and the label of a testing laboratory. Paint, solvent, rubber cement, and other flammable substances should be stored in metal cans with tight-fitting lids in a well-ventilated area far away from heat sources. Never store flammable liquids in glass, plastic, or makeshift containers.

It's a good idea to place correctly containered liquids in a metal cabinet. Do not store them in the house; the vapors that escape from cans are often dangerous. Rags that have soaked up flammable substances should also be kept in metal containers with tight-fitting lids away from heat sources. Better yet, throw them away.

Be sure to clean up any oil drippings.

Pouring spout
Testing lab label
Spring closure valve
Vapor vent

Install lifesaving devices

Smoke and heat detectors, automatic sprinklers, fire extinguishers, and modifications of attic fans can make your storage areas much safer. Other safety measures include solid-core doors (which slow the spread of fire) leading from a carport or garage into living space, and fire-retardant material covering insulation.

Smoke and heat detectors set off an alarm to alert people to danger, giving them time to escape. Smoke detectors alone, when properly placed, installed, and maintained, offer the minimum level of safety recommended by the National Fire Protection Association. Used in conjunction with a smoke detector, a home heat detector is particularly useful in an attached garage, attic, or basement. Heat detectors react when the air reaches a certain temperature, usually 135° F.

An automatic sprinkler system, typically seen in public buildings, is used with a smoke detector or other automatic alarm. A small sprinkler system provides protection in the vulnerable areas of your home: the garage, attic, and basement.

Sprinklers are designed to slow the development and spread of fire. A drawback of a sprinkler system, of course, is that water might damage valuables.

Fire extinguishers. Fire emergencies require quick action. Keep a multipurpose chemical fire extinguisher (see drawing) in or near your garage, attic, or basement. Make sure that the extinguisher carries the UL label of approval and is inspected yearly.

The only times you should try to put out a fire by yourself are when you're near the fire when it begins, or when you discover the fire in its early stages. And, of course, you must know how to use an extinguisher. Don't be overly ambitious in the face of fire; your personal safety comes first.

An attic fan can be a lethal instrument if a fire starts anywhere in your house while the fan is in operation. Air currents speed combustion, and can turn a small fire into a raging one in a few seconds. To eliminate this hazard, fit the louvered shutters on fans with fusible links, and equip fan power circuits with an automatic cut-off switch activated by a fire detection system.

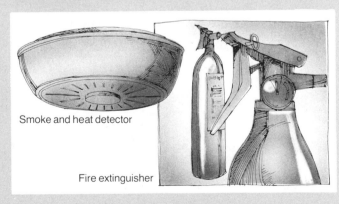
Smoke and heat detector
Fire extinguisher

Custom-fit Unit

Side-wall storage in narrow garage

The tapered shape of the storage wall pictured on the facing page solves the problem of fitting both the car and a sizeable storage unit into a narrow garage. It takes advantage of potential storage space in the upper part of the garage.

The shelves are narrow enough near the base to let a car door swing open. But at the top near the ceiling joists, they extend more than 2½ feet from the wall. Rectangles made of ¼-inch-thick hardwood paneling fit over the openings to each of the 12 shelves, giving the unit a finished, uncluttered look.

Although your own garage may have a different ceiling height or direction of ceiling joist, the principles of building a similar unit remain the same.

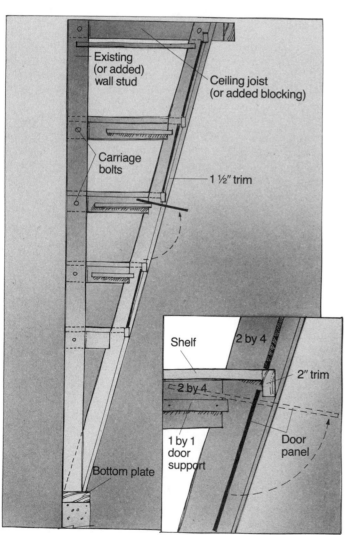

Triangular framing along wall

As the drawing at left shows, 2 by 4s angle outward at a 15° angle from the bottom plate of the garage wall. At the base, each 2 by 4 bolts to the side of an existing (or added) stud and angles up to join a ceiling joist (or added blocking). The 2 by 4s at each end fit on the inside face of the studs and join the joist with a cross-lap joint.

Shelves of 1 by 12s varying from 13 to 16 inches apart rest on 2 by 4 supports, which are bolted to studs at the rear and fit in notches cut in the angled 2 by 4s in the front. The shelves are notched in the front and back to fit around the angled 2 by 4s and the wall studs; on the front side, they stop 1 inch short of the outside edges of the 2 by 4s.

The ends are closed in with ⅜-inch-thick plywood. Trim ripped from 1 by 12s cover the exposed edges of the shelves and angled 2 by 4s.

Door panels of plywood are unattached, swinging open and then sliding in. They rest on 1 by 1s nailed to shelf supports. Each door leans outward from the base and rests against the back of the horizontal trim piece. The width of each door is ⅛ inch less than the opening; height is ½ inch greater.

Leaning tower of cabinets

Angled 2 by 4s anchored to studs at the bottom and to ceiling joists at the top support a spacious, neat storage system designed to take advantage of unused space in a narrow garage. Sturdy shelves, shown above, can be adjusted to your needs and to garage door clearance.

Workshop Basics

Consider safety first, then organize for project efficiency

The four major components of an efficient home workshop are the workbench, storage units, proper lighting, and adequate electrical wiring and outlets. (For a discussion of lighting and wiring considerations, see pages 48–49 and 66.)

The focus of your workshop should be a large, stable workbench. Many kinds are available premade, or you can make your own from a 2 by 4 frame and plywood or hardboard top. The area beneath a workbench is ideal for drawers, cabinets, boxes, and shelves.

Storage units and stationary power tools should be ordered in a way that reflects the sequence of a typical project. Similar tools and materials should be grouped together so that you can find them easily. Large power tools mounted on casters can be rolled out from a stor-age closet or cabinet, or away from a wall, then back again when the work is done. Wall cabinets are best for portable power tools because they protect the blades and working parts from damage and keep children from making dangerous mischief.

Besides tools and projects in progress, you'll want to store materials: leftover lumber, metal scraps, or bulk lumber from a special sale. Leftovers can be stored in a rolling box with a hinged top. Shelf brackets fastened to every other wall stud will handle light lumber. For heavier loads, assemble "ladder racks," like the ones used at lumberyards, from 2 by 4s and lag screws. Tough fiber storage tubes help pigeonhole and protect lengths of pipe or moldings. And if you're pressed for space, look to the rafters or ceiling joists.

Within easy reach

Storing tools where they're easy to retrieve—and put away—makes woodworking more pleasurable, as well as safer. Careful storage also keeps equipment in good condition for many years.

Along with lockable cabinets and drawers, this workbench has wall cupboards backed with pegboard for hanging small hand tools. Power tools stay on the countertop, each near its own electrical outlet.

Pristine platform workshop

Elevated on a 4½-inch-high concrete slab at the rear of the garage, this workshop makes efficient use of walls and floor space. Hand tools on the pegboard panels are conveniently within reach. Mounted on the left wall is a cabinet with small drawers for organizing nails, screws, hooks, and other supplies. A wall-mounted strip with outlets every 15 inches provides electricity for power tools on casters. The outlets are controlled by a key-operated switch, keeping youngsters from playing with the equipment. Architect: R. Gary Allan.

Workshop Hand Tools & Supplies

Maintaining order for a miscellany of small items

Hammers, paint cans, motor oil, nails, picture hooks, electrical fuses, extension cords: home maintenance supplies get out of hand fast without neat organization. And a home workshop can also mean woodworking, crafts, art, or darkroom supplies to store. What you need are storage containers and units that corral easily lost small items in specific, accessible places. The ideal workshop should combine both open and closed storage.

Hand tools are among the most bothersome workshop storables. The popular pegboard and hanger system (see pages 7 and 53) is best suited for visible, hands-on storage. You can also buy individual wall racks for small tools like screwdrivers and pliers.

Though less accessible, closed units protect tools from rust and dust. One space-saving closed unit is a shallow cabinet with sturdy double doors: line the cabinet back and both doors with tools.

Less-often-used storables, such as paint, brake fluid, and turpentine, can go on shelves installed high on the wall or suspended overhead or between ceiling joists. Graduate your shelf depth and spacing to fit the containers—gallons, quarts, and pints—and make sure that the labels are visible.

Drawers—plenty of them—are a blessing to any workshop owner. Build them into your work counters or an open frame, or recycle old bedroom dressers or kitchen units.

Dream home for fasteners

Fasteners of every size, type, and description can easily be spotted inside carefully labeled bins. Hinged doors in the top cabinet unit flip up for access, down for protection and neat appearance. The base cabinet is headquarters for painting supplies, and on the countertop are parts drawers—for even more fasteners.

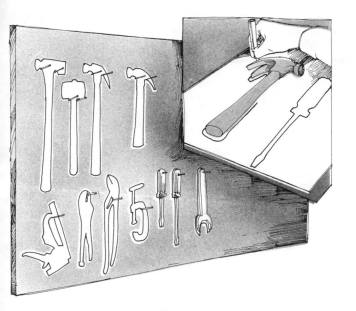

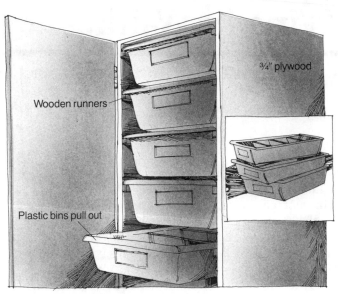

Instant guide to what goes where

It's no small task to keep hand tools in order and accounted for, especially when several family members share the same workshop. These simple silhouettes will help.

The simplest way to make silhouettes is to hang your tools in the ideal order, then outline each one with a broad-tipped indelible felt pen. Or lay each tool on heavy white paper and trace its outline. Carefully cut out each silhouette and glue it to the wall as shown. The glued-on silhouettes will last longer if you coat the entire board with clear sealer.

Slide-out supply bins

These sturdy plastic bins—purchased from office, restaurant, or school suppliers—are just right for home maintenance or crafts supplies. Build a plywood frame, then attach pairs of small wooden runners to both side walls as shown. Bins slide or lift out for easy access. For extra protection or just to be fancy, add a hinged door to the entire unit.

Cutlery trays, though less rugged, also make serviceable drawers or fine workshop drawer inserts.

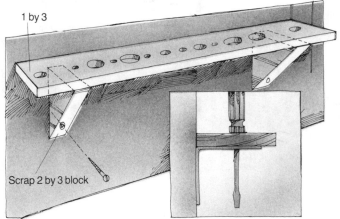

Natty solutions for nuts, bolts, nails

Jars, empty coffee cans, and cigar boxes can help save your workshop from chaos. House these containers on narrow shelves lipped with 1 by 2 trim. Jars for nails, nuts, and other items unscrew from their own lids, which are fastened to the bottoms of the lipped shelves.

Between-stud shelves with 1 by 4 or 1 by 6 strips across the fronts are also ideal for small storage.

Quick-reach tool rack

One simple way to keep small hand tools such as screwdrivers, files, or chisels instantly accessible is to build a tool rack at the rear of your workbench. Drill holes through a length of 1 by 3, large enough for each tool's shank to pass through, but too small for the handle. Attach your rack to the wall with L-braces or triangular blocks made from scraps of 2 by 4.

Wine in Waiting

Laying aside a few valued bottles—or aging by the case

If you're serious about your wines, you'll soon want an organized, stable environment (see pages 58–59 for wine storage details) for your collection. Racks or bins are the key to organizing your wines.

Will you store a few bottles for ready consumption or a by-the-case collection that requires bottle aging? For relatively few bottles, commercial accordion or cubbyhole racks are commonly available at department stores and at some wine shops. Diamond-shaped or triangular bins are traditional for long-term storage (see photo, page 59); the typical bin has a capacity of one to one and a half cases. Wine bottles of any size up to a magnum (2 quarts) may be stored on cabinet shelves or open shelves 14 inches deep.

When it comes to designing your own racks, remember two things: racks must be sturdy (one case of wine weighs about 40 pounds), and bottles should be stored on their sides to keep corks moist.

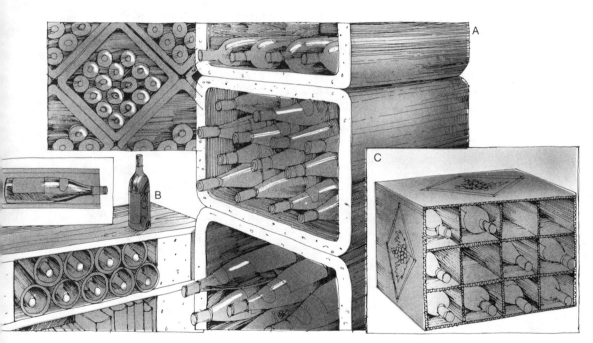

Vintner's classics, easy to re-create

Whether you want storage for a modest supply or a lavish one, these simple ideas may be all you need. Rectangular chimney tiles (A) handle a case or more apiece, but are relatively fragile in larger sizes and shouldn't be stacked too high; round drainpipe tiles or mailing tubes (B) pigeon-hole individual bottles. Of course, the simplest solution for short-term storage is to turn a divided cardboard wine box on its side (C).

Each slot stacks a case

This stylish vertical slot system is fashioned from vertical 1 by 10s faced with 1 by 3s shaped at the top so that bottles slide up and out. The platform on top displays the contents—up to one case—of each slot below. Make the basic unit 4 feet high; the number of slots is up to you.
Architect: Ron Bogley.

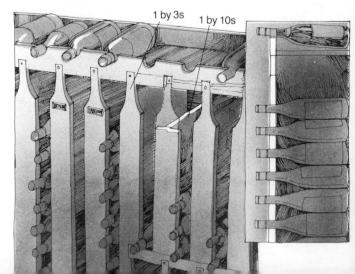

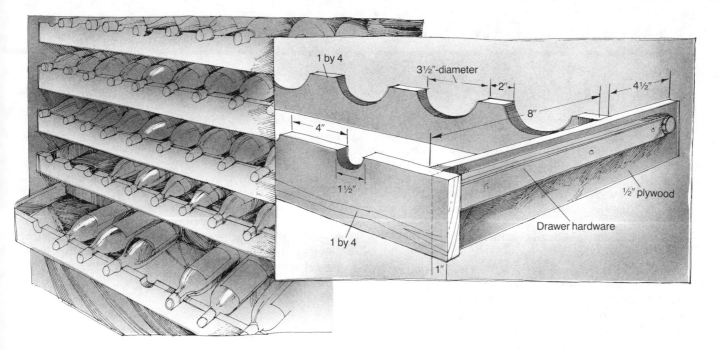

Wine by the drawerful

This handy rack is like a chest of open drawers for wine. To build it, first shape front and rear rails as shown, then connect them with plywood side strips. Mount your new drawers (they shouldn't be more than about 3 feet wide) inside a frame on heavy-duty drawer hardware. The drawers shown are 14 inches deep. Fasten your frame to a wall or to the ceiling for stability. Design: John Hamilton, George Kelce.

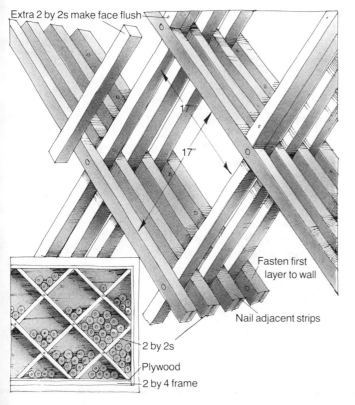

For copious collecting

A large-capacity, diamond-shaped bin system can be built by crisscrossing successive layers of 2 by 2 strips. Rip the 2 by 2s from fir 2 by 4s; seal, stain, and varnish; then assemble. Fasten parallel 2 by 2s to the wall at a 45° angle, as shown (use masonry nails for masonry walls, screws for wood stud walls); then nail on successive layers, each one perpendicular to the last. Eight layers of 2 by 2s provide bins approximately 12 inches deep. To provide additional support for your system, and to keep wines off a damp or dusty floor, position your bins atop a base of 2 by 4s and plywood, as shown.

Your bin system might stretch from wall to wall and from floor to ceiling, but it can be as modest as you like. For a finished look in a smaller unit, enclose the bins within plywood or fir sides and top. The bin size shown holds two cases. Architect: Neil M. Wright.

Wine Cellars for Vintage Care

Why create a wine cellar? For one thing, you'll always have a special bottle on hand when friends drop by. But perhaps more important, by purchasing young wines or sale wines in bulk, then letting them mature in your own cellar, you'll save the appreciable markup that dealers tack on for each year that wines age on *their* shelves. Moreover, many fine wines disappear from the market long before they're mature. A wine cellar or storage area can rapidly save you more money than it cost to build.

Where does a wine cellar go? An attractively finished basement is ideal both for a booming collection and for candlelight tasting parties. But there are other spots—a crawl space (see page 79), a garage corner, an outdoor shed, even an excavated hillside "cave."

Constructing a smaller wine cellar room within a basement or other larger space normally entails building walls, insulating walls and ceiling (see drawing, page 26), then adding racks or bins for wine. A vacant closet or even some unused cabinets form ready-made cellars for small collections.

Regardless of your cellar's size or location, remember four factors for successful wine storage: temperature stability, peace and quiet, absence of light, and bottle positioning.

Temperature: keep it cool and stable

For the optimum aging of wine, it's best to keep your cellar between 50° and 60°F/10° and 16°C; 58°F/14°C is generally regarded as ideal. Some experts, however, wouldn't pale at the idea of storing wines at room temperature — 65° to 70°F/18° to 21°C. Temperature *stability* is more critical than precise temperature: wine can tolerate slow temperature changes over a period of days, but rapid or extreme fluctuations will cause damage.

Insulation is the key to temperature stability. Masonry—the building material for most basements— insulates well. Earth is an excellent natural insulator, which is why so many wine cellars are built below ground level. You don't have a basement? Search the house for an area that stays naturally cool (the north side of the house is shadiest) or that can be vented to a naturally cool crawl space or outside area.

Your cellar should not be near the furnace, heating ducts, or water heater. Insulating the walls heavily (the more the better) will stabilize temperatures. And don't forget the door — it should be solid-core with double weatherstripping. In cool climates, you can leave cool (usually north or east) basement walls uninsulated. Where it's warm, you might choose a power fan or air conditioning unit with an automatic thermostat to keep the wine cool. Though it does consume energy, an air conditioner might be needed only two to three months a year if the cellar is well insulated, and it needn't be overly powerful. Cellar humidity, although not critical, is best around 50 percent. If your cellar is too damp, the labels may fall off your bottles — resulting in a real guessing game.

Peace and quiet

The conditions required for storing wines may sound like a sickroom atmosphere, but wine should not be disturbed. Protect it from sources of vibration such as stairways, washers, and dryers. Sturdy wine racks will help (see pages 56–57); in earthquake country, bolt your racks to fixed walls.

Shut out the light

Direct sunlight and other sources of ultraviolet light may harm wines (specifically, the yeast organisms still alive within the bottle), so make your cellar lightproof. But don't forget good artificial light for those times when you're hunting for that special bottle or hosting a wine-tasting party.

Keep bottles on their sides

Efficient wine racks are the key to organizing your cellar space. For specifics on racks, see pages 56–57. A genuine cork is the traditional sign that a bottle of wine deserves special care. The cork breathes slightly, so it must be kept moist by the wine inside to prevent air or airborne organisms from entering and spoiling the wine.

Store bottles on their sides or at a slight tilt from the horizontal, with necks toward you for easy access. To help sort out the Beaujolais from the Zinfandel, hang small labels around the necks, or label each slot in your rack. Keep a complete log of all your wines and their locations.

A simple corner cellar

Wooden grid panels, fore and aft, allow prize wines to rest at their preferred angle. Counter is handy for uncorking bottles and pouring wine. Architect: Kenneth Lim.

Elegant enough for entertaining

This wine cellar is much more than a wine storage room—the owners enjoy their converted crawl space so much that they have dinner parties here. From the table, guests can admire the triangular wine bins, each of which holds about a case of wine. A serving alcove in the wall opposite the bins is fitted with a rack for wine glasses. The brick floor and rough redwood paneling add to the atmosphere and help insulate the cellar. Design: Jean Chappell.

Garages,
Attics &
Basements

Turning troublesome spaces into work-for-you places

Closet within a closet *takes advantage of normally wasted space along attic eaves. The small access door opens from the master bedroom closet. Architect: James Jessup.*

Space below the basement stairs *is fitted with shelves and hooks; floor space is open for bulky items.*

Garage corner *lends plenty of wall space for bicycles, hand tools, and camping gear. The cutaway workbench with shelves underneath is a bonus. Architect: Wendell H. Lovett.*

Garages

Maximizing storage, yet leaving space for the car

A loft for lightweight items, *simple racks for tools, and roomy utility shelves help organize this garage. All of these features stretch storage space even when the car's inside. The tool rack is made from 1 by 4 rails fastened to studs. For loft-building help, see page 65. Design: Steve Wolgemuth.*

You can't find your best pair of hedge clippers. Ah!—you spy them hanging on a nail in the corner of what has become a jungle—the garage. Up, down, and around you go, clearing a path to the corner. As you balance among a garden rake, birdcage, mattress frame, and broken lawn chair, reaching for the clippers, you stumble and fall onto a pile of laundry next to the washing machine. The clippers are still in the corner.

Clearly, you're out of storage space in your garage or carport, and it's time to do something about it. Consider organizing your belongings, improving your present storage facilities and adding new ones, or extending the building.

As you tackle your garage storage problems, think "clean up and look up"—this can be your byword for discovering and using your garage's storage potential. A thorough cleanup alone can drastically increase your garage's capacity. And once your belongings are sorted through, you'll be able to make better use of existing and added storage units such as shelves, drawers, pegboards, and roll-outs.

But don't forget to look up. Overhead storage—cabinets, platforms, lofts, and ledges—can be used to tame your garage jungle and create room for a much needed laundry center, workshop, or potting table. Overhead storage is also feasible in carports, which call for secure, weatherproof storage units.

If you're already organized, this section will show you how to improve your garage—and the time you spend in it—with better heating, lighting, ventilation, and other amenities. And if you can't possibly fit in another paint can or tricycle, you'll find some ideas here on how to increase storage space by extending the garage itself.

Your garage's or carport's storage potential

With building costs multiplying as quickly as your storage inventory, you may well turn to your existing garage or carport with fresh hopes. Its length and width determine the structure's basic amount of available space, of course, but other factors count, too. Here are some questions to consider: How high is the roof? Is it flat or peaked? How large is your car? Does it need year-round protection?

Garage dimensions. Garages are nominally termed "one-car," "two-car," and "three-car." The size of a one-car garage begins at about 10 feet by 20 feet—small, but you can probably squeeze some good storage space out of it. You're in luck if your one-car garage has a peaked roof. Two-car spaces run upward from 18½ feet by 20 feet; 25 feet square is ideal. If you have a three-car space, you have a head start on storage.

Garage and carport types. The design of your garage or carport affects its storage potential. Garage walls are usually built from wood framing and sheathing, cement blocks, or prefabricated metal panels. Building materials have little influence on storage capacity, but it's easier to attach storage units to wood frame walls than to masonry or metal. Wood frame walls also allow shallow storage between studs.

A carport's open structure is a different story. Because carport storage is more exposed to weather and theft, you'll want to limit storage of valuables to lockable weatherproof units; install them either along the carport's perimeter or overhead.

Gable and hip roofs (see drawing below) are tops for storage. Shed-roof structures also provide some overhead space between the rafters and ceiling line. In a flat-roofed garage, you're limited to the space between the top of your head or vehicle and the ceiling.

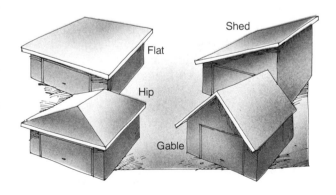

Subcompacts and limousines. The sizes of your automobiles directly affect the available floor space in a garage or carport. Fortunately for the storage-needy, average car dimensions have been shrinking (see drawing at right above for sample dimensions). Adapt

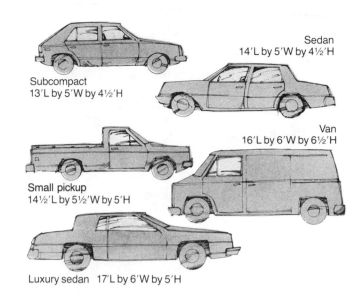

Subcompact
13'L by 5'W by 4½'H

Sedan
14'L by 5'W by 4½'H

Van
16'L by 6'W by 6½'H

Small pickup
14½'L by 5½'W by 5'H

Luxury sedan   17'L by 6'W by 5'H

your storage plans to the size of your vehicle or vehicles, but keep in mind that some day you might want to sell your home to a family with two vans.

Clearance. In your garage or carport, clearance is the space needed around the car when the car is parked inside; it affects how much room you'll have to work with when planning where to put storage units, appliances, and worktables.

See the drawing below for minimum clearance recommendations around typical vehicles. To calculate how much storage space you have to work with, drive your vehicle or vehicles into place. Then measure the distance from each vehicle to the ceiling, walls, rafters, and other obstructions. Subtract the recommended clearance figures, and you have the bottom line—the real storage potential.

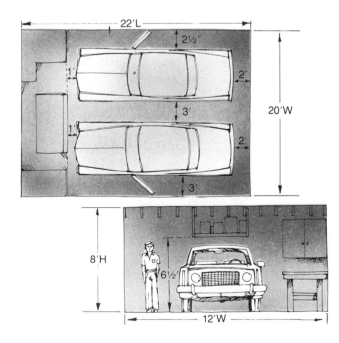

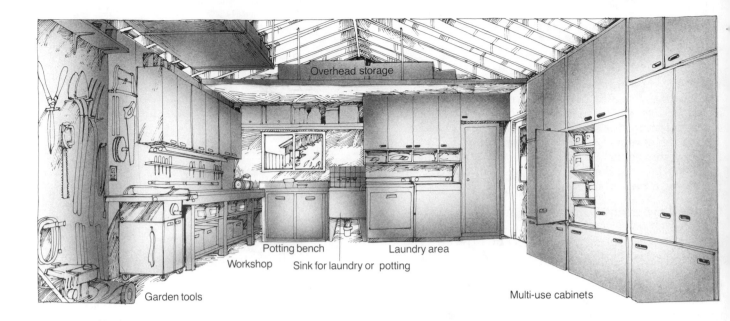

Overhead storage

Potting bench

Workshop

Sink for laundry or potting

Laundry area

Garden tools

Multi-use cabinets

The multi-use garage and carport

After you've assessed your usable storage space, take stock of what you need to store. Do you want to make room for that laundry center, workshop, or potting bench? Efficient overall planning, plus storage units especially designed for your garage or carport, will open up more space than you might imagine.

Coordinating your garage layout

The keys to an efficient garage layout are 1) using all available space, leaving minimum clearances next to, behind, and above vehicles; and 2) grouping items that go together—gardening supplies, for example.

Because most storage problems stem from a lack of floor space, you'll do well to raise storage units above the ground whenever possible. You can hang them high on a wall or suspend them from the joists or rafters. Or you can build an "upstairs" loft.

The items you use most often should, of course, be close at hand. Awkward spots and places that are inaccessible when the car is inside (such as rafter space) are best for seasonal or long-term storage.

Plan hanging shelves or wall-mounted cabinets around the contour of your car's hood and roof (see clearance diagram, preceding page). To ensure safe parking, attach a tennis ball to a cord with a fishhook or eyescrew, and hang the ball so that it will nudge your windshield when the car is properly parked; or fasten a length of 4 by 4 to the garage slab to "curb" the front wheels when the car is in place.

Some garage work areas to consider include these: a laundry center with sink and cabinets (see pages 38–39); a home workshop, with places for hand and power tools (pages 52–55); a house maintenance center for paint brushes, spare plumbing and electrical parts,

brooms, solvents, and cleaners; a potting center with workbench, mounted cabinets, and tilt-out bins; a garden maintenance area where you can gather such tools as the lawn mower, rake, clippers, and weeders; and a mudroom and closet for boots, rain gear, and other outdoor or seasonal clothes (see pages 20–23).

Position such areas for convenience and good working conditions. An outdoor maintenance area, for example, should be handy to the garden or yard.

Storage units for the garage

Here's a brief guide to storage units particularly suited for the garage (see drawing on facing page).

Between-stud shelves. Most garage walls are of wood frame construction; the vertical studs are spaced 16 or 24 inches apart, center to center. The shallow, uniform area between studs is ideal for storing miscellaneous small items like nail jars, engine oil, and paint cans.

Open shelves. Build freestanding frames for shelves or hang shelf units (those with backs) from the wall. You can also use adjustable tracks and brackets, L-braces, individual brackets, or continuous brackets attached to studs to hold up shelves. If your garage walls are of brick or concrete block, back shelves against the wall, hang them from ceiling joists, or use special masonry fasteners (see pages 78–79 for types and installation tips).

Cabinets, drawers, and closets. Enclosed units keep dust and moisture out, and help to organize easily lost small items. Large tools, lawn mowers, and cleaning supplies fit into vertical closets. Recycled cabinets from a remodeled kitchen are perfect for the garage. Securely locked, enclosed units keep children safe from garden poisons and sharp tools, and guard against theft. Sliding doors, roll-down window shades, or tilt-out bins make large units more accessible in tight places. For more on cabinets, see page 10.

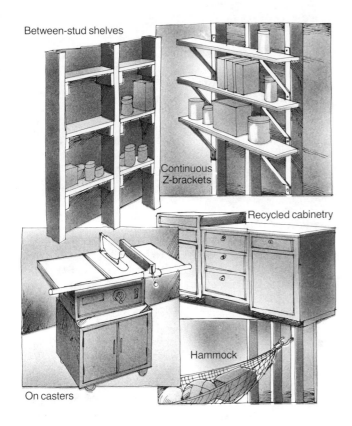

Between-stud shelves

Continuous
Z-brackets

Recycled cabinetry

Hammock

On casters

Building a loft. An overhead loft is an effective means
to increasing storage space—especially in a cramped
one-car garage—and it's comparatively straightfor-
ward for you and a helper to build. To construct the
simplest type of loft, take advantage of existing ceiling
joists, adding more joists as necessary. Lay a ½ or
⅝-inch plywood "floor" on top of the joists (use
⅝-inch sheets if you're going to be using the loft for
heavy storage).

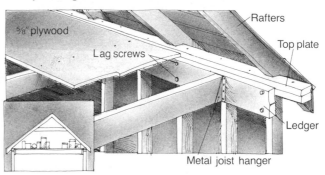

⅝" plywood

Rafters

Top plate

Lag screws

Ledger

Metal joist hanger

When planning a garage loft, inspect the size and
condition of the existing joists. High-quality 2 by 6s
should be strong enough to support the weight of ordinary storage. But if you plan to walk on the surface
or store heavy furniture in the loft, or if the joists must
span more than 12 feet, they should be stouter than
2 by 6s. Diagonal 1 by 4 braces running between joists
and overhead rafters provide extra support. Ask your
local building department about requirements in your
area. Joists should be spaced on 16-inch centers for
heavy storage.

If you have to add ceiling joists, remember that
ideally they should sit on opposing top plates. If the
top plates are inaccessible, bolt ledger strips to the
wall studs, attach metal joist hangers, and use these
to support the joists.

With a peaked roof framed by trusses (see drawing
on page 70) or low collar beams, install smaller
plywood platforms in the spaces between consecutive
trusses (commonly 24 inches) or beams; support the
platforms with 2 by 4 cleats nailed to the sides of the
trusses.

Access. To gain access to your new loft, use a sturdy
stepladder or utility ladder. For a large loft space, see
page 73 for information on building stairs and other
kinds of access. If you plan to haul bulky, heavy items
up and down, a narrow ladder is not only exasperat-
ing, but also dangerous.

Pulley system. You might consider a suspended
plywood platform operated with pulleys (see page 41)
for garage storage. Here's another option: bend 1-inch-
wide iron straps so that they extend 3 inches under the
platform on each side, and screw them to the bottom
and sides. Attach cable or rope to the strap ends. This
kind of unit should be used for lightweight storage only.

Racks and pegs. Most versatile for hanging storage is
the pegboard hanger system shown on page 7. Oversize carpenter's nails and spikes, or dowels set into
wall studs, can hold garden chairs—even ladders.
Commercially manufactured racks, whether of heavy-
duty metal or vinyl-coated wire, are versatile but
more costly.

Roll-outs. One way to fit storage units, workbenches,
or equipment into a tight garage is to mount them on
heavy-duty casters. Store them close to the wall, then
roll them out onto the main floor when the car is out.

Overhead storage units. Even in flat-roofed garages,
overhead joists—the horizontal cousins of wall studs
—form cubbyholes that are great for small storage,
especially for seasonal or infrequently used items. To
provide easy overhead "shelving," nail boards across
joist bottoms (use heavy nails). A nylon or canvas
hammock draped above head level can be used to
store lightweight items such as seasonal sports equipment and winter blankets.

Overhead platforms

Often the most neglected storage space throughout a
house is the area above your head. Garages with
gable, hip, or shed roofs are ideal for anything from a
perimeter ledge (page 41) to a finished upstairs room.

When putting overhead garage space to work, remember to leave adequate clearance for the garage
door to operate smoothly—and for you and your family to move freely about the garage. In general, any

Carport storage ideas

The two major shortcomings of carport storage are exposure to weather and lack of security; the most common solution to both is to install enclosed cabinets. Build units from exterior-grade ¾-inch plywood, and finish them with tough exterior enamel or polyurethane. (See page 10 for more details on cabinets.) Build units with bases that raise them several inches above the floor; either waterproof the bases or build them with pressure-treated lumber. For greater security, use good locks and hasps (see page 10) and inside-mounted hinges.

The number one spot for carport storage units is between the roof support posts. Attach units to the floor slab, suspend them from overhead beams, or add intermediate vertical framing to hold them up. A long cabinet might have separate doored compartments— one shelved, one with drawers, and one without interior divisions. Units that have doors that slide or that open to the outside leave more clearance inside the carport (see drawing on page 63 for minimum clearances).

If your carport has a pitched gable or hip roof, consider an overhead storage area (see page 65). Lockable plywood chests bolted to a loft "floor," joists, or ledger strips can be used to store valuables (see drawing below).

A small room—perhaps 6 feet by 8 feet—added to the rear of the carport and equipped with windows, electrical outlets, and a small heater, makes a protected "mini-workshop," laundry, or crafts studio. You can fit such a room with shelves, pegboard, and other open storage standbys.

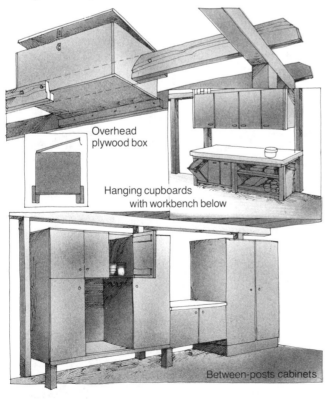

Overhead plywood box

Hanging cupboards with workbench below

Between-posts cabinets

Garage improvements

If your garage (or carport) is to be used for more than parking, it may require specific improvements to ensure that it's safe, comfortable for working, weathertight, and up to code. Consider these possibilities:

Ventilation. To prevent the buildup of moisture, auto exhaust, paint fumes, or shop dust in a closed garage, open ventilation is a necessity. As a rule, there should be 1 square foot of open vent space per 150 square feet of floor area. A laundry must have its own vent system.

Insulation. You might choose to insulate your garage for either of two reasons: 1) to prevent swings in temperature that might damage storage; or 2) to make a heated garage more energy efficient. Put insulation between wall studs and rafters. Choose fiberglass batts, blankets, or rigid board insulation with a vapor barrier, or add a plastic barrier (see pages 70–71).

Lighting. Ideally, you should mix natural and artificial light. To obtain more natural light, install windows and skylights, or replace a large section of a wall, or even the garage door, with translucent panels. Carports are often roofed with rippled plastic sheeting that lets in muted light. By placing garage windows high, you'll save wall space for storage.

Overhead fluorescent shop units are the most efficient for general artificial lighting; one 4-foot double-tube shop unit lights up about 40 square feet. Place individual, adjustable spotlights—incandescent or fluorescent—where direct lighting is needed. Paint the garage walls and ceiling, as well as pegboard storage panels, white to amplify light by reflection.

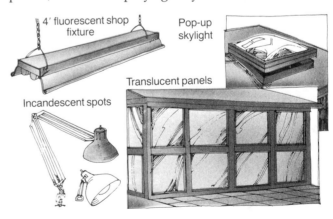

4' fluorescent shop fixture

Pop-up skylight

Translucent panels

Incandescent spots

Wiring. Power tools and garage lighting should be on different circuits; a tool or laundry circuit should be at least 20 amps. Install as many circuits as possible to prevent an overload. A laundry, a workshop, or an electric heater may require up to 240 volts.

Several grounded (three-prong) electrical outlets are a necessity, and continuous power strips are a great convenience. You can run wires either underground or overhead from a power source to a detached garage.

Plumbing. Laundries, photo darkrooms, garden center sinks, hose spigots, and mudrooms may require plumbing improvements. Extending plumbing to a detached garage can be a problem. Remember that outdoor pipes must be placed below the frost line (check local codes), and facilities that require plumbing must be higher than the drainage system. In freezing climates, plumbing systems for unheated garages or carports should be equipped with shutoff valves.

Floors. Concrete slab floors are standard. If you want to use your garage for work or play during the day and for car storage at night, you can protect the floor from oil drippings by laying down a 10-mil layer of polyethylene sheeting. For a more finished look, you might consider vinyl-asbestos tiles; some types take wear and tear from cars surprisingly well.

To insulate and dress up a drab slab, simply cover the floor with straw mats or colorful rugs. You can also paint the slab with special concrete paint, or lay vinyl-asbestos or asphalt tiles in adhesive over the concrete (waterproof it first). If you want to use a covering that requires a wooden base, you can build up such a base over the waterproofed concrete (see pages 78–79 for details). A separate work area within your garage or carport might warrant such treatment.

Heating. Insulation and a built-up subfloor in the work area will help reduce heat loss. To provide heat, you have three options: 1) extend ducts from your central heating system to the garage (not feasible with detached garages); 2) install a separate forced-air unit in the garage (illegal in some areas); or 3) set up a built-in or portable room heater—probably your best choice.

The four types of room heaters are these: electric (baseboard, portable, or quartz type); kerosene; oil or gas wall heaters (designed to fit between wall studs); and woodstoves. Neither a kerosene heater nor a woodstove requires any power hookup, but both need ventilation; a woodstove also requires special fittings and flashing.

Room heaters operate either by convection (they heat the air in a room) or by radiation (they heat objects first). Radiation is most effective in a small area. In general, wall-mounted units are more efficient, but a portable unit can go where you go.

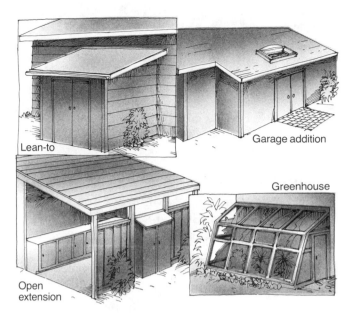

Lean-to
Garage addition
Greenhouse
Open extension

Garage extensions

You've tried all the possibilities, but you just can't fit all your sports gear, garden tools, and lumber into the garage. Before you build a new structure—shed, carport, or garage—consider a simpler garage extension.

Extension types. An extension represents a smaller investment in both time and money than a new structure, and takes less space. Among your options (see drawing above): a roof extension for sheltering a car, boat, or RV—or for storage and work space in milder climates; a lean-to with outside access; a glass greenhouse version of the lean-to (consider a prefabricated unit); or a garage addition. If you're ambitious, you can also convert a one-car to a two-car garage.

Building tips. An extension borrows the garage's framework for part of its structural support. A lean-to is essentially three walls and a roof—the fourth wall is the garage. More elaborate additions entail cutting a door between the garage and an added room, or "punching out" an entire wall. In such cases, be sure to preserve adequate structural supports (headers) for the remaining garage framework. When any structural alterations are required, consult a contractor or architect for recommendations, and have your plans checked out by local building inspectors. Building codes may place limits on extension materials, height, setback from the property line, and foundation type.

Normally, an extension is built over a poured concrete slab that has been tied into the garage slab. However, a more solid foundation, extending below the frost line, may be required in severe climates. Your new extension must be weathertight: provide a sound roof and install flashing where the extension adjoins the old garage roof or siding. Select a design, materials, and colors that match or complement your garage and house.

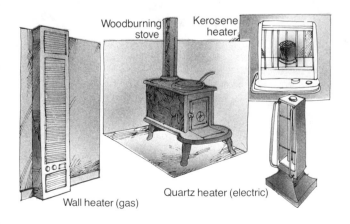

Woodburning stove
Kerosene heater
Quartz heater (electric)
Wall heater (gas)

Attics

Taking the mystery out of access, sloping walls, air vents, and floors

An attic is like a treasure chest—it's usually filled with a few treasures, some disappointments, and a little mystery. Grandfather's steamer trunk, your summer camping gear, and holiday decorations are your treasures. But how do you take the mystery out of storing—and finding—prize possessions within that oddly shaped space?

Attics are scarce in modern housing, particularly in the West. If you grew up with an attic or recently acquired an older or custom home with an attic, you'll welcome solutions to the storage problems posed by attics. These pages offer ways to create a great storage area that's warm, dry, accessible, and even pleasant to visit.

Even if you don't have a formal attic, you may still have a low crawl space above the ceiling that you can convert into a handy storage area.

These are the biggest problems confronting those who wish to make good use of attic space: the awkwardness of sloping walls, sharp roof peaks, and unfinished floors; temperature fluctuations—stifling heat in the summer and icy air in the winter; dampness and humidity from roof leaks and improper air circulation; and insufficient access from below. The following sections treat these problems individually. Overcoming them is something many homeowners can do themselves; refer to the *Sunset* book *Basic Carpentry Illustrated*.

Anatomy of an attic. *The classic attic triangle is shaped by opposing roof rafters rising to a ridge board at the peak, and by floor joists—which double as ceiling joists downstairs—that span the outer house walls. Collar beams sometimes brace opposing rafters, or are added as ceiling supports. Plywood sheets or "1-by" strip boards laid atop the joists serve as flooring. In addition to the open floor space, use these three key storage areas: along the sloping walls, against the gable walls, and along the ridge line.*

An attic overview

An attic's shape—and its capacity for storage—depend on how steeply the roof is pitched (attic height) and on the house's dimensions (floor space). Steep roofs make the best attics, flat roofs none at all. For a living space, a room should normally have a 7½-foot ceiling over at least one-half of the available floor space. For storage, though, you can use whatever space is accessible. Even a minimal crawl space, common in newer homes, has usable storage space.

Organizing your attic

Familiarize yourself with the attic vocabulary explained in the drawing on the facing page. Then add two more terms: *organization* and *accessibility.*

An attic's layout needn't be stylish or fancy, but it should be orderly. The goal is to organize the attic so that you can easily find everything. Arrange related objects in one place, and store those you use often where they're easy to reach. To save a lot of teeth-gnashing, label covered items and boxes with permanent ink on white tape for identification, and keep an inventory of everything in the attic.

Those small, fragile keepsakes requiring extra protection from moisture, dust, and insects should be carefully packed in sturdy boxes and sealed; cover furniture with mattress pads and wrap with polyethylene.

Fitting storage to the attic

An attic's configuration is usually a challenge for orderly storage. How do you deal with sloping walls, corners you have to crawl into, triangular gable walls, and the high but narrow ridge line overhead? Here are some tested ideas; see pages 6–11, too, for general information on storage units.

Sloping walls. You can either shape storage units to conform to eave spaces or give up on the eaves and build vertical units. A 4-foot-high knee wall unit with cabinet doors, recessed drawers, or even a curtain across the front is an efficient way to use eave space (see drawing below). Knee wall units should not be deeper than your reach, unless they're large enough to be walk-ins.

Simpler solutions? Shelves hung with rope or chain, or items hanging from a closet rod, use the force of gravity to square off attic space. Or between adjacent rafters, horizontal 1 by 12s create another version of "between-stud" shelves for out-of-the-way storage.

Gable walls are good spots for a combination closet to store seasonal clothes, toys, and sporting goods. Shelves are easy to fit on a gable wall: install track and bracket hardware for shelves (see drawing below), or place shelves or cabinets along the base of the wall.

Articles that would be damaged by extremes of heat or cold (artwork, for example) shouldn't be stored against a gable wall unless it's insulated. This is particularly true if the gable wall is on the north side of the house or if it's exposed to direct sun for substantial periods. Also, be sure not to block any vents in the wall (page 71).

Along the ridge line. Cut off the triangular peak with rope-hung or chain-hung shelves (accessible from the sides), or hang storage from long nails, hooks, and pegs fixed high on the rafters. A closet rod or simply a long 1 by 2 fastened to opposing rafters will support garment bags full of seasonal clothes. If there's a ridge vent (page 71), don't block it.

To form an "attic within an attic"—a scaled-down version of the loft platform on page 65—place boards or plywood between existing collar beams or between beams you've added yourself. Such a platform should be used for lightweight storage only.

Sloping walls   Gable walls   Ridge line

Cramped quarters. Many newer homes, particularly in the West and South, were built with relatively flat roofs that leave only a minimal attic or a crawl space. Usually, even a crawl space has some usable storage in the middle and at the gable ends. You can at least lay down plywood around the access hatch. If you can reach the gables easily, build storage cupboards and a catwalk (page 72) leading from the hatch.

Truss framing presents an obstacle to increased attic use; the trusses integrate rafters, collar beams, and sometimes ceiling joists into single framing members, usually spaced 24 inches apart. Trusses may not be removed or cut into, so storage must be built around or between them. Access will often be a trial, as you have to crawl through the spaces within trusses. But don't give up—lay down plywood (see below) and make the most of the space.

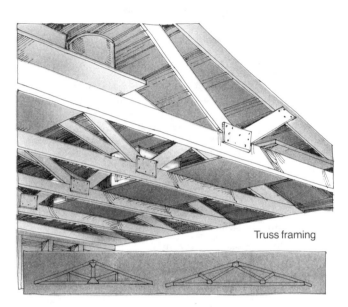

Truss framing

Solving attic problems

Attics revive that old cliché "Out of sight, out of mind." Often you won't notice an attic's problems until you open up the space for storables that demand dry, stable conditions.

Your major enemies are swings in temperature and moisture. If the space is improperly vented or insulated, an attic's temperature might soar to 150° in August, then plunge below freezing in January. Moisture enters the picture as humidity from downstairs condenses on cold attic walls, or—more trying—through a roof leak (for information on making repairs, see the *Sunset* book *Roofing & Siding).*

To eliminate swings in temperature, install insulation between the roof rafters and along gable walls. Add a vapor barrier to prevent humid house air from condensing inside the attic. To improve ventilation, consider adding gable vents, soffit vents, ridge vents, turbine vents, and fans.

Attic insulation—the "balancer"

Insulation slows the transfer of heat from one space to another through a solid surface—wall, roof, or floor. Attic insulation is a "balancer"—it prevents warm air from escaping through the roof in winter, and slows down the accumulation of heat from outside in summer. An "R-rating" is given to all standard building materials—the higher the number, the more effective the insulation.

How much insulation does your attic need? Climate and personal choice are factors: check with the building department for the optimum R-rating where you live.

Where does it go? To make an attic suitable for storage or living space, insulation should be placed between the roof rafters and used to line gable walls—not incorporated into the attic floor as is common. You could insulate behind knee walls—ending the storage space there—instead of the lowest rafters. If your attic floor, or the ceiling below, is already insulated, so much the better; such insulation slows down humidity and heat exchange and deadens sound.

Insulation types. In unfinished attics the most common types of insulation are blankets or batts of spun fiberglass or rock wool, and lightweight rigid boards of compressed fiberglass, polystyrene, or urethane. Blankets and batts are sized to fit common framing gaps of 22½ inches and 14½ inches. Panels are available in the following sizes: 4 feet by 8 feet, 4 feet by 4 feet, and 2 feet by 8 feet. Different thicknesses have different R-ratings. Blankets are easier to install, but boards have a higher R-rating per inch of thickness. Some codes require that insulation be covered with ½-inch gypsum wallboard or a layer of another fire-retardant material.

Vapor barriers. It's necessary in all but the driest climates to install a vapor barrier to prevent humid house air from condensing inside attic walls and roof materials. Blankets and batts are commonly sold with a vapor barrier of foil or kraft paper; if your insulation doesn't have this protection, cover it with polyethylene sheeting (at least 2 mils thick), foil-backed wallboard, or asphalt-covered building paper. Normally, vapor barriers should face in toward the attic.

Attic ventilation

For a simple solution to heat buildup in summer, and humidity and condensation in the winter, try good ventilation. *Natural ventilation* takes advantage of thermal air movement and wind pressure; *power ventilation* uses an electric fan to push or draw hot air up and out of the attic through vents near the ridge line.

The key to proper ventilation is the placement of the vents. The lower drawing on the facing page illustrates the various options for placing vents—but you won't need all those vents. You'll need about 1 square foot of

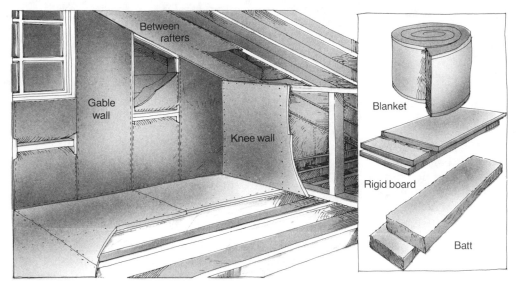

Insulate the shell. *If you're developing attic storage or workspace, provide attic insulation between rafters and inside gable walls. Check your building department for the optimum local "R-rating," then choose from blankets, batts, or rigid boards. Buy insulation with an attached vapor barrier, or add polyethylene sheeting—2-mil or thicker. (The vapor barrier faces inside.) Cover insulation with fire-retardant wallboard or paneling.*

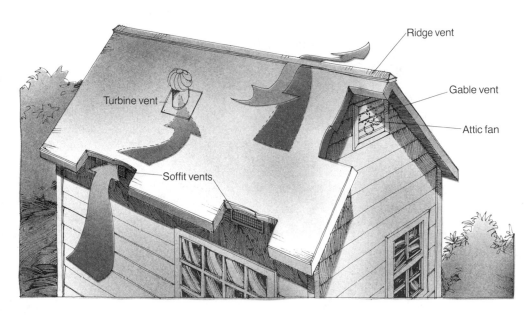

Attic ventilation. *Natural air movement is the key to attic vent placement. Cooler air enters low, pushing rising hot air out the top. Low soffit vents coupled with ridge or gable vents are standard. For problem cases, an electric fan in a downwind gable expels hot air quickly. Slotted turbine vents set up a natural vacuum when the wind blows.*

open vent space (don't count screens or slats) per 150 square feet of floor area.

Gable vents are set in the gable walls, as close to the ridge line as possible. They're usually installed in pairs: one facing into the prevailing wind, the other downwind. A breeze entering one vent pushes hot attic air out the other. Gable vents are often combined with soffit vents. To prevent icy winds from blowing through your attic, close or cover a windward vent during the winter.

Soffit (eave) vents are openings at the attic floor level, below the rafter overhang, that bring cool air into the attic. This air is drawn up by warm-air convection, which forces hot air out vents near the ridge line.

Ridge vents are very efficient, but they're troublesome to install. They release hot air from the roof peak, and

because they're two-sided, they'll always vent in the downwind direction. Ridge vents require extensive complementary soffit venting below for good results.

Turbine vents. When the wind is blowing, the slotted ball atop the vent rotates freely, creating a vacuum that draws attic air up and out. The vent remains open when the wind doesn't blow.

Electric attic fans are powerful tools for pushing hot air out of an attic. A fan is inserted into a cutout in the gable wall, then wired; it's usually paired with an opening in the attic floor that draws air from the house below. Some fans are equipped with a thermostat that conveniently monitors their operation. The disadvantages of electric fans—aside from the effort it takes to install them—are that they consume energy and make noise; some fire codes prohibit their use (see page 49).

Upgrading your attic

If your attic is properly insulated and ventilated, you're ready to attend to three other big considerations: your attic's floor, lighting, and accessibility.

The attic floor

Is your attic floor ready for storage or heavy traffic? If the floor joists are exposed, the answer is a loud "no." *Don't* walk or place storage in the areas between joists —that's your downstairs ceiling, not intended to support weight. For flooring, you can choose between an attic "catwalk" and a finished floor.

A catwalk is a narrow weight-bearing surface extending the length of the attic and possibly to areas under the eaves. With a catwalk you can gain access to the whole attic area without balancing on joists or installing a complete floor.

A catwalk—or a portion of one—is usually built of plywood laid right on top of the joists. Be sure the joists are strong enough—see "A new attic floor," below. Standard plywood sheets 5/8-inch thick are usually adequate, provided you can fit the large (4 feet by 8 feet) sheets up into the attic. If you can't fit standard plywood sheets through the hatch, the stairway, or a dormer opening, cut the sheets down to a manageable size or use strip lumber (1 by 6s should be adequate).

A new attic floor. Attic floor joists, which are of course also the ceiling joists for downstairs, may not be built to support the weight of human traffic, heavy storage,

or furniture. Your first task is to inspect the joists. Check two things: the spacing of the joists—which should be 16 inches center to center (or 24 inches if the joists are stout enough); and the joist dimensions— joists should be at least 2 by 8s for heavy use, even more stout for long spans. Check with building department officials for requirements in your area.

See the drawing below for details about installing new joists, if necessary, and laying a floor. About floors: for simple utility and strength, 5/8-inch or 3/4-inch plywood is the best choice. Plywood is easy to lay, adds rigidity and strength to the floor structure, and is usually squeakproof. Top-grade plywood isn't necessary for attic floors. However, special subfloor panels with tongue-and-groove edges are stronger than standard plywood, though they cost more.

Lighting

Light fixtures don't have to be fancy in the attic, but they should provide illumination where it's most needed. Well-placed electric lights can save you a lot of anguish when you're looking for small items under the eaves or atop a ridge line shelf. One main attic light should be operable from a switch below; individual lights can be turned on by switches or pullchains as you move about the attic.

Attic access

Is your attic readily accessible? How do you plan to use it? If it's for light or seasonal storage only—especially in minimal crawl spaces—a trap door and folding ladder will probably be adequate. Heavier storage requires

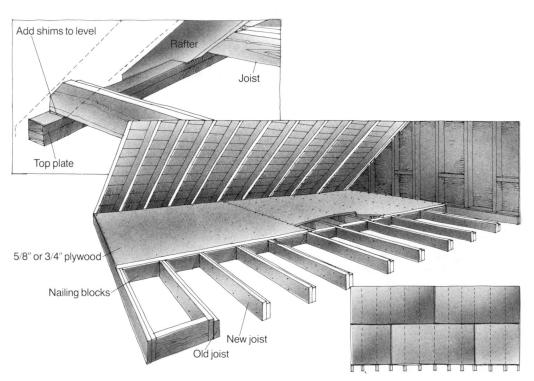

Add shims to level

Rafter

Joist

Top plate

5/8" or 3/4" plywood

Nailing blocks

New joist

Old joist

Laying a floor. *If your present joists aren't up to the task of supporting stored items, you'll have to add new ones. Lay new joists next to old ones (if the original spacing is correct); nail the new joists to the old and to the top plate or bearing wall at each end. To level the new joists, slip small wood blocks or shims beneath them as necessary.*

Then it's on to the plywood floor. Lay the sheets lengthwise across the joists; panel ends should meet midway over a joist for solid support. Stagger rows so that no two adjacent joints line up. Adding nailing blocks between joists or installing tongue-and-groove plywood strengthens edges.

a sturdy ladder or stairs, as well as a larger opening for lugging mattresses, dressers, and chairs up and in. If you'll be using the space frequently, you'll almost certainly want a fixed stairway.

Stairs or ladders adjoining a wall will be sturdier, safer, and less obtrusive than those placed further out in a room. Remember, though, that stairways are often required by code to have a minimum of 6½ feet of headroom, so a stair opening in the attic can't be tucked under the eaves.

The access opening. Here are the three rules for an attic opening: 1) the opening must be large enough for you and your storage to fit through without undue gymnastics; 2) you should have sufficient overhead clearance when you step up into the attic; and 3) the ladder or stairway should not interfere with traffic patterns or take up too much space below.

A door-size opening will admit most large storage. Width is the critical dimension, though. Homeowners with limited crawl spaces can make do with a push-up hatch smaller than door size.

Look for ways to provide attic access from out-of-the-way spots. If your garage is attached, you may be able to get into the attic from the garage. You could also remove the ceiling from a large closet, install a ladder, and convert a crawl space above into a "storage loft."

Ladders—fixed and fold-down. Fixed ladders and fold-down stairs are best for occasional traffic and light storage. Fold-down stairs, available from building suppliers or well-stocked hardware stores, swing up into the ceiling to close, leaving open floor space below; they also demand little clearance above. Their disadvantages: they usually provide no hand support and they lack stability. Look for a ladder with minimal bounce at the hinges.

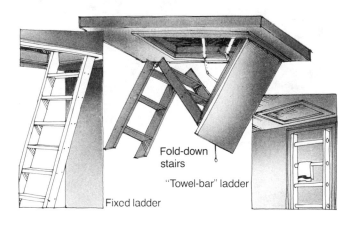

Fixed ladders are more stable, especially when fastened to a wall. They range from traditional structures to door-mounted rungs that double as towel bars (see drawing above). In general, the heavier the intended use, the more sturdy the ladder should be. A ladder's biggest drawback is its steepness; it's difficult to climb up and down with full hands.

Planning your staircase. A well-crafted main staircase is a carpenter's showpiece, demanding the same attention to detail as fine cabinetry. But, an unadorned flight of attic utility stairs is much easier to build than it may look, and it doesn't require fancy materials or many tools. The key is in the planning.

First, consider your available space and the total rise and total run to be covered; then choose your basic stair type and dimensions accordingly. The three basic types, as shown below, are straight-run, "L"-type, and "U"-type. Straight-run stairs are the easiest and cheapest to build; L and U-types are better in tight spaces and for avoiding obstructions. Spiral or "winder" stairs, a fourth type, take up even less space, but they're awkward and dangerous for transporting storage goods up and down; some local codes ban their use altogether.

A typical stair assembly consists of stringers, risers, treads, and railings. Design factors, which are commonly subject to building codes, include riser height, tread depth, stair angle, and stair width. The drawing below illustrates the major elements. Check local codes for specific requirements in your area.

Stairways may be open or closed, or a combination of the two. Open sides should be equipped with handrails above vertical banisters or a solid side guard. On a closed side, a rail can be wall-mounted with metal brackets. Manufactured assemblies are common, but a 2 by 4 rail and supports are sufficient.

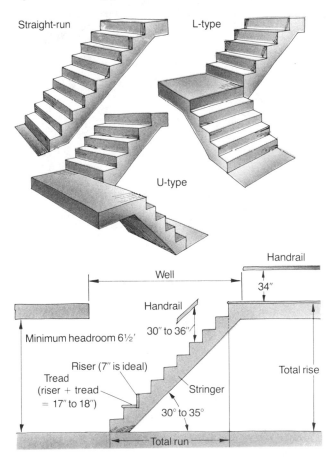

Basements

Getting on top of what's down under: ideas for dry storage

Like the Rock of Gibraltar, a basement should be an impregnable fortress, impervious to weather, water, and rodents. If your fortress is crumbling under the attack of any or all of these enemies, you're probably wondering how to guard your storage.

In the following pages, we show you how to solve moisture problems, whether from sweating pipes or outright leaks, and how to control basement temperatures by using insulation, heating, and air conditioning. Darkness—another common basement foe—can be overcome by the addition of new lights (the *Sunset* book *Basic Home Wiring Illustrated* tells how).

Depending on your needs, it may not be necessary to improve your entire basement. Instead, consider sectioning off an area with easy access and focus your best efforts there.

All kinds of storage units—closets, cabinets, shelves, and racks—have a place in the basement. You can use masonry fasteners to attach these and other accessories to brick and concrete walls. You may also want to install a combination of such units beneath the stairs.

Even if you don't have a basement, you might have a crawl space between the floor joists and the ground below. There are lots of possibilities—including further excavation—for utilizing this area.

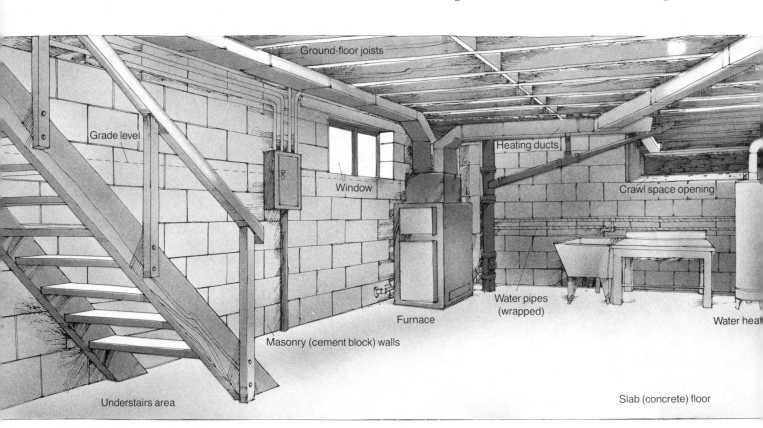

The view down under. *A full basement extends underneath an entire house, and reaches from the slab level to the first floor joists above. Foundation walls—commonly poured concrete or masonry blocks—form the perimeter. Basements are prone to seepage, condensation, and temperature problems, but once these are controlled, basement space is great for storage. Prime storage spots include along the walls, between overhead floor joists, and beneath stairs.*

A basement overview

A basement, loosely defined, is the area between the base of a house's foundation and the floor joists that support the living space above. In the case of a "full" basement, the concrete slab and foundation walls form an enclosed, defined room—but one usually left unimproved by the builders. A full basement has sufficient headroom for a livable space, usually 7½ feet.

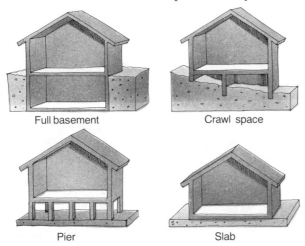

Full basement

Crawl space

Pier

Slab

In many newer homes, the foundation is made shallow to save money and labor, and perhaps to avoid problems with the underground water table. In such cases, only a minimal foundation wall extends above the footings, so basement space is greatly reduced. This kind of mini-basement, or *crawl space,* can still be very useful for storage (see page 79). Split level homes often have both a full basement and crawl space.

Exceptions to the usual basement scheme are pier and slab foundations (see drawing above). Slab foundations are unusable for storage. Pier foundations afford some space, but it's open to the elements, insects, and animals—as well as theft. Hardy storables such as firewood would be fine here; for other types of storage in a pier foundation, use enclosed, lockable units (see "Carport storage ideas," page 66).

Simple basement storage solutions

What kind of storage can you create in your basement without going to very much trouble and expense? If you're lucky enough to have only minor moisture and pest problems, note the precautions that follow.

The structure of your basement may offer ready-to-use storage space: look underneath the stairs, overhead, and around and between ducts. With masonry fasteners you can attach shelves, hooks, and hangers to concrete or brick basement walls.

Moistureproof storage. Waterproofing or dehumidifying may be more expensive than it's worth if the moisture problem is minor and your storage hardy. For damp, unimproved basements, choose metal storage units instead of wood—metal won't swell and warp (though it might rust). Don't pile up containers— let air circulate around them. And don't install closets and cabinets on the floor or against an uninsulated masonry wall; instead, raise them 3 to 4 inches off the ground on a treated wooden base, and fur them out (see page 78) from the wall at least an inch. Heavy polyethylene sheeting placed below and behind storage is an added protection (see drawing below left).

If your basement is subject to occasional flooding or standing water, consider placing loose items on a makeshift raft to float through any unexpected deluge.

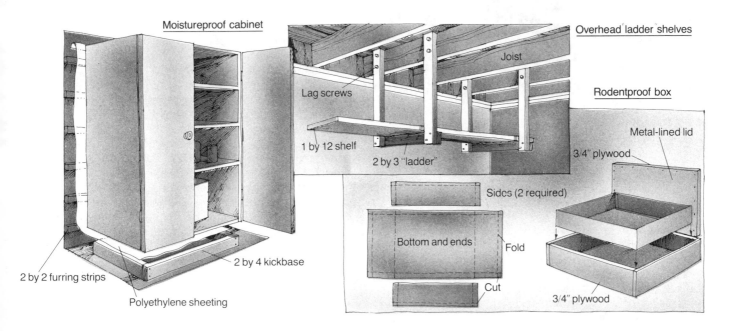

Moistureproof cabinet

2 by 2 furring strips

Polyethylene sheeting

2 by 4 kickbase

Lag screws

1 by 12 shelf

2 by 3 "ladder"

Joist

Overhead ladder shelves

Rodentproof box

Metal-lined lid

3/4" plywood

Sides (2 required)

Bottom and ends

Fold

Cut

3/4" plywood

Rodentproof storage. A basement with a dirt floor is a rat's delight. A good cement wall-and-slab foundation certainly helps keep rats and mice at bay. Most rodents enter through rotted sheathing (just above the foundation wall), dilapidated vent screens, and vent pipes; check these regularly. Metal containers, taped shut, or plywood boxes lined with sheet metal (see drawing on page 75) will keep rodents away from stored items.

Ideas for overhead storage. An unfinished basement is "roofed" with the floor joists and subfloor materials of the rooms above. The spaces between exposed joists, and the clearance between your head and the joists, are excellent for storing small goods. Pick spots that are free of girders, ducts, and wiring.

Nail plywood or boards across several joists to create overhead shelves; two strips in line make a rack. Shelves suspended with rope or chain or "ladder shelves" (see drawing on page 75) are easy to make.

Understairs storage. A frequently wasted space, the wedge-shaped area under stairs offers the space-conscious homeowner a place to build tailored shelves, roll-out bins, cupboards, or a closet. Straight-run stairs offer access from one or both sides; L or U-type stairs may provide several individual cubbyholes.

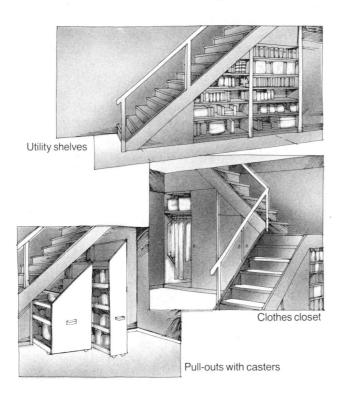

Utility shelves

Clothes closet

Pull-outs with casters

Attaching storage units to walls. If you've solved the moisture problem, basement walls are prime spots for shelving, pegboards, and hanging cabinets (see pages 6–11). It's easy if you have wood stud walls inside the foundation wall, because the units can be attached with standard woodscrews, nails, or lag screws. If you're fastening directly to masonry, see page 79.

Dealing with moisture and temperature

Here's a game plan for beating moisture buildup and temperature fluctuations, the major opponents of basement storage.

Moisture buildup

Correct diagnosis is the key to solving basement moisture problems, which range from the subtle drip of condensation to a running stream. Where does the water come from and how does it get in?

Most basement moisture problems are the result of improper drainage away from the house and foundation. When water builds up near the foundation, hydrostatic pressure eventually drives it to seep through or actually crack masonry walls or floors. Your best course of action is to prevent moisture buildup at the source. These are the most common culprits:
• *Clogged gutters* that concentrate water and cause overflow near the house walls.
• *Downspouts* that aren't connected to drainpipes or tiles to lead water away from the house.
• *Improper grading*—less than 1 inch of drop for each of the first 10 feet away from the house.
• *Flowerbeds* that pool and store water.
• *Window wells* around basement windows that lack drainage or proper caulking or weatherstripping.

· If you can actually *see* water leaking through your basement wall, you'll probably have to stem the flow of water at its source; see the preceding list and the drawing above right for pointers. The alternative is waterproofing the wall itself from the outside—a messy and costly job.

A serious flow of moisture can't simply be plugged up from inside the basement, but many minor ones can. Here's how:

Stopping seepage. Masonry sealers, primarily of Portland cement, chemical combinations, or both, are designed to stop seepage. Follow the manufacturer's instructions closely; most require a clean wall and two coats. The powder types, less convenient than the liquids, can be applied to a wet wall—which is, alas, often what you'll have to work with.

Stopping minor leaks. Common sites of leaks are between masonry blocks, in stress cracks, and where the foundation wall meets the floor slab. Portland cement —or heavy-duty patching mixtures containing Portland cement—can be pressed into a crack after it's been enlarged with a cold chisel. Again, follow the instructions provided by the manufacturer. Some compounds are formulated for use on active leaks.

Condensation occurs when humid interior air meets a colder surface—an outside wall or cold-water pipe. Sweating pipes are one tipoff; wrap them with insulating tape or special jackets and a vapor barrier. To test

Stopping the flow. *Basement water buildup can usually be traced to familiar outside problems.*

Be sure that gutters are adequate and in good condition. Downspout flow should be steered at least 10 feet from the house to drain or dry properly; provide drainage for window wells, too.

Flowerbeds that pool water next to the house should be moved, or at least sloped for a distance of 6 to 8 feet to hasten runoff; for proper grading in general, provide a drop of at least 1 inch for each of the first 10 feet away from the house.

Labels in illustration: Clogged gutter; Downspout flow; Window well; Flowerbeds; Improper grading

whether your problem is condensation or seepage, tightly tape a square of thin metal or aluminum foil to the foundation wall, and leave it for a few days. If moisture builds up on the wall side of the foil, it's seepage; on the basement side, condensation.

Insulating basement walls (page 78) will eliminate most condensation problems. Even opening a window helps. If the problem persists, the answer is often an electric dehumidifier. To be effective, a dehumidifier usually requires an air temperature of at least 60°.

The water table blues. At some level below the ground lurks the water table. Its depth varies with the topography, season, and soil, among other factors. An excavated basement may suddenly "fall" below the water table after a heavy rain, causing floor seepage or actual flooding. To find out if you're getting seepage from below, tape a small square of plastic to the basement floor. If the floor beneath the plastic is wet after a few days, seepage is occurring.

Water table problems are difficult to remedy. If the problem is slight, you can waterproof the floor and build a new floor above it (see pages 78–79), or simply elevate your storage units. If the problem is more severe, either embed perforated drain pipe around the perimeter of the floor (a laborious project) or install an automatic sump pump to at least handle flooding.

Temperature: the ups and downs

Ideally, most of your basement should be warm and dry, but you may want to plan some cooler space for a wine cellar—and if you're a gardener, you may be wishing for cool and even humid storage for root crops. Wall off a separate, insulated area—large or small—adjacent to an outside wall for your cold storage. Then heat the remaining basement space.

Cooling. Basically, you have two cooling options: natural and mechanical. Natural cooling takes advantage of outside air and ground temperatures to cool the air, and an insulated space to maintain the coolness. Construct a simple room on the basement's north or east side; insulate the new inside walls (see page 78 for tips on building and insulating walls) and the ceiling above the room to confine the cold air and to prevent warm air from entering. Vent the space to the outside (see food storage on pages 26–27, for details). A natural cooling system might involve a manually controlled vent with a thermostat you must regulate.

For food or wine storage, you may need a more reliable mechanical cooling system. Mechanical units include thermostat-controlled vent fans, window air conditioners, or even an old refrigerator (its door removed) recessed into an inside wall (otherwise, heat from coils would dilute the cooling effect). If the outside air temperature is above 40° for a significant part of the food storing season, or if you want to create a wine cellar in a climate with temperatures commonly above 60°, investigate mechanical means for cooling your basement.

Heating. Your basement or crawl space may already be heated—at least indirectly—by your house's central heating system. If not, check the system's capacity, and if possible run new ducts to the basement space. If you don't have a central heating system, consider an independent source of heat: a gas, electric, or kerosene heater, portable or built-in. See page 67 for more information.

Basic basement improvements

After you've conquered any moisture problems your basement might have, you can move on to other improvements that will make it weathertight for storage or multipurpose use—like a garage, a basement often doubles as a workshop, crafts studio, or laundry room. You'll find here the basic techniques for insulating and "furring out" masonry walls, and for building a subfloor. For more improvement ideas, see "Garages," especially pages 66–67.

Beefing up basement walls

Two basic ways to build up masonry walls (see drawing below) are with furring strips or standard 2 by 4 framing. Furring strips—2 by 2s or 1 by 3s—are attached directly to masonry walls with paneling adhesive, or with hammer or gun-driven masonry nails (see facing page). Walls built from 2 by 4s "float" in front of masonry walls—or can be positioned anywhere within the basement. They provide a better "dead" space for condensation control, as well as extra room for thicker insulation and for wiring. They are, however, more expensive and complicated to build than furring-strip walls. (See the drawing below for examples of both types.)

Types of insulation commonly used on basement walls include rigid polystyrene boards, fiberglass blankets, and fiberglass batts. If the insulation you choose doesn't include a vapor barrier (pages 70–71), add a complete layer of polyethylene (at least 2 mils thick) over the studs and insulation. Rigid board insulation and the vapor barriers on fiberglass types are flammable and should be covered with ½-inch gypsum wallboard or another fire-retardant material.

The soil itself is a good insulator. It's usually not necessary to insulate more than 2 feet below grade in many areas or below the frost line in others; check with your local building department.

High and dry basement floors

If you can't cure your cold, leaky basement floor, build another one above it (see drawing on facing page).

For the best results in problem cases, first cover the old slab with asphalt. Be sure to plug any floor drains. Floor framing of 1 by 4 sleepers (see drawing on facing page) is attached with masonry nails (see below right) to the slab. Add shims or wood blocks below the sleepers to level out a sloping or wavy floor. If your new floor is to be of plywood sheeting, be sure the sleepers are spaced on 16 or 24-inch centers. Insulation between sleepers is optional—it's not strictly necessary when the slab is below grade.

With the sleepers in place, spread 4-mil polyethylene sheeting (for a vapor barrier) over their tops, overlapping and taping all edges together. Next, add another layer of 1 by 4s above the first, "sandwiching" the sheeting. Then lay your subflooring— plywood or "1-by" floor boards (see page 72).

A simpler flooring job, if your slab is dry and level, entails brushing on a chemical sealer, then laying tiles —asphalt or vinyl-asbestos—directly on the slab.

Masonry fasteners

Fastening storage units, brackets, and structural framing to masonry is a challenge. Fortunately, a good selection of tried-and-true hardware and techniques is available. The composition of the wall or floor you're working with and the type of fixture to be attached determine what kind of fasteners you should use. Some tips: always attach fasteners to solid masonry, not to the mortar between segments; cement block foundations, because of their hollow construction, require toggle bolts or very short plugs; and always wear

Two types of walls. *Furring-strip construction is less expensive and easier to build than standard 2 by 4 walls. The 2 by 4s provide better condensation control, though, and room for wiring and thicker insulation.*

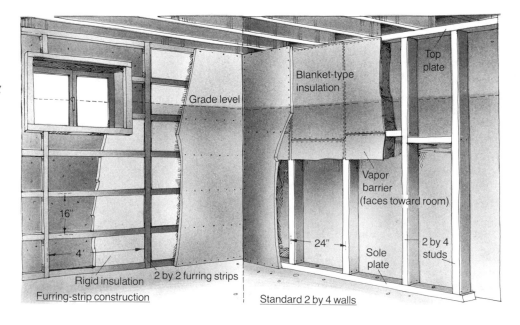

Grade level

16"

4'

Rigid insulation

2 by 2 furring strips

Furring-strip construction

Blanket-type insulation

Top plate

Vapor barrier (faces toward room)

24"

Sole plate

2 by 4 studs

Standard 2 by 4 walls

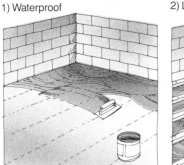
1) Waterproof

2) Lay 1 by 4 sleepers

3) Add polyethylene sheet and 1 by 4s

4) Lay subflooring

Follow these four steps *to build a floor in your basement.*

safety glasses when drilling holes in masonry or driving masonry nails.

Expansion anchors include fiber and plastic plugs, and lead expansion shields and plugs. Use fiber or plastic plugs for lightweight installations, where you'd normally use woodscrews. Expansion shields, which secure lag bolts or machine screws, are for heavy jobs—hanging large shelf units or cabinets from walls, or anchoring the sole plate of a new wall to the floor.

All expansion anchors are installed in a similar manner. Drill a hole the diameter of, and slightly longer than, the plug in the wall or floor. Use either a star drill and hammer, or an electric drill equipped with a carbide-tipped bit. Tap the plug in. Insert the screw or bolt through the fixture to be attached, and drive it into the plug.

Masonry nails. Driven with a hammer or a .22-caliber cartridge-powered stud gun, masonry "cut" nails, pins, and studs are excellent where strength isn't critical, because they're simple to install. Use them for fastening furring strips to a masonry wall and for hanging lightweight brackets and accessories. Stud guns, commonly available for rent, can fire pins through a 2 by 4 sole plate into a concrete floor to anchor a wall.

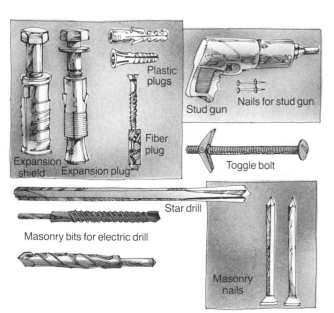
Plastic plugs / Stud gun / Nails for stud gun / Fiber plug / Expansion shield / Expansion plug / Toggle bolt / Star drill / Masonry bits for electric drill / Masonry nails

Toggle bolts. Hollow cement block foundation walls demand toggle bolts. Drill a hole in the wall just large enough for the wings (see drawing) to pass through when compressed. Thread the bolt through the fixture to be mounted, attach the wings, and slip the assembly through the hole. Once through, the wings will spring open, then pull up against the back of the wall when the bolt is tightened.

Crawl space improvements

Though you're desperate for storage space and lack a full basement, if you have a crawl space you may still be in luck. As long as you can negotiate at a crawl and sit up without bonking your head, the space is usable.

If your crawl space is less than 4½ feet deep—or in any case if it inspires feelings of claustrophobia—you'll need to enlarge it by excavating.

Access. If you need to provide entry to your crawl space from above, where is it convenient? An out-of-the-way kitchen pantry or a large hall closet, perhaps? A ladder or a steeply angled ladderlike set of stairs is your best route of descent. The door itself may be a simple trap or a larger double door.

Excavating can be messy as well as awkward, evoking memories of prison escape movies. For cement or asphalt surfaces, you'll need a pick, cement chisel, or jack. Excavate only the area you'll need, which could be as small as 3 feet deep and 5 feet square. Be careful that no water pipes or sewer lines are in the area—look over your house's plans before starting to dig.

If the water table rises above your excavation, you'll end up with a pool of water instead of a storage area. Check with the local building department for underground water levels in your area.

Flooring. A dirt floor can be left as is or covered with new cement, asphalt, sawdust, wood chips, pebbles, or plastic sheeting. A cement floor is framed with a wooden form, then poured using a shovel and wheelbarrow from above or inside (see the *Sunset* book *Basic Masonry Illustrated* for more detailed information). You can insert anchor bolts for stud frame walls in the cement while it's wet.

INDEX

COMBINED INDEX

A comprehensive index to all three volumes appears on the following pages. This is in addition to the individual book indexes which appear on page 80 of each title.

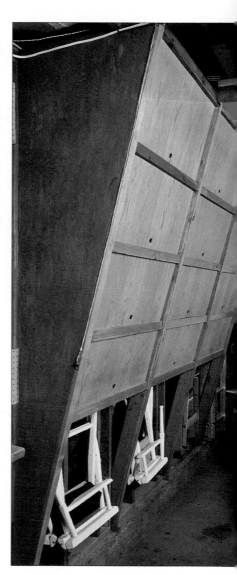

KITCHEN STORAGE

BEDROOM & BATH STORAGE

GARAGE, ATTIC & BASEMENT STORAGE

Combined Index